Deng Xiaoping

Portrait of a Chinese Statesman

Studies on Contemporary China

The Contemporary China Institute at the School of Oriental and African Studies (University of London) has, since its establishment in 1968, been an international centre for research and publications on twentieth-century China. *Studies on Contemporary China*, which is sponsored by the Institute, seeks to maintain and extend that tradition by making available the best work of scholars and China specialists throughout the world. It embraces a wide variety of subjects relating to Nationalist and Communist China, including social, political, and economic change, intellectual and cultural developments, foreign relations, and national security.

Volume in the Series:

Art and Ideology in Revolutionary China, *David Holm*
Demographic Transition in China, *Peng Xizhe*
Economic Trends in Chinese Agriculture, *Y. Y. Kueh and R. F. Ash*
In Praise of Maoist Economic Planning, *Chris Bramall*
Chinese Foreign Policy: Theory and Practice, *edited by Thomas W. Robinson and David Shambaugh*
Economic Reform and State-Owned Enterprises in China 1979–1987, *Donald A. Hay, Derek J. Morris, Guy Liu, and Shujie Yao*
Rural China in Transition, *Samuel P. S. Ho*
Agricultural Instability in China 1931–1990, *Y. Y. Kueh*
Greater China: The Next Superpower?, *edited by David Shambaugh*

Deng Xiaoping

Portrait of a Chinese Statesman

Edited by
DAVID SHAMBAUGH

CLARENDON PRESS . OXFORD
1995

Oxford University Press, Walton Street, Oxford OX2 6DP

Oxford New York
Athens Auckland Bangkok Bombay
Calcutta Cape Town Dar es Salaam Delhi
Florence Hong Kong Istanbul Karachi
Kuala Lumpur Madras Madrid Melbourne
Mexico City Nairobi Paris Singapore
Taipei Tokyo Toronto
and associated companies in
Berlin Ibadan

Oxford is a trade mark of Oxford University Press

Published in the United States
by Oxford University Press Inc., New York

British Library Cataloguing in Publication Data
Data available

Library of Congress Cataloging in Publication Data
Deng Xiaoping: portrait of a Chinese statesman / edited by
David Shambaugh.
p. cm
(Studies on contemporary China)
Includes bibliographical references
1. Teng, Hsiao-p'ing, 1904–   2. Heads of state—China—Biography.
I. Shambaugh, David L.   II. Series: Studies on contemporary China
(Oxford, England)
DS778.T39D46 1995   951.05'8'092—dc20   94–48627
ISBN 0–19–828933–2

1 3 5 7 9 10 8 6 4 2

Printed in Great Britain
on acid-free paper by
Biddles Ltd.,
Guildford & King's Lynn

Contents

List of Contributors

DAVID SHAMBAUGH is Senior Lecturer in Chinese Politics at the School of Oriental and African Studies, University of London, and is Editor of *The China Quarterly*. A specialist in Chinese domestic politics, military affairs, foreign relations, and the international politics and security of Asia, his books include *The Making of a Premier* (1984), *Beautiful Imperialist* (1991), *American Studies of Contemporary China* (1993), *Chinese Foreign Policy: Theory and Practice* (1994) and *Greater China* (1995).

JUNE TEUFEL DREYER is Professor of Political Science at the University of Miami, Coral Gables. An expert on the Chinese military, she has also published widely on Chinese politics and minority affairs. Her books include *China's Forty Millions* (1976), *Chinese Defense and Foreign Policy* (1988), and *China's Political System* (1993).

BARRY NAUGHTON is Associate Professor in the Graduate School of International Relations and Pacific Studies at the University of California–San Diego. A specialist in the Chinese economy, he has published widely on Chinese industrial policy, finance, and problems of the transition to a market economy. He is the author of *Growing Out of the Plan: Chinese Economic Reform, 1978–1992* (1995).

LUCIAN W. PYE is Ford Professor of Political Science emeritus, Massachusetts Institute of Technology. He is also former president of the American Political Science Association. He has published extensively on Asian and Chinese politics. His many books include *Communications and Political Development* (1963), *Warlord Politics* (1971), *The Spirit of Chinese Politics* (1968), *The Dynamic of Chinese Politics* (1981), *Chinese Commercial Negotiating Style* (1982), *Asian Power and Politics* (1985), and *The Mandarin and the Cadre* (1988).

MARTIN KING WHYTE is Professor of Sociology and Chinese Studies at the George Washington University. He has published extensively on various aspects of Chinese urban and rural society, and is currently engaged in research on ageing and inter-generational relations. His books include *Small Groups and Political Rituals in China* (1974), and with William Parish *Village and Family Life in Contemporary China* (1978) and *Urban Life in Contemporary China* (1984).

MICHAEL YAHUDA is Reader in International Relations at the London School of Economics and Political Science, University of London. An authority on China's foreign relations and the international politics of Asia, his books include *China's Role in World Affairs* (1978) and *Towards the End of Isolationism: China's Foreign Policy After Mao* (1983).

BENJAMIN YANG is a Research Fellow at the John King Fairbank Center for East Asian Research at Harvard University. A specialist in Chinese Communist Party history, he is author of *From Revolution to Politics: Chinese Communists on the Long March* (1990). He is presently writing a biography of Deng Xiaoping.

Introduction: Assessing Deng Xiaoping's Legacy

David Shambaugh

Deng Xiaoping has been one of the world's pre-eminent leaders of the late 20th century. Deng's impact will be felt well into the next century as China looms as the world's next superpower as a result of his reforms.

Deng's life spanned the century, involving him in many of the major events of modern China's revolutionary development, although his activities were primarily noticeable during the 1980s and early 1990s. Deng was born during the waning years of the last imperial dynasty. He had a fairly typical peasant upbringing in rural Sichuan before being dispatched to bustling Chongqing and then abroad for study. Like many other would-be revolutionaries, Deng experienced the proletarian life of Paris and received Comintern training in Moscow. From his return to China in 1927 until the Chinese Communist Party (CCP) seized power in 1949, Deng's exploits were the militant revolutionary activities of the time: urban underground organization; peasant uprisings; public propaganda and political indoctrination among Red Army troops; the Long March; and numerous battle campaigns during the anti-Japanese and civil wars. After 1949 Deng served initially as a regional administrator in his native south-west, before moving on to a succession of key Party, government and military posts in Beijing prior to the Cultural Revolution. By 1954 he was one of the inner circle of CCP leaders, and as such had a hand in virtually every key policy and event from 1954 to 1966. Like so many other CCP elites, he came under vicious attack during the Cultural Revolution and endured six years in internal exile. The mid-1970s saw him rise again to the pinnacle of power only (again) to fall suddenly just before Mao's death. With the fourth political "rehabilitation" of his career in 1977 Deng set about deconstructing the Maoist state and constructing his comprehensive programme to reform China and bring it into the front ranks of world powers.

Deng's career was certainly not without its blemishes, the Tiananmen massacre being the most noteworthy. His legacy will be complex and his historical verdict no doubt mixed. Yet there is no denying that Deng was responsible for a monumental transformation of one-fifth of humanity, awakening China from its socialist slumber with the prospect of an unprecedented future.

Deng Xiaoping pursued many goals during his lifetime, but none more central nor persistently than strengthening the Chinese nation-state. Deng was a staunch nationalist who sought to restore China's wealth and power. This quest of Deng's was not unlike that of previous Chinese reformers during the 19th and 20th centuries: creation of a modern industrial base; transformation of China's agrarian social structure; attainment of a materially comfortable standard of living for the populace; reclaimed national independence, dignity, and freedom of manoeuvre in foreign relations; a strong national defence and maintenance of territorial integrity around China's borderlands; and attainment of great power status. In these respects, Deng's vision for China shares an essential continuity along a historical spectrum of Chinese reformers dating from the late Qing reformers Li Hongzhang and Kang Youwei. Deng was not the first Chinese leader with these goals during this century, but he was the most successful in realizing them.

Deng Xiaoping inherited from Mao Zedong a stagnant economy, alienated society and paralysed polity. He will bequeath to his successors a robust economy and rejuvenated society, but antiquated political system. China's political system is antiquated partly for reasons common to Leninist party-states, but also because of Deng's steadfast refusal to create meaningful channels of political participation for China's citizenry. In significant ways Deng was a true Leninist. Unlike Mao who assaulted the commanding heights and tore asunder the Communist *apparat* during the Cultural Revolution, Deng sought to rebuild the party-state. Deng believed, like other Chinese reformers before him, that a strong state which monopolized political power was essential to economic development. His view was reinforced by the East Asian developmental model.

Yet, at the same time as Deng rebuilt the party-state from its fractured condition of the Cultural Revolution, he also sowed the seeds of its potential demise. His economic reform programme and the autonomy from state control that he created for Chinese from many walks of life inexorably decreased the Party's previous hegemony. In the wake of Tiananmen Deng and the Chinese leadership sought to refurbish the instruments of Orwellian state power – subjecting the society to considerable coercion, propaganda and economic austerity – only to realize that these instruments had dulled as a result of the 1980s reforms. From the collapse of Communist regimes across the globe in 1989–91 Deng drew the lesson that only material gain can ultimately save socialism. Of course, he also concluded that tight political control and the loyal support of the security services were important elements, but without material gain no degree of coercion could ensure the Party's survival. Consequently, in 1992 Deng reignited radical economic reform. The results were impressive indeed: 12.8 per cent GNP growth in 1992. Foreign direct investment poured into China at unprecedented levels. But overheating, inflation, corruption and many other negative manifestations resulted. At the time these articles were written the full impact of this latest reformist phase has yet to be felt – either for the Communist Party or for Deng himself.

Deng Xiaoping ruled very differently from Mao Zedong. Deng did not rely on coercion, charisma or ideology, but preferred to rule through formal Party institutions and Leninist norms. Only late in life did he, like Mao, grow distrustful of the party-state he had created. When this occurred in 1991–92, like Mao, Deng circumvented his chosen successors and the bureaucracy by taking his case directly to the people during his famous Southern Tour (*nan xun*). Not a populist by nature, Deng was acting out of frustration with his chosen successors.

At the same time, it must be recognized that (unlike Mao) Deng

Xiaoping trusted in the entrepreneurial spirit in Chinese culture, and did much to remove state strictures from people's lives. In this sense he shares a legacy with free-marketeers Ronald Reagan and Margaret Thatcher. Getting the government "off the backs" of average Chinese, in order to free their essential commercial instincts, will be one of Deng's most enduring legacies. He rolled back much of the intrusive apparatus that had intimidated a vast nation and provided the stimulus for the realization of the Napoleonic prophecy of the awakened Chinese giant. In doing so, however, he unleashed powerful centrifugal forces in society that are progressively undermining Leninist rule and Communist Party control. In this respect Deng may be remembered more like Mikhail Gorbachev. This is true of many the world's great reformers, who satisfy the people's cravings only to create new and insatiable desires. Deng's lasting contribution was to stimulate the revolution of rising expectations.

One does not know when Deng Xiaoping will "go to meet Marx" (as he once noted in meeting a visiting dignitary), but it is not too early to offer a preliminary assessment of his life and times. Such an assessment is, of course, conditioned by its temporal perspective. An assessment of Deng in the mid-1990s varies considerably from what one would have written in the aftermath of the 1989 Beijing massacre (for which Deng was primarily responsible), at the height of the Cultural Revolution, or during the Long March.

History and historians will ultimately cast judgments on Deng Xiaoping, and therefore the chapters that follow hold no pretence of definitiveness or ultimate verdict, but at the same time offer careful, comprehensive analysis and reasoned judgments by some of the world's leading China specialists and Deng-watchers. They are the product not only of lengthy and detailed research that draws upon unprecedented sources and data, but also grow out of an intensive three-day workshop held at the School of Oriental and African Studies (University of London) in May 1992, and at the 1993 annual meeting of the Association of Asian Studies in Los Angeles.

The eminent political scientist and sinologist Lucian W. Pye opens the Special Issue with an introductory discussion of Deng Xiaoping in the context of Chinese political culture, and Benjamin Yang follows with a detailed biographical study of Deng's pre-1949 years. The subsequent articles are organized along various key dimensions of Deng Xiaoping's professional persona: *politician* (David Shambaugh), *economist* (Barry Naughton), *social reformer* (Martin King Whyte), *soldier* (June Teufel Dreyer) and *statesman* (Michael Yahuda).

This volume was originally published as a special issue of *The China Quarterly*, which was very well received. It is hoped that, while preliminary, the analyses will contribute to a broader understanding of Deng's life and times, and begin to assess his place in the scales of history.

An Introductory Profile: Deng Xiaoping and China's Political Culture*

Lucian W. Pye

Perhaps never in human history has an established society gone through such a total transformation, without a war, violent revolution or economic collapse, as did China with the ending of Mao Zedong's reign and the emergence of Deng Xiaoping as paramount ruler. The *leitmotiv* of Mao's China was orthodoxy, conformity and isolation, a whole people walking in lock-step, seemingly with only one voice, repeating one mindless slogan after another. All Chinese appeared to be united in a state of egalitarian autarky. To have read one newspaper was to have read them all, to have heard one official's briefing was to have heard them all. In amazing contrast, Deng's China was a congeries of elements, not an integrated system at all, with regional differences suddenly surfacing, some urban centres vibrating to the currents of international commerce, its youth in tune with the latest foreign fashions, while the great rural masses were re-establishing bonds with their ancient folk cultures, and nearly everybody rejoicing over the ending of Maoist orthodoxy and politics by mass campaigns. Above all, economics and politics seemed to be adhering to different rules, so that there was openness here, controls there. All the different voices saying different things made it hard to hear any one authority giving vision and guidance. And as the people scrambled to look after their private selves, corruption seeped in, and while the government did not seem really to expect people to obey all its orders, it also acted erratically, sometimes with cruel violence – a "fragmented authoritarian" system in Kenneth Lieberthal's well-chosen words.

Politics in Mao Zedong's China was theatre, and there was constant drama, albeit in a tiresome Chinese style. The Chairman was a master manipulator of public sentiments. Political life was an incessant stirring of emotions, as the whole society careered first in one direction and then another. But in the implementation of public policy, Mao's record was unimpressive, especially the appallingly cruel treatment of people. No other Chinese ruler matched him in the numbers of people killed, banished from their homes to rural exile, imprisoned both in the gulags and in caste-like categories of class identities, and who starved in policy-produced famines.[1]

The reforms associated with Deng Xiaoping constituted a profound revolution. In modern times the Chinese have proclaimed one

---

* I wish to thank David Shambaugh and David Zweig for their comments on an earlier version of this article.

1. Western scholars still need to review, in a constructive spirit, why so much of their work on the Mao era, even when the horrors of the Cultural Revolution were not hidden matters, was both factually wrong and contrary to common sense. John Fairbank did publicly confess that he had been grossly wrong in his evaluations of Mao's rule. Harry Harding has also provided leadership for a self-examination of the field on several occasions, including in his, "Reappraising the Cultural Revolution," *The Wilson Quarterly*, Vol. IV, No. 4 (Autumn 1980) and "From China with disdain," *Asian Survey* (October 1982), pp. 934–958.

"revolution" after another, but with only modest actual progress or change; but with the more humble label of "reform," Deng's rule brought a real revolution. Yet, in Deng's China there was no visible leader, no conductor, indeed no orchestra. Everyone of course knew the name of the paramount leader, but he rarely made a public appearance. State policy was, however, extraordinarily beneficial to the Chinese people. In contrast to policy under Mao, China experienced genuine economic progress: living standards dramatically improved, people became freer to move about to seek to better themselves, and instead of hearing only empty promises, they could begin to see substantive advances in their lives. China at last began to take on some of the appearances of a modern society, albeit still a less developed one.

The changes from one era to the other seemed nearly miraculous, and it is therefore understandable to ask how far Deng Xiaoping should personally be credited. The short-hand convention, but really a lazy form of analysis, is to hold a leader responsible for whatever happened when he was in power. While his partisans will credit him for everything that was good, his enemies will do the same with all that was bad. The adversarial logic of politics being what it is, the partisans will attribute any failures to real or fancied enemies who stood in the way of their hero.

Unquestionably the Chinese people were immensely better off under Deng's leadership than they had been under Mao. Yet, any serious evaluation of Deng's personal place in history must credit him with only those developments, both good and bad, for which we can find his fingerprints. How much of the great transformation was directly the product of his efforts, his specific design, and his exacting orders? To what extent has he received credit for what was the actual work of others, such as Hu Yaobang and Zhao Ziyang? How many of the changes should be seen as wonderful expressions of the genius of the Chinese people once they were liberated from the constraining follies of the ideological madhouse that was Mao's China? There is also the more profound historical question of the extent to which the dramatically visible changes were in fact the product of long and imperceptible processes that suddenly surfaced.[2]

In the contributions which follow the authors will seek to evaluate Deng Xiaoping's place in history according to the standards of his various public roles and in terms of his accomplishments in different

2. The collapse of Communism and the sudden end of the Cold War has challenged the social sciences to explain how just such imperceptible, historical processes can culminate in dramatic instant change. The diplomatic historian John Lewis Gaddis writing about the sudden and unexpected end of the Cold War notes that in the physical world change does not necessarily come about gradually: "Metal fatigue reveals its effects all at once: bridges do not collapse gradually, nor do airplanes decompress unhurriedly. Faults in earthquake zones lock themselves into place for decades at a time, releasing accumulated strains rarely but, when they do release them, very dramatically." See John Lewis Gaddis, "Tectonics, history, and the end of the Cold War," Occasional Paper, Mershon Center, Ohio State University, 1992, p. 3. And so it is at times with change in social and political systems. The strains in China may have been there for decades, and hence the explanation of cause becomes tricky because the relationship between the long-run imperceptible processes and the immediate dramatic events is hard to fathom.

areas. This introduction is an overview evaluation from the perspective of Chinese political culture. It must, however, be acknowledged at the outset that it is far from easy to arrive at firm answers about Deng's eventual status, particularly because he chose to operate in quiet ways often out of the public eye. Deng was like the Chinese magician who, in his unassuming manner and dress, is no different from his audience and whose prattle suggests that he is quite as surprised as the audience at the wonders taking place – not at all like the Western magician who is as much the centre of attention as the feats he performs. The extraordinary and dramatic changes in China would seem to have called for a larger-than-life charismatic leader-magician who could project his persona so as to captivate the imagination of a whole population. Yet, consider the astonishing fact that Deng rarely appeared in public and almost never used the mass media personally.

Indeed, there was something strange, almost unnatural, in the way Deng Xiaoping brought television to China so that more than 560 million people could watch it every day; but then, during the years when he controlled the state's propaganda apparatus and had an urgent agenda for change, he unaccountably shunned using what is manifestly the most powerful technology yet invented for mobilizing public opinion. Imagine what a Gandhi, a Nehru, a Nkrumah, or any other modern national leader, trying to educate his public into new ways, would have done if any one of them had available to them the reach of China Central Television, CCTV. Western political consultants would have advised Deng to exploit vigorously his access to television to get across his message of change. The potential pay-offs that Deng had earlier denied himself were dramatically demonstrated in January 1992, when he was persuaded by his faithful secretary (*mishu*) Wang Ruilin and his two daughters, Deng Nan and Deng Rong, to make a trip to south China during which he briefly appeared on television. The act electrified the whole country, suggesting to the Chinese that politics had been again turned around, and the way was opened for the publication of a spate of articles praising ever more economic liberation and reform. Indeed, it seems undeniable that at any time in the late 1980s and early 1990s Deng could have severely set back his political opponents by openly attacking them with the novel power of television, but he never made such a public move. If he truly wanted to overwhelm the so-called "hardliners," his leftist enemies, and open the way to the uninterrupted successes of the reforms, why had he not years before mounted a concerted campaign in the new electronic medium, thereby mobilizing the Chinese people who were craving progress?[3]

3. The basic nature of the Chinese political process is wonderfully revealed by the contrast between the introduction of the modern print media and television. Chinese political culture quickly and comfortably incorporated newspapers and magazines because they reinforced, first, the Chinese tradition that politics is an insider's game at which the public can only get a glimpse and must guess about, and secondly, the longstanding Chinese preference for government by an intellectual elite. The print media also brought the negative consequence of exaggerating more than ever the gap between words and deeds, between ideas and realities, basic to Chinese politics, as leavened by intellectuals. In contrast, television ran into

The reason was simple: Deng was behaving like a conventional Chinese political leader. This apparent self-denial was only peculiar from a Western point of view. What Deng did was totally normal according to standard Chinese practices. The great leaders of traditional China were all supposed to have unassuming manners and private virtues, and none of the oratorical skills or the larger-than-life posturing of Western leaders. China does not have the finger-pointing, sword-waving, horseback-riding statues which fill parks in Western cities. Deng's quiet approach to leadership conformed to important norms in traditional Chinese political culture, a political culture that was shaped by the role model of mandarin bureaucrats and semi-divine, superman emperors, leaders who all operated out of sight, secretly behind the scenes.

Thus to understand Deng's accomplishments in the context of Chinese culture it is necessary to start with an extraordinary paradox: for although Deng Xiaoping was the paramount leader during what has been China's most revolutionary period of change, his style of leadership was more traditional than that of other recent Chinese national leaders. Deng's style of behind-the-scenes leadership and his non-use of television was indeed an extraordinary example of the supremacy of culture over both structure and rationality in responding to new technologies.

The Chinese Tradition of Leading from Behind the Scenes

For politicians who live by the principle that the name of the game is public exposure, it is hard to conceive of a political environment in which leaders consciously shun the limelight and build walls around themselves to escape prying eyes. Yet Chinese political culture traditionally operated on the premise that omnipotence lies in the mystery which invisibility evokes. The workings of the world of the mandarinate were hidden from the eyes of commoners. No one was supposed to look upon the personage of the emperor, for even high officials were expected to bow their heads and hold before their faces tablets which implied ritualistically that they were not looking at the August One. The potency of invisibility springs from some very primitive human instincts which undoubtedly go back to the universal childhood experience of parents who are attentive and omnipotent even when unseen. The Bloodworths vividly describe this feature of traditional Chinese political culture:

---

footnote continued

trouble, first, because it is the Chinese tradition for leaders to work behind the scenes and not out in the open. China has no tradition of orators. Secondly, as the Gulf War dramatically illustrated, television confronted the Chinese authorities with an unsolvable dilemma: if CCTV used foreign footage of the fighting it would lose all control over what the Chinese public was shown, but if it used only Chinese material it would have nothing visual to show. Censorship and the screening of ideas becomes exceedingly difficult with television. For an excellent analysis of the difficulties the Chinese have with television, see L. Sophia Wang, "The Chinese television coverage of the Persian Gulf War," unpublished manuscript, Joan Shorenstein Barone Center, John F. Kennedy School of Government, Harvard University, June 1992.

The enlightened ruler cultivates the art of being a terrifying, actionless, fathomless blank, notes Han Fei Tzu. He is "so still that he seems to dwell nowhere, so empty that no one can see him." He "reposes in non-action above, and his ministers tremble with fear below." He drains the wise of their wisdom, the worthy of their virtue, the brave of their valor. Their role is to work. His is to personify all their wisdom, virtue, and courage and enjoy the success of their efforts.[4]

In all cultures the mystique of authority rests upon the illusion that in spite of the obvious fact that there is very little difference in people's physical strength or other attributes, rightful leaders are still somehow different from all others. The magic of authority resides in the minds of a public who are eager to show deference to their needed leaders. With cunning wisdom, the world of Chinese officialdom long operated on the principle that the best way to exploit such fantasies of omnipotence was to keep top leaders largely out of sight. Leaders could thus be imagined to be figures who were actually responding to the Will of Heaven and were at one with the cosmic forces of nature. The Chinese logic that the greater the leader the more invisible the personage contributed decisively to the total failure of the Chinese to develop the arts of oral persuasion, rhetoric and oratory as nurtured and admired first in Athens and Rome and then in parliaments and congresses. Modern Chinese national leaders risked diminishing their aura of greatness by speaking publicly, an activity generally left to lesser figures who could not hope to raise their prestige by engaging in the shrill shouting and barking that passes for oratory in China.

Deng's refusal to mount the political stage and exploit the manifest powers of modern mass media technologies thus conformed to a long-standing Chinese tradition. And it was not just the Chinese people who have assumed that, even though they had little to go on, they in fact did know all that was necessary to fathom Deng's goals, values and political methods. China-watchers in the West also claimed to understand this non-public man. Indeed Deng's image as a superman was oddly most vivid for those who were the most removed from the realities of his rule. Thus Deng's popularity, like Gorbachev's, was greater with Westerners than it was with his own people. *Time* magazine twice chose Deng as the Man of the Year even though in the two stories in praise of him the editors could provide no empirical evidence that he had actually caused what they found good in China at the time, or that he believed what they thought he believed. In the 1 January 1979 issue, the editors mistakenly thought that Deng was going to be to Hua Guofeng what Zhou Enlai had been to Mao; and in January 1986 they believed that Deng's ambition was to race ahead of Gorbachev in ridding his country of Communism.

Since Deng Xiaoping did not operate as a public figure in the open, people had to assume that his greatness lay in his ability to manipulate events from behind the scene, much like a puppeteer. But how did he do it? Seeing the man in person provides no clues. He enters the room at the

---

4. Dennis and Ching Ping Bloodworth, *The Chinese Machiavelli* (New York: Farrar, Straus and Giroux, 1976), p. 75.

slow, unanimated pace in which great authority is expected to move in China, the exact opposite of the vigorous American politician or executive. He is surrounded by his assistants, all of whom seem a head taller than him. It is said that he is five feet tall, but that is surely an exaggeration. He awkwardly greets his guests; his handshake is limp, without life, almost as though the nicotine stains had taken all the strength from his fingers. As he settles into an overstuffed chair his sandalled feet barely touch the floor, and indeed hang free every time he leans forward to use the spittoon. His provincial Chinese haircut seems to bring out the contours of his skull and makes his head seem even bigger, an impression that is exaggerated because he seems to be almost without a neck. He doesn't bother to communicate any emotion. Even when he throws back his head for a ritualized, cackled laugh there is no sign of real feelings. As a host he makes a feeble pass at being jovial, but he is not warm; indeed, he seems oblivious to the uses of charm. When he speaks of enemies, such as the Soviet Union or the Gang of Four, it is without animus but in a straightforward, low-key manner. He is known to rattle off statistics in the manner of Chinese cadres who strive to suggest by exaggerated precision that they are in command, or at least that they have good memories. He has an atrocious Sichuan accent which makes his words slur together in a gargle. Like Mao, who in his old age became unintelligible to all but his faithful interpreters Nancy Tang and Wang Hairong, Deng in his last years usually had his aides at hand (primarily his daughter) to make his utterances into intelligible communications. To the observer he reveals not a hint as to how he was able to manipulate people and lead a huge nation. There are few signs of liveliness of mind, of wit or humour, and no sustained, systematic pursuit of ideas, only cryptic remarks, short-hand indications of positions or opinions, or dogmatic assertions of policy positions. And a tendency to back away if any point is pressed by his interlocutors for greater clarification.

People come away from meeting Deng Xiaoping with different reactions. Not surprisingly, many are convinced that they have discovered that what they wish for China is also what Deng wants. For some, however, the most lingering impression is the absence of any signs of affect, no hints as to his understanding of how emotions work. What he has to say is straightforward enough, but there is no attempt to reach out and to win over others by the bonding powers of sentiment. Equally there is no attempt to awe his audience, or to capture its imagination. One could call his approach business-like; it is, however, not surprising that Henry Kissinger, who is peculiarly sensitive to the workings of personal chemistry in diplomacy, concluded that Deng was a "nasty little man."

Deng the physical man in no way communicated the secret of his greatness because the mystique of what was special about him lay in what could not be seen. However, by doing almost nothing to cultivate his public image or persona, Deng went well beyond the traditional avoidance of public posturing by Chinese leaders. It was not just that he discouraged any suggestion of a cult of personality; he actually seemed to work at creating his anonymity.[5] He rarely attended any of the grand international meetings where he could have rubbed shoulders with other world leaders. In contrast to the way international figures sought out meetings with Mao Zedong, Deng managed China's foreign affairs, as Yahuda's contribution shows, with a less personalized form of diplomacy.

Within the sphere of Chinese leadership, he could easily have been the Premier or Party Chairman after the removal of Hua Guofeng from those posts, yet he chose to be merely a "Vice-Premier," a designation that created awkward protocol problems for the world of diplomacy – precisely because everyone knew that he was in fact the supreme leader. And eventually, presumably in order to gain even greater power, he abandoned all posts and offices, to be just a common citizen who happened also to be the paramount leader. As such he must have been the most powerful private person in all of Chinese history. But the point was that any formal office would have limited his powers. People were thus free to imagine him as being truly omnipotent, far more in command than if his powers were only those assigned to a particular position or job.

Yet, by not having a formal rank and office Deng also was able to avoid accountability. No assigned post, no set responsibilities; and therefore risk-taking became possible. This puppeteer was truly invisible, for he did not appear to have his hands on any recognizable levers of power, and yet he was happily freed from all the customary standards for evaluating performance. How can one criticize someone who was an elderly private citizen, who played bridge with his cronies twice a week, went swimming regularly, happily chain smoked, and played with his grandchildren every day? But in the end accountability could not be entirely avoided, and consequently when things did go wrong, as with the Tiananmen massacre, Deng became the target of diffuse and equally unbounded blame by both foreigners and Chinese.[6]

Coming to Power in the Wake of the Cultural Revolution

To understand how this seemingly ordinary and unassuming man could have so dramatically changed the lives of nearly one and a quarter billion people it is helpful to begin by asking how he became the paramount leader in the first place. He was neither popularly chosen nor legally designated. What happened was that several factors in Chinese political culture helped to produce a vague and indeterminate process which

5. In the run-up to the 14th Party Congress Deng did seek an image boost by publishing *Mao Zedong and Deng Xiaoping on the Chinese Condition* which contained 88 articles, 64 by Deng and only 24 by Mao. Also at the time, Deng's face appeared on a huge poster in Shenzhen and the exhibition at the Beijing Military Museum had a large painting of Deng and Mao together, a theme repeated in other displays. *Boston Globe*, 10 August 1992, p. 9. David Shambaugh's contribution utilizes the large number of Chinese books which praise Deng's theories.

6. The mood of alienation and profound depression about China's prospects which was pervasive among Chinese intellectuals both before and after Tiananmen is sensitively and accurately captured by Perry Link in *Evening Chats in Beijing* (New York: Norton, 1992).

without much turmoil yielded the unarticulated consensus that Deng Xiaoping should be China's supreme decision-maker after Mao.

First of all, Deng's elevation was furthered by the extraordinary and instinctive deference Chinese give to old age and seniority, a propensity which underlies the Chinese tendency to have a semi-permanent gerontocracy. By merely being one of the Party elders, a Long March veteran, a colleague of Mao Zedong, Zhou Enlai, Zhu De and all the other heroes of the Party, Deng was enveloped with the aura of unchallengeable authority and thus automatically anointed as a leader. As long as the old men were around, it was unbecoming for younger ones to push ahead.

The Chinese respect for age was, however, a two-edged sword for Deng: it helped him to power, but in time it also worked to complicate his policy efforts. First, he discovered that real authority could not be transferred to his designated successors, Hu Yaobang and Zhao Ziyang, as long as he continued to hover in the background as the senior, all-powerful figure.[7] The power associated with age overwhelmed the limited authority associated with official designations. Secondly, Deng was thwarted in his attempts to get the other Party "elders" to retire to "advisory" posts and thereby fade away because, like his own power, that of the Ancient Ones was not derived from their official posts but from their seniority in the Party.[8]

The authority of age thus reinforced the Chinese way of not distinguishing between status and power. People with high status are simply powerful figures, regardless of their formal positions or offices. Therefore Deng's status as the Senior Great One meant that his views and preferences had to be respected over the views of those who merely had official positions, and the power inherent in status ensured that there could be no real retirement for those who were known to be important.

In speculating about Deng Xiaoping's ultimate place in Chinese history one needs to keep in mind that Chinese respect for age is, in a peculiar way, countered by a powerful cultural propensity to give only lip-service respect to the dead while easily ignoring their last wishes, if these happen to be inconvenient. A culture without a strong legal tradition has no way of irrevocably enforcing the last wills of the deceased, and in China it was enough merely to show ritual respect to the spirit of the dead. Furthermore, the Chinese rule is: "Speak no ill of the elders – until after they die." The treatment of Mao confirmed this rule, for he was totally above criticism until after his death, and then it became commonplace to fault him, especially for his last years – when he was, ironically, the elder

7. On Deng's relations with Hu Yaobang see: Uli Franz, *Deng Xiaoping* (Boston: Harcourt Brace Jovanovich, 1988), pp. 141, 236 ff., and Harrison Salisbury, *The New Emperors: China in the Era of Mao and Deng* (Boston: Little, Brown, 1992), ch. 47. On Deng's relations with Zhao Ziyang see: David Shambaugh, *The Making of a Premier: Zhao Ziyang's Provincial Career* (Boulder, CO: Westview, 1984); Willy Wo-Lap Lam, *The Era of Zhao Ziyang* (Hong Kong: A.B. Books, 1989), Zhao Wei, *The Biography of Zhao Ziyang* (Hong Kong: Education and Culture Press, 1989); and Franz, *Deng Xiaoping*, pp. 273–76.

8. Deng initially established the Central Advisory Commission as a way of getting the Old Guard to retire, but instead it became an institutional base for maintaining their power, and so Deng had to abolish it at the 14th Party Congress.

beyond criticism. With very few exceptions Chinese heroes honoured in life were seen after their deaths to be flawed men with feet of clay. In other cultures time seems to work to enlarge the reputation of deceased heroes, but in China the popular images of Sun Yat-sen, Chiang Kai-shek and Mao Zedong have all shrunk with time. This helps to explain the Chinese paradox of having living leaders who are bigger than life-sized, but of not having an established pantheon of great heroes. Thus almost certainly Deng will be criticized after his death, particularly because, unlike Zhou Enlai, he had few endearing qualities.[9]

Deng's rise to power was facilitated by the situation in which China found itself after Mao's death. In particular he benefited from the two most profound but paradoxical legacies of the Cultural Revolution. That decade of horror had shattered whatever illusions the Chinese public had about the potency of ideology and above all it left them profoundly cynical about Marxism. Yet, it also taught the Chinese that the dangers of anarchy were very real and thus it worked to intensify their deeply-held cultural fears of disorder and *luan*. As a consequence they wanted an end to ideological politics but they also remained fearful of unpredictable change and hence sympathetic to heavy-handed authoritarian ways, even to the point of tolerating and rationalizing the need for repression. This distinctive combination of attitudes provided the basis for legitimacy for the Deng era. The Chinese people had clearly had enough of grand collective visions and were ready to focus on private concerns, but at the same time they wanted political stability and public order. For the authorities this meant the need to keep their own power struggles muted, as invisible as possible, but it also gave them justification to use force to repress political dissent.

Thus, Deng caught the Chinese public's imagination by becoming leader at a time when all Chinese wanted to rid themselves of the memories of the Cultural Revolution. Nobody associated with the horrors of that awful period of Chinese history could have effectively ruled the country. It was others who got rid of the Gang of Four before Deng was rehabilitated, but once he was back in Beijing he was universally seen as an innocent and victimized comrade, and hence a deserving hero who was in addition associated with the "good years" before the "lost decade." His son Pufang had been nearly killed and was permanently crippled by the Red Guards when he was thrown from a fourth floor window at Beijing University. Deng's younger brother was driven to suicide for being related to the "Number Two Capitalist Roader." Thus, at a time when revulsion over the Cultural Revolution dominated public sentiments, it did not take much skill for Deng to push aside those who were close to Mao when the Chairman plunged the country into disaster. So Deng

9. Although it was far from a scientific sample survey, a 1990 graduate student exercise of interviewing Chinese students studying in America revealed that nearly one quarter of them expected that the Chinese public's response to the announcement of Deng's death would be widespread "smashing of little bottles," and over one half believed that there would be general joy. Needless to say, the Chinese students in America are disproportionately dissidents who are particularly angered at what happened on 4 June 1989.

could quietly go about removing, first, the hapless Hua Guofeng, whose claim to leadership rested solely on Mao's mumbled words, "With you in charge, I'm at ease." Then it was equally easy to purge such others as Wang Dongxing, the head of Mao's bodyguards, Wu De, the Mayor of Beijing, Ji Denggui and anyone else who was tainted with bad memories of the Mao era.[10]

The Chinese public welcomed Deng's straightforward, no-nonsense, business-like style of speaking whatever was on his mind. After the years of Mao's hyperbole and decades of Aesopian language on the part of all Chinese leaders, it was as though a window had been opened to let in fresh air when Deng spoke out. He did not seem to have a hidden agenda, and he was not trying to be clever. At last there seemed to be a degree of honesty and down-to-earth common sense in China's political language. Over time, as Deng settled in as paramount ruler, his language did revert at times to the old Communist mode. He began to make preposterous boasts about Chinese socialism surpassing the advanced industrial countries, while slipping more and more into cryptic slogans for guiding the country's business. Thus, for example, after the collapse of the Soviet Union, Chinese officials, in seeking to carry out both domestic and foreign policies, had to try to make sense out of Deng's dictum that "One Cold War is over, two new ones have started." And after his 1992 spring visit to South China his one-sentence pronouncement that "Markets are good" was reminiscent of Mao's dictum, "Communes are good," which set off the frantic establishment of communes during the Great Leap period.

As the reforms began to take shape under his formal guidance, Deng seemed to be operating without any set plans or a complete vision as to exactly what he wanted for China. Rather, he was primarily responding to the universal desire of the Chinese people to escape from the stifling effects of Mao's rule. All Deng had to do was to revive one of Mao's epigrams, "Seek truth from facts," and add his own, "Practice is the sole criterion of truth," for him to be seen as heralding a new day for China.[11] The Chinese public had had enough of impossible dreams, and as they came out of their times of folly they were jolted into an awareness that China was not leading the world into the wonders of Communism but rather it was stumbling far behind not only the West but all of its Asian neighbours.

Thus in sum, much of the change associated with Deng's elevation to power came about because he was willing to tolerate what once had been taboo. The idea that some sections of the population could get rich first was revolutionary only because it so blatantly contradicted the norms of Mao's China. Similarly the formula of "one country, two systems" was shocking given the previous paramountcy of ideological orthodoxy.

10. The details of these events are covered in David Shambaugh's article.

11. Since the Tiananmen massacre some Chinese intellectuals in their efforts to discredit Deng have made a point of identifying both epigrams as Mao's creations. Of course Mao himself got the first slogan from Zhang Zhidong and a long line of Confucian scholars.

Several other changes were repeats of earlier formulas or policy attempts, but this time they were allowed to achieve fruition. The idea that science and technology might be the driving force for China's modernization goes back to the Self Strengtheners, the 1898 Reformers and the May Fourth era, and the decision to adopt the household responsibility system in agriculture was another try at what Mao had once said was a good idea.[12]

Deng thus became the symbol of the times at a moment in history when China had to break out of its isolation, abandon its absurd ideological rhetoric and let in a little common sense. While this process was taking place, Deng did benefit from the Chinese mystique about leadership. In the imperial tradition the Chinese assume that there is always a superior figure who is responsible in a vague way for whatever is happening in the country, and even in nature. The emperor-figure is thus ritualistically bound to the country's fate, but not in the precise and indelible way greatness is established in Western cultures. The Chinese measure of greatness is limited almost entirely to private virtues, not public skills.

Yet, it is puzzling why Deng's traditional Chinese approach to leadership was so effective in the post-Cultural Revolution environment. The behind-the-scenes leadership style of the mandarin-bureaucrat was designed to be effective when there was an entrenched bureaucratic state and a society that was hierarchically ordered and well established. The post-Cultural Revolution China, in contrast, was in a state of disorder after Mao had disrupted both the Party and the government and shattered all manner of public institutions. Yet, there were two key features of Chinese culture that paradoxically made the mandarin administrator's role an effective one even in such circumstances. First, the period of disorder had left the public intensely anxious to find stability and order, and for the Chinese this meant seeking hierarchical arrangements. People wanted to know who they should look up to for guidance and thus they needed a clear sense of who was superior and who was inferior. Secondly, their reaction to their state of anxiety was to adhere ever more strongly to their basic communitarian or group-oriented values. That is, they wanted to belong to some sheltering group. This combination of seeking out their assigned group or collectivity and, once in their respective offices, factories, schools, neighbourhoods or communes, of spontaneously arranging themselves in their proper hierarchical slots, meant that a remarkable semblance of order was restored in record time immediately after Mao's death. People who only a year or so before had passionately clashed with each other (some who had even killed each other's friends) were now able to settle down and work together in offices and factories.[13]

---

12. These and other details of the economic reforms are analysed in Barry Naughton's contribution to this issue.

13. Anne F. Thurston has captured the emotional state of Cultural Revolution survivors in *Enemies of the People* (New York: Alfred A. Knopf, 1987).

Deng's basic approach of not trying to command and control the total scene but of allowing a great deal of independence and autonomy, and above all of delegating authority, met the needs of the situation. The public could feel that even though they could not see him at work, Deng as their paramount leader was in full control. The public mood and the objective circumstances in China when Deng came to power were ideally suited for the restoration of the basic essence of the traditional Chinese style of government: in which the topmost leaders could solemnly proclaim an ideology which required only lip service; lesser officials could freely practise feigned compliance, and as long as they did not challenge the ideology they could do what they thought best for themselves and their communities; and the masses could pursue their own interests as they operated in their face-to-face small groups. In a phrase, it was a form of authoritarianism tempered with anarchy.[14]

Deng as Master Administrator – Chinese Style

Thus when Deng took command the mood of the country demanded a change from most of what Mao had stood for. Deng's approach to government was that of the behind-the-scenes manipulator, the master administrator. To the Western mind, imbued with the principle of rule by law, the concept of an administrator suggests careful, indeed exaggerated attention to regulations, details, processes, procedures and forms, while remaining impersonal, unreachable to special pleading and totally task-oriented. In China, coming out of a very different mandarin-magistrate tradition, the ideal administrator, while possessing some of these qualities, was primarily the skilled master of human relations. The key to manipulating power was knowing how to read human character so as to spot individual strengths and weaknesses, with the ability to control subordinates, manipulate superiors and play off equals. In this way mandarin-administrators could build *guanxi* networks and exploit particularistic relationships – while always pretending to propriety and correctness according to a moralistic ideology. When they turned their attention outward to deal with the public they followed two somewhat contradictory rules of behaviour. They were expected to be benevolent toward the people and sensitive to their basic wishes and desires. Yet, they were also called upon to be personally involved in the punishment of wrong-doers. Unlike the Western bureaucratic administrator, the Chinese mandarin had to prove himself capable of not just ordering penalties but of actually supervising extremely harsh, indeed cruel, forms of torture.

14. Much of the best work in Chinese political economy points to the extent to which successful enterprises and communities disregarded official policies as they maximized their private interests. See in particular, Dorothy J. Solinger, *From Lathes to Looms* (Stanford: Stanford University Press, 1991); Elizabeth J. Perry and Christine Wong (eds.), *The Political Economy of Reform in Post-Mao China* (Cambridge, MA: Harvard University Press, 1985); Andrew Walder, *Communist Neo-Traditionalism: Work and Authority in Chinese Industry* (Berkeley: University of California Press, 1986).

In following the Chinese administrative tradition Deng was, as Shambaugh's contribution fully documents, above all the master of the insider's art of personnel management. As for his approach to the public, Deng was sensitive to the people's wishes, and in particular he understood their craving for economic progress and improvements in their material well-being. He knew that people wanted a better life for themselves and their families, and that they would respond enthusiastically to material incentives. But in the Chinese tradition he also accepted the need to be ruthless in administering punishment if necessary. Throughout his career Deng cultivated an image of toughness, of being anxious to make hard choices, to take on challenges, to prove that he was not afraid of a fight. Westerners generally find it hard to reconcile Deng's sympathy for the people's welfare with his posture of toughness. Deng gained a reputation for toughness early, while carrying out the land reform programme, by egging on the peasants into killing landlords, because, as he said, once they had blood on their hands they would be loyal to the Party.[15] In inner-Party struggles he had the reputation of being the hard-headed, aggressive investigator of misdeeds – as in his report on the Gao Gang–Rao Shushi conspiracy – and of standing up to the Soviet leadership in polemical battles. And of course, there was his "Three Don't Be Afraids" speech during the Tiananmen crisis in which he told the Politburo that they should not be afraid of foreign opinion, public reactions or the shedding of blood.

It was, however, in the way he played the insider's game that Deng was the quintessential Chinese administrator. He understood that power lay in the management of officials. Yet he was also almost unique among Chinese leaders in his understanding that it was possible to delegate responsibilities while staying in total command. His distinctive leadership style was to find the right person for each job and then to step back and allow the appointee to perform, a very untraditional Chinese practice. It was second nature for him to leave it to lesser officials to work out problems on their own.[16] As Secretary General of the Party during his formative years in the leadership ranks, Deng had to manage ten different departments and keep track of the personnel files of the top cadres. Mao's style was that of reigning and ruling, of withdrawing from daily operations for long periods, but then coming in and troubling himself with all manner of petty details. Deng, in sharp contrast, rarely intervened in details, except in making personnel appointments. Thus, much of the specifics of the economic reforms can be credited to Zhao Ziyang, and the cultural opening to Hu Yaobang.

All of these characteristics of Deng as the behind-the-scenes administrator suggest an extraordinarily self-confident and secure personality. It is time to look into his development as an individual.

---

15. Salisbury, *The New Emperors*, p. 28.

16. In the more legalistic West, officials are motivated to supervise their subordinates closely because supervisors can be punished for the mistakes of their subordinates, whereas under the principle of rule by men in China there has been more tolerance for human failings.

Fitted to the Mould Early in Life

The early years of great men are generally filled with hints of later developments, but there is usually much that is contradictory. What is astonishing in the case of Deng Xiaoping is that nearly everything in his life story pointed in the one direction that was to be his destiny. The progression of his personal development followed a remarkably smooth and uninterrupted path of maturing in which he easily and comfortably responded to his environment at every stage. There were no crisis points at which to make hard and painful choices. He seems to have simply gone along hand-in-hand with the inevitable. He eventually arrived at the pinnacle of national power and in the process he came to his distinctive leadership style without any noticeable periods of self-doubt or confused uncertainty as to who he really was or what he should try to become. At every stage along the way his environment provided a definition of his identity, and he accepted each definition as his natural right.

The childhoods of Deng Xiaoping and Mao Zedong were uncannily similar on the surface but there were very important differences in psychological development. Both were the eldest sons of the leading families in their respective rural communities. Deng came from the most prominent family in his native village of Paifang but, unlike Mao's newly prospering rural family, the Deng family had a long tradition of scholar-ship and public service dating back to the Ming dynasty. Benjamin Yang notes that his father, Deng Weiming, was a community leader in every respect: the biggest landowner, chief of the Elder Brother Society, supervisor of the county security force, and spiritually the leader of the "Religion of Five Sons," a sect which blended Confucianism, Buddhism and Taoism for the purpose of improving people's secular behaviour.[17] Deng's father was prominent enough to place him on good terms with the Governor of Sichuan province.

Every indication is that Deng Xiaoping had a very secure and sheltered childhood in a large, warm and nurturing family.[18] Deng's first years were spent in a setting in which everyone knew him and treated him well. Harrison Salisbury took the trouble to visit Paifengcun in 1988 and found some villagers who remembered Deng as a "sunshine boy" who enjoyed turning somersaults down a path for nearly a third of a mile.[19] Even as a child Deng was inordinately small, and he had to learn early to compen-sate with wits and determination for his lack of physique.

Deng's father, quite unlike Mao's, was anxious for him to get a good education and he instilled in Deng the idea that he could go far in life. Deng Weiming had four wives, the second Deng's natural mother who died in 1927. Deng did not attend the funeral; he did not know the third

17. See his article in this volume.
18. On Deng's childhood, see: Salisbury, *The New Emperors*, ch. 4; Han Shanbi, *Deng Xiaoping pingzhuan (An Analytical Biography of Deng Xiaoping)* (Hong Kong: East–West Culture Co., 1988), Vol. I, pp. 23–42.
19. Salisbury, *The New Emperors*, p. 27. Salisbury's respondents must have been report-ing the local folklore for there could not have been many villagers who had vivid memories of the boyhood of an 88-year-old man.

wife but brought the fourth, Xia Bogan, to Zhongnanhai to live with his family after the Communists came to power. She became such a part of the family that she was taken with them to Jiangxi when he was exiled during the Cultural Revolution.

It is not clear what if any significance should be attached to the fact that the family were Hakkas, a minority ethnic group in which women generally do the hard physical labour. They never bound their feet and the men have fewer behaviour constraints than is customary with other Chinese – freer, that is, to deal with the "big things" such as to talk politics, gamble and feud with others. It may be marginally significant for explaining Deng's readiness to delegate responsibility to note that Hakka men still leave to their womenfolk more control over household matters, including money, than in most Chinese families where husbands feel the need to supervise the entire household. It may not be entirely irrelevant that Deng's closest *mishu* or secretary-aide was also a Hakka.

Although it seems that Deng must have had a happier childhood than Mao, in later years Mao enjoyed being the local hero and made repeated visits to his birthplace at Shaoshan, whereas Deng never returned to his native village once he left Paifengcun as a mere 12-year-old to go to Chongqing to be educated under the supervision of a tutor.[20] As he did throughout his life Deng simply closed the book on one period and went on to the next. His unsentimental nature, which was developed early, reinforced his tendency to be totally absorbed in his immediate preoccupations which, as noted, were central to his administrative style. He never looked back, and not only did he not attend his mother's funeral but he never made an effort to clarify the facts about his father's murder. His father was brutally killed in 1940, possibly by "bandits," but also possibly by local Communists engaged at that time in attacking landlords, or even possibly by an enemy of the provincial warlord. In any case, Deng never tried to solve the mystery.

After the establishment of the People's Republic and during the Maoist years of ideologically labelling everybody according to his or her family background, Deng had very good political reasons for blanking out his origins. Not only was his family rich and for many generations well established, but so was his wife's. Throughout China people from far more modest families were having a hard time as they were classified as having "bad" backgrounds. Thus, in a very real sense Deng became a man who had to mask the realities of his origins and to act as though he had no real roots. This compelling need no doubt psychologically reinforced his tendency to focus all his energies on the present and the future and not to look back. To understand Deng's behaviour at times it is necessary to keep in mind that people who have to deny their origins can tend to become aggressively defensive about any challenges to their identities. Eventually they may develop vulnerable egos. Deng was protected from such a reaction because he had such a well-structured

20. At 16 Mao also went away to school, but it was to live with his mother's family and at a school at which he was by far the oldest student. Deng lived with a tutor whom his uncle had selected for him, and did not really attend a school with other students.

ITEM ON HOLD

e: Deng Xiaoping : portrait of a Chinese statesman / edited by David Shambaugh.

thor:
umeration:
ronology:
py: 1
m Barcode:

0 2 2 0 9 0 1 3

n Being Held

ron Barcode:

3 0 0 1 9 0 5 4 8

ld Expires: 4/19/2015
kup At: Kelowna Circulation Desk
tron Comment

state bureaucracies. In particular he was troubled by the influence that Party cadres, who were strongly ideological, had on the state bureaucracy. Deng was doubly motivated to achieve such a separation of authority, first, because he basically wanted to break from the politics of ideology, and secondly for an even more pragmatic reason, that he had more support and followers in the state system than in the Party leadership where the balance of power had been tilted more to high officials with sentimental feelings for the Mao era.[41] As both Martin King Whyte and David Shambaugh explain in their contributions, Deng sought to rule through the bureaucracy even as he was intolerant of bureaucratic practices.

All of this is to say that it would be wrong to think of Deng's attacks on bureaucracy as being totally new to the Chinese political tradition. Yet, there were some characteristics which were distinctive and more removed from tradition. Therefore in evaluating his place in history it is necessary to take note of some of these.

A first significant difference in Deng's style was the unemotional and detached manner in which he treated the other leaders and the lesser officials. Although he knew personally and had worked with all the top leaders, he was surprisingly impersonal and often cold and distant in his personal dealings with them. His view seemed to be that if one man could not do the job, there would always be someone else who could take over. This made it possible, as David Shambaugh details, for Deng to remove even people with whom he had long and close working relationships. The ease with which he abandoned his closest associates and picked successors, especially Hu Yaobang and Zhao Ziyang, is shocking when judged by most standards of political loyalty.[42] It is true that Mao also had a record of abandoning those he was closest to, but these breaks were usually followed by political and emotional fireworks. Deng simply dropped people when they became a liability, and he did so without treating them as either enemies or sinners. His reserved and somewhat detached approach meant that he had no truly close friends or deeply committed enemies. Whereas Mao had a vivid sense of friend and foe, Deng was more even-handed and less given to emotional responses to the behaviour of others. People who failed in their jobs did not have to be

41. For an analysis of how Deng Xiaoping was able to exploit his base in the State Council to out-manoeuvre Hua Guofeng who at the time had a majority of support in the Standing Committee of the Politburo, see Dorothy Grouse Fontana, "Background to the fall of the Gang of Four," *Asian Survey*, Vol. 22 (March 1982), pp. 237–260; Lowell Dittmer, "Bases of power in Chinese politics: a theory and an analysis of the fall of the 'Gang of Four'," *World Politics*, Vol. 31 (October 1978), pp. 26–60.

42. At the 14th Party Congress in 1992 Deng again abandoned a close personal friend and political supporter when he allowed Yang Shangkun and Yang Baibing to be dropped from the Central Military Commission even though Yang Shangkun had been his "alter ego" and Yang Baibing had declared that the PLA would "provide armed escort (*baojia huhang*)" for Deng's reforms. It was speculated that the Yangs had accumulated too much power and too many enemies, and so "when various factions counter-attacked to bring the Yangs down, Deng Xiaoping let things take their natural course." He Zi, "Yang jiajiang shishi neimu," ("The inside story about General Yang's decline in power"), *Zhongguo shibao zhoukan* (*China Times Weekly*), American edition, No. 44 (1992), p. 9.

harshly punished nor was there any need to go to the lengths that Mao did to rectify people's errors.

His consistently impersonal approach absolved him of charges of favouritism. He knew the rules of *guanxi* but he also knew that the fear of abandonment is what gives *guanxi* its sting. Significantly in the succession struggle none of the potential heirs publicly made a point of being a close personal follower of Deng. Several, of course, identified themselves with the reform policies which Westerners associate with Deng, but they all seemed to distance themselves from Deng as an individual. In part they were no doubt aware that once Deng died the mystique of his authority would rapidly decline, but they also were probably reacting to his detached manner, and to his erratic "pragmatism" in policy directions. Over the years Deng has left a trail of sudden policy reversals, especially as he vacillated about the speed of the economic reforms and even more the degree of political liberalization, and thus anyone who committed himself to Deng at one point could have been made to look foolish at the next – as did happen to many foreign observers who went overboard in praising Deng before the Tiananmen massacre. Mao of course made even more dramatic policy zigzags, but he always had an emotional justification, usually in the context of fighting "enemies," and hence his reversals had the legitimacy of being tactical manoeuvres. Deng's changes were done without passion or tactical justification.[43]

Deng's impersonal manner in personnel matters was matched by a very straightforward, uncomplicated and brisk style of decision-making. Decisions seemed to come easily to him. There was no agonizing beforehand and no soul searching afterwards. What had to be done should be done quickly in order to move on to the next issue. Bo Yibo tells of how Zhou Enlai once contrasted Deng Xiaoping's and Liu Bocheng's approaches to decision-making: "Comrade Xiaoping's style is that of 'lifting something heavy as if it were light' while that of Comrade Bocheng is 'lifting something that is light as if it were heavy'."[44]

Numerous examples can be cited of Deng's increasingly brisk decision-making after he became China's paramount ruler, unconstrained by any formal office. Not untypical was his resolution of the bitter dispute which arose when the Ministry of Foreign Affairs, sensitive to Western concerns, objected to the PLA's Polytechnologies sale of DF-3 missiles to Saudi Arabia. When representatives of the two parties met Deng for his final decision, he waved aside their formal presentations, and asked only one question: "How much money will you be making?" The Polytechnologies officers replied, "two billion dollars" to which Deng merely said,

43. Liu Binyan made the point that people could not identify with Deng because of his elusive character and policy contradictions in an essay in the *Ming Bao*, 4 June 1992, p. 5; reported in *Inside China Mainland*, Vol. 14, No. 8 (August 1992), p. 25–28.

44. Bo Yibo, *Lingxiu, yuanshuai, zhanyou* (*Leaders, Marshals, Comrades-in-arms*) (Beijing: The Central Party School Publishing House, 1989), pp. 119–120.

"Bu shao na" (not a little).[45] The case was thereby closed, nothing more needed to be said. (It may not be entirely irrelevant that Polytechnologies Inc. is run by Deng's son-in-law, He Ping.[46])

Thus, Deng's brisk decision-making sometimes degenerated into compulsiveness and impatience. For a leader who was reputed to be the total pragmatist and whose main slogan was "Seek truth from facts," he could be quite casual with data and ready to make decisions before all the evidence was collected and analysed.[47]

These tendencies all contributed to Deng's practice of focusing almost entirely upon the present situation without being affected by memories of the past or ranging speculations about the future. Indeed, he had almost tunnel vision as he concentrated solely on immediate realities and set goals. This also meant he was able to discount in his own mind the costs of past policies. For example, in belittling the impact of the December 1986 crackdown on students on world opinion, Deng cited the example of closing down Democracy Wall and the arrest of Wei Jingsheng in 1979: "A few years ago we punished according to law some exponents of liberalization who broke the law. Did that bring discredit on us? No, China's image was not damaged. On the contrary, the prestige of our country is steadily growing."[48]

The combination of even-handedness and grace in decision-making did not, however, always produce stable policies under Deng's guidance. When power is operated largely behind the scenes and through personal relationships there is a tendency toward jerky and unexpected movements in public affairs. Small changes in personal relationships can create political earthquakes, and for no reasons visible to outsiders. Events do not necessarily follow the logic of what is publicly known. Indeed, many of the unexpected ups and downs of Chinese politics, the high expectations and sudden disappointments, or developments that did not continue, which characterized some of the Deng era, can be traced to the ways in which small changes in the inner elite relationships were played out in the public arena. Required to operate according to the logic of personalized power relationships, a top Chinese leader, such as Deng Xiaoping, cannot tell his associates that his public persona makes it impossible for him to

45. John W. Lewis, Hua Di and Xue Litai, "Beijing's defense establishment: solving the arms export enigma," *International Security*, Vol. 15, No. 4 (Spring 1991), p. 96.

46. John Pomfret, "Chinese army now major U.S. arms merchant," *Washington Post*, 4 March 1993, p. A18.

47. I had the personal experience in 1974 of asking Deng Xiaoping what the population of China actually was. He replied that they did not know what it was. I said that I thought that was hard to believe, given the administrative abilities of the Party and the government, but Deng reacted as though I was innocent and naive. He patiently explained that in China local authorities report all kinds of numbers, some thinking it good to have a high number because it might give them more rations and benefits, while others would deflate their numbers because they were worried that they would be assigned higher quotas and made to pay more to the state. So according to Deng it was best not to take any government statistics seriously, and especially not to worry about what China's population figure actually was. Policy should be geared to what seems to be a reasonable figure.

48. *Beijing Review*, 29 June 1987, p. 15, as cited by Merle Goldman, *The Seeds of Democracy in China* (Cambridge, MA: Harvard University Press, forthcoming).

do their personal bidding. The politician whose power is manifestly derived from his public image can always inform his colleagues that, "I would love to do it your way, but I just cannot because that would mean going against my public position – I am sure you can appreciate my situation and forgive me." This formula, so typically that of a democratic politician, is simply not available to a Chinese leader whose power depends upon his behind-the-scenes relationships.

Deng's aloof manner in his personal relations did, however, allow him to practise some complicated manipulations of support and withdrawal. Thus, for example, he did not stand up for his old friend Peng Zhen at the beginning of the Cultural Revolution, but then quickly rehabilitated him in 1975, and in doing so recaptured Peng's trust enough for Peng to feel the need to reciprocate in supporting Deng's rehabilitation in 1977. Using a different tactic, Deng in 1979 surprisingly elevated Hu Qiaomu to head the Chinese Academy of Social Sciences even though Hu had taken the lead in denouncing him when he was first under attack during the Cultural Revolution. The appointment left Hu unsure of exactly where he stood, and the uncertainty became even greater when Deng left Hu exposed as he ran increasingly into criticism.

Deng's coolness in personnel matters and decision-making was matched by an equally aloof manner toward criticisms of his policy decisions. If he had to make apologies for his errors in order to get back into power, as he was forced to do at least five times, he could be fulsome, but when he was politically secure he brushed aside any criticisms. Others might make excuses for him, but Deng himself generally ignored most critics and treated the past as over. He was, for example, the one who thought up the idea of sending intellectuals down to the countryside in the Anti-Rightist campaign, an idea Mao enthusiastically embraced, but even when he needed the support of the intellectuals he never felt any obligation to express remorse. And of course, the Tiananmen massacre could not have happened without his assent, but afterwards he never found it necessary to justify or explain his position.

This detached style suggests a supremely self-confident personality, a person who believes that he belongs at the top, not because he had an urgent mission, but simply because he belongs there and it would be unjust if he were not at the centre. Hence his willingness to grovel and to go through the required rituals of self-criticism in order to be restored to his rightful place.[49] After the arrest of the Gang of Four, the still purged

49. An example of the self-degradation Deng was willing to suffer to get back into power was his self-criticism during the Cultural Revolution, which included such statements as: "Whenever I think of the damages caused by my mistakes and crimes to the revolution, I cannot help but feel guilty, shameful, regretful, and self-hateful. I fully support the efforts to use me as a negative example for lasting and penetrating criticism in order to eradicate the evil influence left by me over long years…. No punishment is too much for a man like me. I promise that I will never seek to reverse the verdict on me and I will never be a remorseless capitalist roader. My greatest wish is to be able to stay in the Party and I am begging the Party to assign me a tiny and insignificant job at an appropriate time … I warmly cheer the great victory of the Great Proletarian Cultural Revolution." Deng Xiaoping's Autobiography, 5

Deng wrote Hua Guofeng and the Central Committee an obsequious letter, seeking reinstatement, in which he stated:

I support with all my heart the decision of the Central Headquarters to appoint Comrade Guofeng Chairman of Central Headquarters and the Military Command. I rejoice over this decision, which is of great significance not only for the party but also for socialism itself. With respect to politics and ideology, Comrade Guofeng is the most appropriate successor to Chairman Mao.... Like the people, I rejoice with all my heart over this important success and must cry out over and over, "Hurray for the victory!" By these brief words I try to express my deepest feelings. Long live the great victory of the Party and socialism![50]

These flattering words apparently did not turn Hua's heart or head so that exactly six months later Deng sent another letter both in praise of Hua and admission of his own failings: "Without reservation, I support not only the latest speech of Chairman Hua at the labor conference, but also his directional line ... I support fully and completely the manner in which Hua Guofeng attacks the problems and tasks."[51] He went on to ask that his first letter of praise be publicized to the whole Party, and then he pledged Hua Guofeng that he would be a dutiful and obedient subordinate, doing whatever the new Chairman commanded. Yet, within a year after Hua let him come back he went against his word, and saw to the removal of the leader to whom he had pledged his loyalties. He acted as though his behaviour was normal politics and without any sign of embarrassment.

Of course, people will say all kinds of things under trying conditions, but in Deng's case it is significant that he rarely tried to use a crisis to tip the account in his favour. He had no apparent need to tidy up the past or to make his record prettier. It is true that he fought to get the Party to "reverse the verdict" of the first Tiananmen incident of 1976, but that was necessary if he was to get back into a leadership position. As a consequence of this strange lack of any need for self justification there are many grey and even possibly scandalous spots in his career which he has never taken the trouble to explain away. There are, for example, confusing and contradictory accounts of Deng's role in such events as the Seventh Army incident of 1931, and his dismissal as Party secretary in 1933 after being attacked at the Jiangxi Party work conference as a member of the Deng–Mao–Xie–Gu "anti-Party clique," all of which raise troublesome questions, but Deng himself has done nothing to try to clear up the record.[52] Even when he acknowledged the dark spots in his career he could be so half-hearted that he left the

---

footnote continued
July 1968. Mimeographed copy of Red Guard materials available in the Fairbank Center for East Asian Research Library, Harvard University.
    50. Franz, *Deng Xiaoping*, p. 256.
    51. *Ibid.* p. 259.
    52. The details of these events are covered in Benjamin Yang's article.

suspicion that the worst interpretations might be right. In a self-criticism letter he sent to Mao Zedong dated 3 August 1972, for example, Deng wrote: "One of the biggest mistakes I have made in history is my leaving the Seventh Red Corps, an act which was an extremely grave mistake politically, though it was justifiable procedurally."[53] The formula of stressing the difference between "politics" and "procedure" suggests the mind of an administrator who uses the shield of proper process to defend against substantive criticisms, but not a real answer to right one's name in history. Deng's tendency not to personalize friends and foes makes it hard to judge what actually were his feelings about various members of the top leadership. Outsiders, in order to fathom the workings of Chinese politics, have tended, for example, to draw a sharp line between Deng Xiaoping and Chun Yun and to treat them as though they were committed enemies, but Deng himself has never classified Chun as either friend or enemy.

The Meaning of Pragmatism and Modernization with Chinese Characteristics.

It has been conventional to summarize Deng Xiaoping's political philosophy with the single term, pragmatism. Yet, of course, pragmatism has many different meanings.[54] In some cultures it is a euphemism for the ways of a corrupt politician who has no principles and is concerned only with his own self interest. In a slightly more respectable version, pragmatism suggests an operational code in which there are no higher values, nothing is sacred, and everything is up for "sale" if the price is right. Deng earned the label largely because of his Two Cat theory which suggested that he was unencumbered with ideological constraints and thus would be able to focus on efficiency as his guiding principle.[55] And to a large degree this was a fair judgment as far as economic policies were concerned. By restoring the reign of common sense and abandoning the more egregious follies of Mao's economic policies, Deng did preside over a transition to a more efficient economy. Certainly he was not ideologically troubled by the differences between the public and the private sectors of the economy; the rule was simply "getting rich is glorious."

But even in the economic realm there were limits to Deng's pragmatism. He replaced the elitism of ideologues with an equally elitist view of technocrats as people with almost magical powers to bring about eco-

53. Mimeographed copy available at the Fairbank Center for East Asian Research Library, Harvard University.

54. I have characterized what is distinctive in Chinese pragmatism in ch. III, *The Mandarin and the Cadre: China's Political Cultures* (Ann Arbor: Michigan Monographs in Chinese Studies, 1988).

55. Evidence of Deng's personal attachment to his Two Cat theory is to be seen in the large 1984 painting by Chen Liantao, a renowned Chinese artist, of two cats, one white and one black, that hangs conspicuously in Deng's residence, and which reportedly he refused to give to his daughter, in spite of her begging for it. "Deng Xiaoping he 'Shuang mao tu' " ("Deng Xiaoping and his 'Two Cat Picture' "), *Renmin ribao* (overseas edition), 18 November 1992, p. 8.

nomic development. One can read Deng's *Selected Works* and find no evidence that he appreciated the true functions of markets and entrepreneurs, or even the basic rationale for price reform. What one finds instead is his strong faith in technocrats, technology and people's preoccupation with material betterment – all of which could be consistent with continuing the state enterprises, but trying to make them more efficient. In this respect Deng might properly be classified with some of the leaders of the developing East Asian countries from South Korea to Singapore who found a positive role for state intervention in speeding up economic development.

There were, however, other significant limits to Deng's pragmatism. The most important become self-evident when one takes away the division between economics and politics. Politically there were certain values which he would not sacrifice even for the sake of economic efficiency, the most important being the organizational integrity of the Party and its monopoly of political power.

At a more subtle level Deng's pragmatism was constantly compromised by his impatience. Time and again he would push ahead without regard to timing and pace. Although his initiating of the "Pedagogical War" with Vietnam was well-timed domestically for securing his return to power, it was a reckless move in terms of foreign policy. Also, much of the disagreement between Deng and Chun Yun on economic policy revolved around the pace of the reforms – Deng wanting, for example, a 12 per cent growth rate in 1992 and Chen Yun advocating 6 per cent to avoid inflationary pressures.

That still leaves open the question of Deng's motivations about political power. Did he have only a "pragmatic" objective of power for power's sake? Or did he have a more "sacred" mission for which he felt it essential to monopolize all power? The more one probes for hints of Deng's real political objectives the more it seems that he was in many ways surprisingly ambivalent about change for China. On the one hand, he wanted to see China wealthy in a materialistic sense and strong internationally, but on the other hand he also feared that China could be robbed of its essence and contaminated by foreign influences. Deng's ambivalence was thus similar to that of the 19th-century first generation of Chinese reformers who came up with the idea of adopting Western technology while preserving essential Chinese values, the old *ti-yong* formula.[56] But in Deng's case there was one critical difference: the *ti* he would protect from the "spiritual pollution" of "bourgeois liberalism" in building his "socialism with Chinese characteristics" was in fact already a foreign import, Marxism–Leninism. However, just like the turn-of-the-century reformers who thought it should be possible to welcome Western technology while preserving Confucianism, so Deng believed that it would be possible to have economic development based on Western

56. For a comparison of Deng Xiaoping with the leading conservative Chinese reformers, see: Paul A. Cohen, "The Post-Mao reforms in historical perspective," *The Journal of Asian Studies*, Vol. 47, No. 3 (August 1988), pp. 518–540.

capitalistic methods while preserving in the political realm the Four Cardinal Principles of Marxism–Leninism.

The *ti-yong* formula never worked and for precisely the reasons that the Conservatives who opposed the 1898 Reform movements pointed out: it is impossible in practice arbitrarily to separate values and to erect a high wall between the mental state that goes with understanding modern technology and the socio-political sentiments of modernity. Indeed, the formula had it the wrong way around, in that modernization calls for the acceptance of universalistic values associated with the world culture, though adapted to the local, parochial conditions. The *ti* has to be the universal values, and it is the *yong* that should be related to Chinese realities. In a strange way the Deng goal of seeking "Socialism with Chinese Characteristics" may turn out to be a half-step in the right direction in that it acknowledges that the universal should be a foreign import that can be adapted to Chinese conditions. Maybe in time as the bankruptcy of socialism sinks into the Chinese consciousness, the formula will be changed again, to "Modernization with Chinese Characteristics," which might finally put China on a steady path to progress.

In the articles which follow the various authors judge, from different perspectives, Deng's likely place in history. In general terms, however, his ultimate standing will depend, in the last analysis, very much on what happens in the next stage of Chinese history. Deng's standing will be decisively influenced by both the immediate reactions at the time of his death and the more long-term prospects of his policies. In the short run much will depend upon whether his successor chooses to establish his own legitimacy by identifying himself with Deng, much like Hua Guofeng sought to identify with the memory of Mao, or whether he will seek to distance himself from his predecessor, as Deng did when he made the Gang of Four the sole villains for all the horrors of the Cultural Revolution, thereby shielding the system itself from fundamental criticism. With respect to the second possibility it is significant that credible reports in Hong Kong said that Deng removed Yang Shangkun and Yang Baibing because he had been informed by Jiang Zemin that the two brothers had plotted to announce at the time of the patriarch's death that Deng was solely responsible for the Tiananmen massacre, thereby removing that haunting issue from subsequent Chinese politics.[57]

With respect to the more long range developments, events in China could go in quite different directions. It is not entirely impossible that Deng's efforts to have economic progress without political liberalization

---

57. *The Standard*, Hong Kong, FBIS, 6 January 1993, p. 11. Deng gave credence to the plot theory with his November "Three New Don'ts" (*Xin san bu zhuzhang*) speech in which he laid down the law of, "Do not consider revising the verdict on the June Fourth Incident, … do not tolerate bourgeois liberalization, and do not demote or replace any more of those leading cadres who have been affected and treated as 'leftist kings' (*zuo wang*) during the recent 'anti-leftist' campaign." Yan Ming, "Deng Xiaoping de 'Xin san bu zhuzhang" "Deng Xiaoping's Three New Don'ts," *Zhongguo zhi chun* (*China Spring*), No. 118 (March 1993), p. 65.

will not work, and therefore political change will indeed come about. If this were to happen, history will record that Deng opened the way to forces that he could not control. He would then take his place with Gorbachev, men who started processes which went beyond their control, and who consequently will be seen as somewhat failed leaders. It will then be Deng's successor, China's Yeltsin, who will become China's great hero.[58]

Or, it could turn out that authoritarian repression will continue in China in spite of economic advances. This would seem to be Deng Xiaoping's preferred course, but if this should be China's fate, then it would again be Deng's successor who would be acclaimed by history for it would be he who had defied the predictions of modern social science and kept China in an unnatural state of sustained repression.

Between these extreme developments there is the logical, and not at all unlikely, possibility that China will continue to have significant economic growth but only limited modifications in its repressive political system. There might be a revival of the concept of "neo-authoritarianism" as a form of "soft authoritarianism," compatible with continued modernization, in which Deng's successor would play the role of dictator rather than tyrant.[59] If this were to happen judgments about Deng's ranking in history will differ according to whether he is viewed through the perspective of economic progress or through that of human rights. He will be praised in one regard and damned in the other.

The most confident overall judgment one can make of Deng Xiaoping's place in history is that he will be seen as the man of the moment during a brief transition decade in China's slow progression to modernization. He was the man on the spot when the Chinese were ready to turn their backs on the Maoist road to modernity. He was also wise enough to tolerate half the changes progressive Chinese craved. They consisted of those which gave China substantive economic progress. The other half which he refused to tolerate were the political freedoms essential for building a civil society. In the annals of history there is only a small chapter devoted to those who advanced economic progress. The big chapters are reserved for those leaders who brought political freedom and security to their people.

58. For an analysis of Deng Xiaoping's manoeuvring leading up to the 14th Party Congress and of the subsequent prospects for his hopes to have both economic progress and the Party's static monopoly on political power, see: Roderick MacFarquhar, "Deng's last campaign," *New York Review of Books*, 17 December 1992, pp. 22–28.

59. The case for such a future is well argued in Richard Baum "Political stability in post-Deng China: problems and prospects," *Asian Survey*, Vol. XXXII, No. 6 (June 1992), pp. 491–505.

The Making of a Pragmatic Communist: The Early Life of Deng Xiaoping, 1904–49

Benjamin Yang

Ever since Edgar Snow's report 50 years ago, it has been well-known that Mao Zedong's rebellious life started first with his defiance of his father. Mao senior wanted his son to work in the fields, while Mao junior wanted to read books; his father wanted him to stay at home pursuing a practical job, while he wanted to leave home for a better education and a more interesting career. The case of Deng Xiaoping seems just the opposite.[1]

An Aspirant for Sagehood, 1904–27

Deng was born on 22 August 1904 to a landlord family in the village of Paifang, Guang'an county, Sichuan province. There are sources saying that he came from a Hakka lineage originally in northern Guangdong but, even if that is true, he shows no particular evidence of his Hakka background through his ancestral line.[2] His birthplace – the Deng family residence of several generations before and a museum in his honour now – was an elaborate brick and wooden compound located on the flat top of a little hill at the very south-eastern tip of the village. At the time of his birth, the Deng family consisted of his father and two wives, his elder sister and himself. He then had two younger brothers before his biological mother, Deng Dan, died in 1912. Meanwhile, two young ladies were brought into the family as concubines for his father and nannies for the children.[3]

His father and the master of the family, Deng Wenming, could be said to be a full-fledged local elite: economically he was the wealthiest landlord and entrepreneur with the best residence; socially he was the chief of the local Elderly Brother Society; politically he was the village head and later supervisor of the county security force; and above all, spiritually he was the leader of the "Religion of Five Sons" cult.[4]

---

1. Edgar Snow, *Red Star over China* (New York: Grove Press, 1973), pp. 140–49; Ross Terrill, *Mao* (New York: Harper & Row, 1980), pp. 4–17.
2. See Li Huang, *Xuedun shi huiyilu* (*Memoirs from an Ignorant Scholar's Studio*) (Taipei: Biographic Press, 1973), pp. 105–106. Since Li Huang – whose memoirs are full of factual errors – casually mentioned that Deng was from a Hakka family, most Deng biographers have taken this for granted and stress its bearing on Deng's temperament and character. During my visit to Deng's home village, no villagers seemed to know of it. For further on Deng's Hakka background, see Mary S. Erbaugh, "The secret history of the Hakkas: the Chinese revolution as a Hakka enterprise," *The China Quarterly*, No. 132 (December 1992), pp. 937–968.
3. See "Deng Xiaoping's reactionary background exposed," Red Guard pamphlet reprinted in *Deng Xiaoping* (Taipei: East Asian Institute of the National Cheng-chi University, 1978), p. 1; also see "Investigation of the criminal life of Deng Xiaoping," Red Guard pamphlet reproduced in Makoto Yuasa, *To Sho Hei* (*Deng Xiaoping*) (Tokyo: Japanese Literature Press, 1978), pp. 23–24.
4. *Ibid.* It is interesting to note that, according to some local people interviewed, Deng's father was not merely a rural landlord, but also an industrial entrepreneur who owned two mills that made silkware and foodstuffs.

The second child and first boy of the family, Deng was named Xixian or literally "Aspirant for Sagehood," indicating his father's great expectations for him. His father's influence was overwhelming during Deng's childhood. He arranged for Deng to finish primary and secondary school in Guang'an, and go on to Chongqing for senior middle school. Unlike Mao's father, Deng's father did not need, nor want, him to help with manual labour and household chores. He wanted his son to pursue something loftier and greater, something which he himself had not been able to accomplish.[5]

Deng accompanied his uncle, Deng Shaosheng, to Chongqing for high school education in 1918 but ended up enrolling in the Preparatory School for Work-Study in France and left for France shortly after his 16th birthday.[6] Together with 90 or so other youngsters from Sichuan, he embarked on the French cruiser, Andre Lepon, in Shanghai on 11 September 1920 and arrived in Marseilles on 20 October 1920.[7]

Among the Chinese participants in the "work-study" programme in France in the early 1920s were Cai Hesen, Zhao Shiyan, Zhou Enlai and Li Lisan who had been political activists in China and who threw themselves into political movements immediately upon their arrival in France. Cai and Li were deported to China for taking part in the Lyon University protest in October 1921, and Zhao and Zhou founded the Communist Youth League in Europe in June 1922.[8]

Deng was too young to participate in political activities at the beginning. Instead, he tried his best to "work diligently and study thriftily," until he found it practically impossible to do so. His time in Paris, from October 1920 to January 1926 when he left for Moscow, can be roughly divided into two phases. For the first part Deng adhered to the original objective of the programme to work and to study. He stayed in Paris with the Overseas Chinese Society for the first few months waiting for his assignment, then entered a junior middle school in Bayeux in north-west Normandy from January to March 1921, before his finances ran out. He then moved back to the greater Paris area and took various manual jobs such as in the Schneider-Creusot armaments factory and the Hutchinson rubber goods factory. He also attended a few schools such as the College

5. The information on Deng's childhood and early education is primarily based on my own survey in Deng's home village in August 1984; also see Jiang Zemin, "Reminiscences of diligent work and thrifty study in Belgium and France," in *Pufa qingong jianxue yundong shiliao (Historical Materials on the Movement of Diligent Work and Thrifty Study in France*, hereafter *PFSL*) (Beijing: Beijing People's Press, 1981), Vol. 3, pp. 148–150.

6. *Ibid.*

7. These dates are based on the news reports of *Xinwen bao*, 11 September 1920, and *Ou xinwen*, 31 October 1920. Also see Nora Wang, "Deng Xiaoping in France," *The China Quarterly*, No. 92 (December 1982), p. 698. Wang mistakenly gives the date of Deng's arrival as 13 December 1920.

8. See Wang Yongxiang *et al.*, *Zhongguo gongchandang Ou zhibu shihua (History of the European Branch of the Chinese Communist Party)* (Beijing: Chinese Youth Press, 1985), pp. 62–73, 80–102; also see Uli Franz (trans. Tom Artin), *Deng Xiaoping* (New York: Harcourt Brace Jovanovich, 1988), pp. 43–44. Franz's claim that the Chinese Communist organization in France originated in a small left-wing bookshop with Chen Duxiu's two sons is incorrect.

de Montargis and the Lyceum at Chatillon, but none of them ever provided him with more than preliminary courses in French language training.[9]

As he found that his educational prospects steadily diminished, Deng's political career took off. For the second part of his stay in France, from early 1924 to early January 1926, he lived permanently in Paris, working in a Renault factory. During this period Deng became increasingly involved in Communist activities.

Deng left Montargis for Paris in June 1923. He just missed the Second Congress of the Communist Youth League in Europe held in Paris a few days before, but began intensive contacts with the League from that time on.[10] In February 1924, he started working for *Red Light*, the organ of the League, with Zhou Enlai as its founder and editor-in-chief. His initial duties included typing, copying, transcribing and typesetting, and for these he earned from his comrades the amiable nickname of "Docteur du Duplication."[11] With the formation of a united front between the CCP and the KMT back in China, Zhou and many others left for China or the Soviet Union. The Chinese Communist tide in France ebbed, but Deng's role gradually increased. He began contributing articles to *Red Light* and chairing meetings of the Communist Youth League members.[12]

Judging from the several short articles he wrote in *Red Light*, it is clear that Deng was not so much interested in theoretical arguments or national affairs as being involved in partisan struggle with another Chinese organization, the Youth Party and its organ *Herald Weekly*. This struggle ran to such intensity that each side resorted to threatening the other with violent assault and murder and also appealing to the Paris police for intervention on its behalf. On 7 January 1926, informed of an impending police raid the next day, Deng and 20 of his comrades fled Paris for Berlin by train, and arrived in Moscow a few days later.[13]

Upon his arrival in the Soviet Union, Deng first attended the Eastern University and then Sun Yat-sen University, the former being a cadre training school for Soviet Union minorities and would-be revolutionaries from Asian and Middle Eastern countries, while the latter was established

9. See Li Huang, *Memoirs*, p. 106; Wang, *Deng Xiaoping in France*, p. 698; Franz, *Deng Xiaoping*, pp. 44–56.

10. There is no evidence to show that Deng took part in any of the Communist Youth League activities before 1924. He moved from Montargis to Paris in June 1923 and lived in the same building in La Garenne-Colombes where *Red Light* was formally published in February 1924. Logically, Deng joined the Youth League in late 1923 or, more probably, in early 1924.

11. Wang Yongxiang, *History of the European Branch of the CCP*, p. 123.

12. See Wu Hao, "No. 1 report of the Chinese Communist Youth League in Europe," in *PFSL*, Vol. 2, Part 2, pp. 843–48. Wu Hao was the pen name of Zhou Enlai. This uniquely valuable document shows, among other things, that it was against Communist Youth League discipline for its members to join the Communist Party without specific permission. It is therefore unlikely that Deng joined the Communist Party in 1924, as commonly believed.

13. See Xi Xian, "Look at the blatant lies of the reactionary Youth Party," in *PFSL*, Vol. 3, pp. 271–72; also see Xi Xian, "Look at the false news made up by Herald Weekly for the fourth time," in *PFSL*, Vol. 3, pp. 273–74. Xixian was Deng's given name at the time. In my judgment, Deng did not take the given name of Xiaoping until some time in the summer of 1927.

particularly for China and the Chinese revolution. It is most likely that Deng was formally accepted as a Communist Party member in Moscow in 1926.[14] Moreover his classmates included Chiang Ching-kuo (Chiang Kai-shek's son) and Feng Fenong (Feng Yuxiang's daughter).[15] Neither the Eastern University nor Sun Yat-sen University was as academic as their titles indicated. Although Marxist–Leninist doctrines were taught, Deng and his peers were more concerned with the practicalities of making revolution in China than with theoretical studies.[16]

The High Cost of Revolutionary Faith, 1927–33

While Deng was still studying in Moscow the revolution was brewing in China, in the form of the southern alliance of the CCP and KMT against the northern warlords. The successful Northern Expedition caused the split within the northern regime, in which Feng Yuxiang rose up declaring his sympathy with the Nationalist revolution. At this time Feng was in Moscow for several months before returning to China in September 1926. In addition to his interest in Soviet military aid, Feng also sought "political direction," asking for Communists to work with his troops.[17]

At this request, some 30 Chinese Communists were dispatched by the Comintern to Feng's North-western Army. Deng was one of them. The group departed from Moscow by train in late 1926 and reached Kulun, Mongolia in early 1927. After staying there for a month or so, Deng and another two were selected to form an advance team to go ahead of the rest. The three rode in a Soviet truck transporting ammunition back to China. They arrived at Yinchuan, Ningxia, and from there another month-long journey on camels and horseback eventually brought them to the North-western Army headquarters in Xi'an in March 1927.[18] It should be clear from this that Deng did not take any part in the Wuyuan Pledge

14. According to Nie, there were few Party members in Europe and once they came to Moscow, all the League members – presumably including Deng – were "transferred" to become Party members. Nie Rongzhen, *Nie Rongzhen huiyilu* (*Memoirs of Nie Rongzhen*) (Beijing: People's Liberation Army Press, 1983–85), Vol. 1, p. 29.

15. Feng Hongda and Yu Xinhua, "An affectionate reception," *Dangshi tongxun* (*Bulletin of Party History*), Nos. 3 and 4 (1984), quoted in Bang Yang and Zhuo Xiaowei, "White cat or black cat: review of Han Shanbi's Deng biography," in *Tansuo* (*The Quest*), New York (1986), pp. 54, 73.

16. See Wu Xiuquan, "Memoirs of Comrade Wu Xiuquan," in *Zhonggong dangzhi ziliao* (*Materials of CCP History*), No. 1 (1982), pp. 130–141; Zhang Zhongshi, "Reminiscences of studying in Moscow in the 1920s," in *Dangshi yanjiu ziliao* (*Materials of Party History Studies*) (Chengdu: Sichuan People's Press, 1982), Vol. 3, p. 331.

17. James Sheridan, *Chinese Warlord: The Career of Feng Yu-hsiang* (Stanford: Stanford University Press, 1966), pp. 200–210; Gao Xingya, *Feng Yuxiang jiangjun* (*Biography of General Fu Xuxiang*) (Beijing: Beijing People's Press, 1982), pp. 84–106.

18. See the Institute of Historical Documentary Research of the CCP Central Committee, "Brief biography of Deng Xiaoping," in *Dangshi tongxun*, No. 9 (1984); also Zhu Tongshun, "Research on the timing of Deng Xiaoping's return from the Soviet Union during the period of the Great Revolution," in *Dangshi tongxun*, No. 7 (1986), quoted in Bang Yang and Zhuo Xiaowei, "White cat or black cat."

for Feng Yuxiang in September 1926, as many previous biographers have believed.[19]

There also exist numerous exaggerations about Deng's positions in Feng's army, with claims that he was Deputy Director of the political department, Director of Education of the Zhongshan Military Academy, and so on.[20] Actually, he served in Feng's troops, as a political instructor, for only a few months from March to July 1927. Like the other 50-odd Communist agents there, he worked in political propaganda and ideological agitation and did not assume any prominent military positions. Feng, as a warlord, did not entrust Communists with military command, nor did the Communists seem interested in military power at the time. Soon afterwards, the KMT–CCP united front broke apart and Feng had to make a choice. He opted for the KMT and dismissed all the Communists from his troops or, to use his words, "politely sent them away." Each Communist was offered a few silver dollars as travel expenses.[21]

Many of those from the north just quit the Communist Party and returned to their native towns. The southerner Deng opted to travel by train to Wuhan, where the CCP Centre was then located. He found Zhou Enlai and Nie Rongzhen there and was assigned to the Party Centre as a staff member.[22] He served as a record keeper at the Emergency Conference of the CCP Centre on 7 August 1927, in which the Communists formally decided to retaliate against the Nationalists with military rebellions. In late September he followed when the Party Centre moved to Shanghai.[23]

From October 1927 to August 1929, Deng worked as a staff member in the underground Party Centre in Shanghai. When the CCP Sixth Congress was held in Moscow in June–July 1928 he remained in Shanghai as assistant to Li Weihan and Ren Bishi who were left in charge of Party affairs at home.[24]

Soon after the Second Plenum of the CCP Central Committee in September 1929, Deng, under the pseudonym of Deng Bin and together

19. See, for example, Lee Ching Hua, *Deng Xiaoping: The Marxist Road to the Forbidden City* (Princeton: Kingston Press, 1985), p. 40. Lee claims mistakenly that Deng accompanied Feng, along with as many as 98 Russian advisers, back to China on 16 September 1926.

20. *Ibid.* p. 41.

21. Feng Yuxiang, *Feng Yuxiang riji* (*Diary of Feng Yuxiang*) (Beijing: Nationalist History Press, 1932), Vol. 7, pp. 58–77, Vol. 8, pp. 1–60. There is no mention of Deng or the Zhongshan Military Academy in Feng's diary from September 1926 to July 1927, which includes all personal, official and institutional details of the North-western Army at the time. Even the existence of the Zhongshan Military Academy seems questionable, although the diary mentions "Political Department," "Cadres School," "Political School" and "Zhongshan Club."

22. Nie Rongzhen, *Memoirs*, Vol. 1, p. 57.

23. The PRC official version is that Deng became the General Secretary (*mishuzhang*) of the Party Centre in 1927. See Sheng Ping, *Zhonggong renmin da cidian* (*Dictionary of Chinese Communists*) (Beijing: International Broadcast Press, 1991), p. 98; *Zhongguo renmin da cidian* (*Dictionary of Famous Chinese*) (Shanghai: Shanghai Dictionary Press, 1989), p. 45.

24. Li Weihan, *Huiyi yu yanjiu* (*Reminiscences and Studies*) (Beijing: Party History Materials Press, 1986), p. 243. Li recalls that "Deng Xiaoping made notes at all the meetings."

with Gong Yinbing, left Shanghai via Hong Kong and Canton for Nanning as an envoy of the Party Centre to organize armed rebellions in Guangxi. He was formally appointed by the CCP Committee of Guangdong on 30 October 1929 to be the secretary of the Front Committee in preparing a military uprising.[25] Before his arrival, considerable preparation had been done by local Communist cadres like Wei Baqun, previously dispatched Communist agents like Zhang Yunyi and discontented officers within the provincial army such as Li Mingrui. Deng's role was mainly to communicate the Party Centre's line in principle and did not therefore involve much practical operation.

Deng did not personally participate in either the Bai'se Uprising of 11 December 1929 or the Longzhou Uprising of 1 February 1930. He left for Shanghai in late December 1929 to report to the Party Centre and returned to Guangxi in early February 1930. In the next few months Deng stayed in Donglan county experimenting with land reform and mass organization. It was not until the Eighth Army was annihilated and the Seventh Army defeated that Deng directly joined the military leadership as political commissar of the Seventh Army in September 1930.[26]

Deng had always been eager to lead the troops away from Guangxi and go north to join the main units of the Red Army in Jiangxi. The arrival of Deng Gang, another Party Centre agent, in late September 1930 reinforced Deng Xiaoping's position over the military leaders who were reluctant to move. The Front Committee held a conference in Pingma on 2 October 1930, at which a resolution was passed that the Seventh Army should follow the Centre's instructions to relocate. On its way north, the Seventh Army suffered further losses and was reduced from three divisions to two regiments in three months. The troops were separated while crossing the Li River on the Hunan–Guangdong border in early February 1931: the 55th Regiment led by Zhang Yunyi went one way and the 58th Regiment by Li Mingrui and Deng Xiaoping another.[27]

The 58th Regiment entered southern Jiangxi in March 1931 and suffered further attacks from KMT forces. Deng led a small squad to contact the local Party agents in Jiaba. On his return he found the troops had just retreated after a fierce battle. Thereupon, he wrote a note to Li Mingrui, which read: "I assume you have been engaged with the enemy and are now in retreat. As it is impossible for me to catch up with you, please fight your own way through to the Jinggang Mountains and meet

25. See "Announcement of the Guangdong Provincial Committee, 31 October 1929," in *Zuoyou Jiang geming genjudi ziliao xuanji* (*Selected Materials on the Zuoyoujiang Revolutionary Base*, hereafter *ZYJZL*) (Beijing: People's Press, 1984), p. 127. Deng Xiaoping adopted the name of Deng Bin during the Guangxi Rebellion.

26. See "CCP Centre's letter to the Front Committee of the Seventh Army, 20 April 1930," in *ZYJZL*, pp. 232–33.

27. Deng Xiaoping, "Report on the Seventh Army, 29 April 1931," in *ZYJZL*, pp. 409–415.

the Red Army there. I would like to take this opportunity to make a report to the Party Centre regarding the Seventh Army affairs."[28]

Deng then went to Canton and Hong Kong in disguise. He later arrived in Shanghai and submitted a report to the Party Centre on 29 April 1931, which, understandably, said that "the failure of the Seventh Army constitutes a failure of its general line, the focal indication of which is that everything was decided entirely on a military basis instead of according to the masses."[29] Despite his arguments, however, the 14 May letter from the Party Centre pointed to Deng as "the leader of the Front Committee" who should be held the most responsible for the mistake and defeat of the Seventh Army.[30]

There is no doubt that Deng's performance in the Seventh Army was a tragic failure and a black mark on his political career. Subsequently, Deng always avoided discussing that period of his life.[31]

Deng followed the Party Centre personnel to move to the Jiangxi soviet in August 1931, but never returned to the Seventh Army. At about the same time a score of officers of the Seventh Army, Li Mingrui included, were purged and executed in the "counter-counter-revolutionary movement." Fortunately, Deng seems not to have been directly implicated in this incident. Rather, upon arrival in the Jiangxi Soviet he was given the post of Party secretary of Ruijin county.[32]

Deng was the Director of the Propaganda Department of the CCP Jiangxi Provincial Committee in early 1933 during the "Anti-Luo Ming line" movement. Deng was criticized for sympathizing with Luo Ming in implementing "a pessimistic and abolitionist line." Together with Mao Zetan and two others, Deng was also accused of forming a

28. *Ibid.*; Yuan Renyuan, "Reminiscences of the red storms at the right river of Guangxi," in *Renmin ribao* (*People's Daily*), 9 December 1978; "Deng Xiaoping, the deserter," Red Guard pamphlet carried in Keizo Tanagi, *To Sho-hen Sho-ten* (*An Authentic Biography of Deng Xiaoping*) (Tokyo: Elite Press, 1978), pp. 41–42. Despite their differences in approach and detail, these documents all confirm the basic fact that Deng left the troops at his own discretion, not on the order of the Party or army. Surprisingly, some of the most recent Deng biographies still believe that "Deng went secretly to Shanghai to talk to the Party Centre and receive orders regarding his own future" or that "once the Seventh Red Army reached Jiangxi, Deng left Zhang Yunyi in command and headed for Shanghai." See respectively David Bonavia, *Deng* (Hong Kong: Longman Group, 1989), p. 22; and David Goodman, *Deng Xiaoping* (London: Sphere Books, 1992), p. 43.

29. Deng Xiaoping, "Report on the Seventh Army."

30. See "The CCP Centre's letter to the Front Committee of the Seventh Army, 14 May 1931," *ZYJZL*, p. 278.

31. See Han Shanbi, *Deng Xiaoping zhuanping* (*A Critical Biography of Deng Xiaoping*) (Hong Kong, 1985), pp. 107–112. "A brief history of the Seventh Red Army" was compiled under the supervision of Chen Yi in Yan'an in 1942, and alleged that "it is really inappropriate for Deng Bin to have left the troops at that crucial juncture."

32. Deng might have worked in the General Political Department upon his arrival in the Jiangxi soviet, though probably not in as high a position as its deputy director; see Sheng Ping, *Dictionary of Chinese Communists*, p. 98. Some biographers mistake Deng Xiaoping for Deng Ping, the chief of staff in Peng Dehuai's Third Army Corps; see Donald Klein and Anne Clark, *Biographic Dictionary of Chinese Communism* (Cambridge, MA: Harvard University Press, 1970), Vol. 2, p. 821.

"Deng–Mao–Xie–Gu Clique" and conducting anti-Party factionalist activities.[33]

A formal condemnation was issued at the Jiangxi Party work conference held on 16 April 1933. Deng had to submit one confession after another, but without really recanting. "First of all, I realize that I was wrong, and there is no question of that," Deng wrote in one of his confessions, "but secondly, I think that I could not have slipped into factional activities, and there is no serious problem."[34] One sees here a stubbornness and self-righteousness in Deng's personality that would mark his entire career.

To complicate matters, the KMT army seized the county seat of Xunwu. Both the Jiangxi Provincial Committee and the Central Bureau of Soviet Regions passed formal resolutions bitterly criticizing Deng and the three others. Deng was given a serious warning and dismissed from all his leading posts; he was sent to a distant village of Anyuan county as "circular inspector"; and his wife, Jin Weiying (A Jin), divorced him and married Li Weihan (Luo Mai) who had chaired the anti-Deng conferences.[35]

Deng's Star Rises, 1934–37

When the Long March began, Deng edited the army journal *Red Star* and kept records for the Military Council.[36] At the critical Zunyi Conference Deng was chosen by Zhou and accepted by Mao as record keeper.[37] This important opportunity afforded Deng *de facto* entry into the CCP elite.[38]

In early 1935 Deng was sent to the First Army Corps and put in charge of propaganda work. He remained in that position to the end of the Long March. When Edgar Snow interviewed him in mid-1936 in Gansu, Deng was reported to be deputy political commissar of the First Army Corps.[39] In November 1936 he accompanied Zhou Enlai to welcome the arrival of the Second and Fourth Front Armies and was afterwards assigned as deputy to Ren Bishi of the joint forces.[40] With the outbreak of the Sino-Japanese War in 1937 Deng was granted substantial power person-

33. Lo Pu, "The Luo Ming line in Jiangxi"; Luo Mai, "Struggle for the Party's line," in *Liuda yilai (Since the Sixth Congress)*, Vol. 1, respectively pp. 351–55 and 362–68. Lo Pu is another name of Zhang Wentian, and Luo Mai is Li Weihan.

34. See Luo Mai, "Struggle for the Party's line."

35. See Lee Ching Hua, *The Marxist Road*, p. 67; Donald Klein and Anne Clark, *Biographic Dictionary*, p 821.

36. Harrison Salisbury, *The Long March: The Untold Story* (New York: Harper & Row, 1985), pp. 136–143.

37. Benjamin Yang, *From Revolution to Politics: Chinese Communists on the Long March* (Boulder: Westview Press, 1990), pp. 107–110.

38. See *Ibid.*; Keizo Tanagi, *An Authentic Biography*, pp. 51; and David Goodman, *Deng Xiaoping*, p. 47.

39. See Edgar Snow, *Random Notes on Red China, 1936–1945* (Cambridge, MA: Harvard University Press, 1957), p. 137. The actual position of Deng at the time may have been deputy director of the political department of the First Army Corps. As a foreign journalist, Snow might not be so careful about the difference between these two positions.

40. Peng Dehuai, *Peng Dehuai zishu (Autobiography of Peng Dehuai)* (Beijing: People's Press, 1981), pp. 217–18.

ally by Mao in the Eighth Route Army. The Eighth Route Army consisted of three parts: the 115th, 120th and 129th Divisions, formed respectively on the basis of the First, Second and Fourth Front Armies of the Long March.[41] Mao was particularly concerned with the 129th Division which had originally belonged to his opponent Zhang Guotao. To mitigate Zhang Guotao's influence, in August 1937 Mao dismissed Chen Changhao as the political commissar and Xu Xiangqian as commander and substituted Zhang Hao for Chen and Liu Bocheng for Xu.[42] Zhang Hao was a Party veteran, who returned from Moscow to Northern Shaanxi in late 1935 as the Comintern representative and had worked in 1936 as the mediator between Mao and Zhang Guotao. His seniority and neutrality made him acceptable to the rank and file of the 129th Division but at the same time vulnerable to Mao's ever tighter control.[43] Mao would eventually want somebody junior to himself but persuasive enough to indoctrinate the troops. Deng was Mao's choice. In late December 1937 the Eighth Route Army Headquarters telegrammed the 129th Division Headquarters dismissing Zhang Hao as political commissar, while the Party Centre announced the appointment of Zhang as chairman of the National Labour Union Committee. Then in early January 1938, the Military Council appointed Deng political commissar of the 129th Division.[44] Mao's real purpose was to appoint Deng as his man in control of the troops without arousing too much suspicion. From Deng's point of view, the appointment meant the command of one-third of the Communist troops. He was to carry out Mao's political line and remained personally loyal to Mao for many years to come.

Battlefield as Safe Haven, 1937–49

The Eighth Route Army was under the dual leadership of Mao in the Military Council and, as military commander, Peng Dehuai. Under this joint command, a question of military strategy arose: should the Communist troops make it their first priority to fight the Japanese or to avoid fighting in order to preserve and develop their own strength? Mao favoured the latter. While the Eighth Route Army as a whole abided by Mao's strategy, Peng pushed engagement with the enemy – culminating in the "Hundred Regiments Campaign," in which all the Communist troops in North China were ordered to launch attacks on the Japanese-

41. See the Central Revolutionary Military Council, "An order for reorganizing the Red Army into the Eighth Route Army of the Nationalist Army, 25 August 1937," in *Mao Zedong ji* (*Works of Mao Zedong*) (Tokuo: Soso Press, 1984), Supplementary Vol. 5, pp. 101–102. This order appointed Deng deputy director of the Political Department of the Eighth Route Army.

42. See Lee Ching Hua, *The Marxist Road*, pp. 76–77. It is true that Mao did not quite trust Liu Bocheng either, but for different reasons.

43. Yang, *From Revolution to Politics*, pp. 207–212. Zhang Hao is better known under his real name, Lin Yuying, and was actually an uncle of Lin Biao.

44. Su Shijia, "A study of the timing of Deng Xiaoping's appointment as political commissar of the 129th Division of the Eighth Route Army," in *Dangshi tongxun*, No. 34 (1987), quoted in Ban Yang and Zhuo Xiaowei, "White cat or black cat," pp. 62–63, 74.

occupied cities and railways from August to December 1940.[45] Mao received the news of the Hundred Regiments Campaign with mixed feelings. Publicly he sent a telegram to congratulate Peng for this victorious campaign, but at the same time he was deeply worried about the loss of personnel.[46] Deng did not take an active role in the Hundred Regiments Campaign. But neither did he object to Liu Bocheng and the 129th Division participating in the campaign at the time nor complain about Peng Dehuai to the Eighth Route Army headquarters for initiating it. Deng's only comment was that "both the enemy and our own troops suffered considerable losses [in the campaign], with the former larger than the latter by a ratio of 9:7."[47]

In 1942 the Rectification Movement started in Yan'an and soon spread to the entire Party and army. Many high cadres fell as its victims, but Deng did not suffer any attack or criticism.[48] His position as a battle-front commander actually protected him. Some in the Party tried to attack Deng by raising his involvement in the Seventh Army Incident and adherence to the Li Lisan line, but without success.

From 1942 onward, as a result of the Hundred Regiments Campaign and the Rectification Movement which greatly reduced the authority of the Eighth Route Army headquarters, and also because the Sino-Japanese War entered the "phase of protracted stalemate" in which military affairs gave way to political issues, Deng came even more directly under Mao's authority and enjoyed more independence. His writings of that period deal with general Party policies such as governmental administration, land reform, mass organization, economic production, political propaganda and education.[49] It was his responsibility as well as privilege to make regular reports to the Party Centre. He was called back to Yan'an more frequently than other leaders, and would spend long nights in Mao's cave, chatting about personal and political matters. A special relationship of mutual trust and reliance was firmly established between them.

Deng was regarded as a Party man in the eyes of the troops, but simultaneously as a military man in the eyes of the Party Centre leaders. Needless to say, his duty was to keep the political orientation of the army in line with the Party or, more bluntly, to keep an eye on the military for

45. See He Li *et al.*, *Baituan dazhan shiliao* (*Historical Materials on the One Hundred Regiment Campaign*) (Beijing: People's Press, 1982), pp. 10–50. Reading through the various documents contained in this book, one gets a sense that the military commanders were actively for the campaign whereas the political officers seemed less enthusiastic.

46. See Peng Dehuai, *Autobiography*, pp. 234–243.

47. See Deng Xiaoping, "A brief summary of the past five years' struggle with the enemy," in *Deng Xiaoping wenxuan, 1937–1965* (*Selected Works of Deng Xiaoping, 1937– 1965*, hereafter *DX*) (Beijing: People's Press, 1989), p. 35.

48. See James Harrison, *The Long March to Power* (New York: Praeger Publishers, 1972), p. 344.

49. As always, Deng treated the Party and army's policies from a practical point of view: "What does revolution mean? It means to fight against imperialism and feudalism with the latter as the foundation of the former. If we don't fight against feudalism and carry out land reform, we cannot sustain this protracted war, and we cannot succeed in making the revolution." See Deng Xiaoping, "Situations after successfully entering the Central Plain and strategic policies for the future, 25 April 1948," in *DX*, p. 102.

Mao. Deng Xiaoping played this role skilfully, so as not to hinder the work and bruise the feelings of Liu Bocheng and others. Deng also maintained a good relationship of mutual respect and dependence with Liu.[50] It was Liu who was trusted to plan and wage battles.

As the 129th Division advanced militarily and territorially Deng's position grew accordingly in the Party, army and government. Apart from being the political commissar of the 129th division, he concurrently held, among others, the position of secretary of the Taihang Sub-bureau of the Party Centre in the Jin-Ji-Lu-Yu base area. At the Seventh Congress in 1945, Deng was elevated to be a high-ranking member of the Central Committee.[51]

In the wake of the Sino-Japanese War, the civil war between the CCP and KMT continued unabated. Neither of the parties, especially their leaders Mao and Chiang, really believed in any possibility of a peaceful solution at all. While the Chongqing negotiations were still in progress in September 1945, the 129th Division under Liu and Deng started and won the Shangdang Battle in which 30,000 KMT troops were annihilated. For this extraordinary action Liu and Deng won accolades from Mao and the Party Centre.[52]

The first year of the civil war was marked by the Nationalist attack on Communist base areas, especially in southern Shandong and northern Shaanxi from June 1946 to June 1947. To break the deadlock of the KMT attack, Mao and the Military Council favoured a strategy of dispatching troops to thrust deep into enemy territory. Deng carried out such a strategy skilfully. On 30 July 1947, Deng telegraphed Mao at the Military Council: "We have decided to take a half-month's respite and preparation before starting off according to the general strategy.... It is better for us not just to stay at the Yu-Wan-Su border, but to move further ahead to the Dabie Mountains, in order to form a pincer position with the Chen-Xie Corps and create broader and wider mobility. We are ready for striking out far from the rear." The very same day, Deng received Mao's positive response: "If you are determined to leave the rear areas and fight into the Dabie Mountains, we will make sure Chen and Xie have the same determination."[53] A few days later when Deng telegraphed Mao to inform him about the troops' departure, Mao's return message on 10 August 1947 was simple and clear: "You are absolutely right!"[54] As it later proved, the Liu–Deng operation in the Dabie Mountains marked a turning point for the Communist troops, turning a defensive posture to an offensive one.

After two years of engagement, the civil war reached the final stage.

50. Deng said, "For the last five years, we both lived and worked together. We shared the same feelings, and our working relations were also very good." See Deng Xiaoping, "Celebrate Comrade Liu Bocheng's 50th birthday," in *DX*, p. 30.

51. See Wang Jianying, *Zhongguo Gongchandang zushi shiliao huibian* (*Historical Materials of the CCP Organization*) (Beijing: Red Flag Press, 1980), pp. 576–590.

52. Mao Zedong, "On the Chongqing negotiations," in *Mao Zedong xuanji* (*Selected Works of Mao Zedong*) (Beijing: People's Press, 1969, combined volume), p. 1055.

53. See Li Xinzi and Wang Yuezong, *Great Practices and Glorious Thought*, pp. 61–62.

54. *Ibid.*

The KMT forces had lost their offensive momentum and were fast collapsing on all fronts. The focal problem for the military leaders of the Red Army was therefore less one of tactics than of strategic initiatives.

In the grand showdown with the KMT in 1948, the Communist forces were reorganized into four "field armies": the first under Peng Dehuai in the north-west, the second under Liu Bocheng and Deng Xiaoping in the Central Plain, the third under Chen Yi in the east and the fourth under Lin Biao in the north-east. Mao conferred with Chen Yi in June 1948 and decided that the Vice-Commander of the Third Field Army, Su Yu, should lead two army corps of 200,000 to cross the Yangzi into south China behind KMT lines, thus dividing the KMT troops in order to defeat them separately. Instead of accepting his role of marching to the south, Su Yu went to see Mao in person to argue for concentrating the main Communist forces to wipe out the KMT troops north of the Yangzi. Mao was persuaded to change his mind. To make Su's plan easier, Mao transferred Chen Yi temporarily to the Second Field Army and appointed Su Yu as acting commander and political commissar in full charge of the Third Field Army.[55]

Su Yu's strategic proposal to concentrate all forces to fight the KMT troops north of the Yangzi River was eventually realized in the form of the famous Huai-Hai Campaign, in which the combined forces of the Second and Third Field Armies wiped out 550,000 KMT troops in two months from November 1948 to January 1949. In the execution of this campaign, a five-man "General Front Committee" was appointed with Deng Xiaoping as secretary and Liu Bocheng, Chen Yi, Tan Zhenlin and Su Yu as its other members.[56]

Regardless of the Beijing peace talks between the Communists and the Nationalist government, Deng had been busily preparing the river crossing campaign ever since his return from the Second Plenum of the Party Centre in March 1949.[57] He maintained his position as the secretary of the General Front Committee during the river crossing campaign, which took place in April 1949 and resulted in the Communists' capture of the Nationalists' capital at Nanjing and routing of the Nationalist regime.

The formation of the General Front Committee by Mao was based on complicated political, military and personal considerations. The appointment of the younger Deng as its secretary, above Party and army veterans like Liu and Chen, reflected Deng's close relations with Mao.

55. Zhou Hongyan and Yuan Wei, "Investigation on 12 questions about the Huai-Hai Campaign," *Dangshi tongxun*, No. 4 (1985), in Ban Yang and Zhuo Xiaowei, "White cat or black cat," pp. 70, 74.

56. See *Zhongguo gongchandang shigao* (*A Draft History of the Chinese Communist Party*) (Beijing: People's Press, 1985, compiled by the Central Party School), Vol. 4, pp. 144–48.

57. Deng Xiaoping, "Outline operation of the Jing-Hu-Hang Campaign, 31 March 1949," in *DX*, p. 120. Deng's plan was immediately approved by the Military Council on 3 April 1949, which shows that the peace negotiations sponsored by the CCP with the KMT in Beijing on 1–20 April 1949 were just for propaganda purposes. Deng seemed again to have an appropriate understanding of Mao Zedong's thought – its Machiavellian part more than its Marxian part.

Deng took little operational command in either the Huai-Hai Campaign or river crossing campaign.[58] Nevertheless, these military successes brought him great military merit and political capital.

Thus in the course of 12 years the troops under Liu's and Deng's leadership grew from the 129th Division of 6,000 men active only in a few counties in 1937 to the Second Field Army of more than 1,000,000 covering a dozen provinces in 1949. As Deng's accomplishments accumulated, his reputation and influence among the Party Centre was firmly established.[59]

The consistent military successes as well as his own steadfast promotions had created in Deng belief in and reliance on Mao. Close working relations between them were exhibited during wartime and were to continue in the post-liberation years.[60]

Conclusions

It may be too simplistic to apply a retrospective approach to explain somebody's present behaviour entirely on the basis of his past experience. But if Deng is a pragmatic Communist, this personality trait can surely be traced back many decades.

Deng came from a landlord family and was greatly influenced by his father who himself held a kind of pragmatist philosophy. Following a course in search of "sagehood," Deng went to Chongqing and Paris to pursue further studies and eventually to Moscow to become a professional revolutionary. He joined the Communist revolution when it became a popular trend, and he converted to Communism more for personal than ideological reasons. For better or for worse, Deng was never devoted to Communist doctrines from the start, thus making it much easier for him to shake them off at the end.

Deng believed in the Communist revolution as long as it worked well, not only for China and the Chinese people in a broad and abstract sense, but also for himself and his coterie in a more narrow, concrete and subjective sense. Throughout his pre-1949 career Deng Xiaoping developed the traits of a pragmatic Communist, traits that would guide his career and reformist philosophy.

58. See Bonavia, *Deng*, pp. 39–60. Bonavia covers Deng's military experiences with a chapter title of "Strategist." I would suggest that Deng's role was one of political control more than military command, either strategic or tactical.

59. Zhang Guoqi and Li Guoxiang, *Zhongguo renmin jiefangjun fazhan yange* (*Development of the Chinese People's Liberation Army*), (Beijing: People's Liberation Army Press, 1984), pp. 167–69.

60. As for the close relations between Mao and Deng in wartime, see the numerous telegram exchanges between them cited in Li Xinzhi and Wang Yuezong, *Great Practices and Glorious Thought*, pp. 58–90, particularly in the years 1947–49. It should be pointed out that their relationship had always been a delicate mixture of subjective and objective factors, and the practical failures of the Great Leap Forward caused changes in Deng's attitude towards Mao.

Deng Xiaoping: The Politician*

David Shambaugh

"Deng Xiaoping is a man who excels in political affairs, and very few people can match him in that respect."

"Deng is a rare talent. He is known in both military and civilian circles for this. He is like a needle wrapped in cotton. He has ideas. He does not confront problems head-on. He can deal with difficult problems with responsibility. His mind is round and his actions are square."

Mao Zedong[1]

The Contradictions of Deng Xiaoping

Any politician with a career as long and diverse as Deng Xiaoping defies simple designation. Deng Xiaoping the politician has been a complex figure. He has embodied contradictory tendencies and beliefs.

While Deng was a comprehensive reformer, there were limits to each of his reforms. His intolerance of liberalism and direct challenges to Communist Party political hegemony always co-existed with his desire to loosen the Party's control over the economy. It was Deng, an old-style Party organization man reared on the Soviet model of commandist rule, who personally initiated the process of political reform during the 1980s, only to recoil and tighten the Party's grip on the instruments of coercive power in the 1990s. He would not balk at the necessity of using force or coercion in certain instances, yet did much to curtail the arbitrary repression of the Maoist era and enliven the social and professional lives of Chinese from many walks of life. Dramatically improving the standard of living and diversity of life for one-fifth of the world's population, while denying them fundamental political and human rights, will no doubt be Deng's most enduring legacy. In policy-making Deng was pragmatic and made the deals necessary to achieve his domestic goals, yet was often uncompromising in statecraft when he perceived matters of principle and national interest to be at stake. He was consistent in advocating economic reform that adopted market methods, yet he still sought protection of the state sector. Like Gorbachev, Deng believed in

*Aspects of this article were previously presented at Keio University (Tokyo), Institut Francais des Relations Internationales (Paris), the Association of Asian Studies Annual Meeting (Los Angeles), the University of California (Berkeley), and the School of Oriental and African Studies (London). I gratefully acknowledge the many useful comments and suggestions offered by participants at these sessions. I also particularly wish to thank Kenneth Lieberthal, Frederick Teiwes and Gordon White for their trenchant comments on a previous draft. The British Academy/Economic & Social Research Council of the United Kingdom and the School of Oriental & African Studies (University of London) provided funding for research in China on this project, where the Institute of Marxism–Leninism–Mao Zedong Thought of the Chinese Academy of Social Sciences served as my host. I also wish to thank Katie Jukes and Hu Hang for their research assistance. Final judgments and errors are, of course, my own.
1. First quotation from "late 1974" as cited in Department for Research on Party Literature of the Central Committee of the Chinese Communist Party and Xinhua News Agency (eds.), *Deng Xiaoping* (Beijing: Central Party Literature Publishers, 1988), p. 93; second quotation, undated, cited in Harrison Salisbury, *The New Emperors* (Boston: Little, Brown, 1992), p. 328.

socialism and Communist Party supremacy, although he did much to undermine both.

Like so many other Chinese reformers dating from the late Qing dynasty, Deng sought to borrow a variety of methods and technologies from foreign nations and graft them to indigenous structures. Yet what sets Deng apart from his reformist predecessors is that he was able to break out of the confines of the *ti-yong* strategy of selective borrowing (*yong*) while attempting to protect Chinese cultural essence (*ti*). Deng was far more prepared to import anything that would enrich China's productive base without much concern for its corrosive effect on Chinese culture. His Four Cardinal Principles notwithstanding, Deng adopted eclectic methods in his attempt to lift China out of poverty and its feudal past and deliver it into the modern era, with all the attendant accoutrements of great power status.

Studying Deng Xiaoping's Political Behaviour

This article examines Deng's political behaviour over time in order to explain this complexity. It intentionally does not adopt the approach of analysing Deng's policy pronouncements on various issues as indicative of his political style, as there is frequently a disjuncture between word and deed among politicians world-wide. In some cases Deng's speeches[2] do reflect the *content* of his political programme and philosophy and they will be drawn upon in such cases, but on the whole the aim is to study Deng's political *behaviour*: his administrative workstyle, policy agenda, strategies and tactics of rule, sources and uses of power, interactions with colleagues, subordinates and would-be successors, and methods of decision-making and policy implementation. This multi-factor analysis requires studying different periods and events in Deng's career, drawing upon multiple sources of information.[3] A straightforward chronological

2. Bureau for the Compilation and Translation of Works of Marx, Engels, Lenin and Stalin Under the Central Committee of the Communist Party of China, *Selected Works of Deng Xiaoping (1975–1982)* (Beijing: Foreign Languages Press, 1984); and *Deng Xiaoping wenxuan (1938–1965)* (*Selected Works of Deng Xiaoping*) (Beijing: Renmin chubanshe, 1989); Deng Xiaoping, *Fundamental Issues in Present-Day China* (Beijing: Foreign Languages Press, 1987); Deng Xiaoping, *Lun dang de jianshe* (*Theory of Party Building*) (Beijing: Renmin chubanshe, 1990).

3. Many of these sources are primary data, but use has also been made of the existing biographies of Deng. In English these include Uli Franz, *Deng Xiaoping: China's Reformer* (New York: Harcourt, Brace, Jovanovich, 1989); David Bonavia, *Deng* (Hong Kong: Longman, 1989); David Goodman, *Deng Xiaoping* (London: Sphere Books, Ltd., 1990); Salisbury, *The New Emperors*; Chung Hua Lee, *Deng Xiaoping: The Marxist Road to the Forbidden City* (Princeton: Kingston Press, 1985); and Chi Hsin, *Teng Hsiao-ping: A Political Biography* (Hong Kong: Cosmos Books, 1978). Biographies in Chinese include: Department for Research on Party Literature of the Central Committee of the CCP and Xinhua News Agency, *Deng Xiaoping*; Department for Research on Party Literature of the Central Committee of the CCP, *Deng Xiaoping zhanlue* (*The Strategy of Deng Xiaoping*) (Beijing: Renmin chubanshe, 1988); Han Shanbi, *Deng Xiaoping pingzhuan* (*A Critical Biography of Deng Xiaoping*), Vols. 1–3 (Hong Kong: East and West Culture Company, 1984, 1987, 1988); Balike Daineishi, *Deng Xiaoping* (translated from Hungarian) (Beijing: Jiefangjun chubanshe, 1988); Zhou Xun, *Deng Xiaoping* (Hong Kong: Guangjiaojing chubanshe, 1983); Lin Qingshan, *Fengyun shinian yu Deng Xiaoping* (*A Stormy Ten Years*

approach will not suffice analytically, although it might reveal a learning curve in the conclusions that Deng drew from previous experiences for his subsequent workstyle.[4]

The focus is therefore on Deng as an individual politician. While his political behaviour must be viewed in the context of his time in power, this is not necessarily an essay on the Deng *era* in Chinese politics (1978 onward), his reform programme, or even his political legacy from this period.[5] Deng's career in Chinese Communist politics has spanned more than six decades, and his entire professional record is the subject of this analysis. However, because Benjamin Yang's contribution to this volume concentrates on Deng's pre-1949 years, and others assess Deng along a variety of other professional dimensions, this analysis is largely limited to Deng's post-1949 political career.

As the other assessments attest, Deng's career was professionally diverse – working on Communist Party political and organizational matters, the economy, social policy, foreign relations, military affairs, science, technology and educational issues. This professional diversity gave him substantive experience in a variety of issue areas, accumulating the skills of a political generalist necessary for advancement to the pinnacle of Chinese Communist politics.[6] Once at the top Deng displayed

---

footnote continued

with *Deng Xiaoping*) (Beijing: Jiefangjun chubanshe, 1989); Yang Guoya *et al.*, *Ershibanian qian: cong shi zhengwei dao zongshuji* (*Twenty-Eight Years: From City Government Committee to General Secretary*) (Shanghai: Wenyi chubanshe, 1989); Yang Pengyu, *Weidade gaigejia Deng Xiaoping* (*The Great Revolutionary Deng Xiaoping*) (Beijing: Zhongguo xinwen chubanshe, 1989); Yao Chuanwang *et al.*, *Deng Xiaoping zhuzuo zhuanti yanjiu* (*Specialized Research Topics on Deng Xiaoping's Writings*) (Beijing: Renmin chubanshe, 1988); Yang Chunchang, *Deng Xiaoping xin shiqi jianjun sixiang yanjiu* (*Research on Deng Xiaoping's Army-Building Thought During the New Period*) (Beijing: Jiefangjun chubanshe, 1989); Gao Zhiyu and Li Yanqi (eds.), *Deng Xiaoping yu dangdai Zhongguo gaige* (*Deng Xiaoping and Contemporary Chinese Reforms*) (Beijing: Zhongguo renmin daxue chubanshe, 1990); Yao Ping (ed.), *Xin shiqi Deng Xiaoping zhanlue sixiang yanjiu* (*Research on Deng Xiaoping's Strategic Thinking During the New Period*) (Shaanxi: Renmin chubanshe, 1989); Jin Yu and Chen Xiankui, *Dangdai Zhongguo dasilu* (*The Great Theoretical Road of Contemporary China*) (Beijing: Zhongguo renmin daxue chubanshe, 1989); Qing Ye and Fang Lei, *Deng Xiaoping zai 1976* (*Deng Xiaoping in 1976*) (Shenyang: Chunfeng wenyi chubanshe, 1993).

4. For two extremely useful chronologies of Deng's life and career see: Li Xinzhi and Wang Yuezong, *Weidade shixian, guanghui de sixiang: Deng Xiaoping geming huodong dashiji* (*Great Achievements, Brilliant Thought: Chronology of Deng Xiaoping's Revolutionary Activities*) (Beijing: Hualing chubanshe, 1990); and Zhong Hao (ed.), *Deng Xiaoping de lilun yu shixian zonglan, 1938–1965* (*Broad Views on Deng Xiaoping's Theories and Practice*) (Shenyang: Liaoning renmin chubanshe, 1991).

5. To some extent this is done in the other contributions to this volume, but also see Michel Oksenberg, "The Deng era's uncertain political legacy," in Kenneth Lieberthal *et al.* (eds.), *Perspectives on Modern China* (Armonk, NY: M. E. Sharpe, 1991), pp. 309–340.

6. This is a characteristic noted as generally necessary for upward mobility in Chinese elite politics. See, for example, David M. Lampton, *Paths to Power: Elite Mobility in Contemporary China* (Ann Arbor: Michigan Monographs on Chinese Studies, Vol. 55, 1986); Michel Oksenberg and Yeung Sai-cheung, "Hua Guofeng's pre-Cultural Revolution Hunan years, 1949–1966: the making of a political generalist," *The China Quarterly*, No. 69 (March 1977), pp. 3–53; David Shambaugh, *The Making of a Premier: Zhao Ziyang's Provincial Career* (Boulder: Westview Press, 1984), ch. 7.

some similar tendencies to China's previous pre-eminent leader, Mao Zedong,[7] which, as well as the differences, will be contrasted.

Three Paradigms of Analysis

This analysis of Deng's political behaviour draws upon three paradigms, each of which emphasizes different dimensions of leadership style. These models provide a useful framework to study Deng as an individual politician, and in addition it is hoped the case study will be able to refine them in a Chinese and comparative context. It is important to note at the outset that these approaches to studying elite political behaviour are not mutually exclusive; just as leaders employ different methods of rule simultaneously so too must analysts employ different paradigms in tandem.

The first paradigm is the traditional "power base" approach. This method is useful for analysing how a politician moves up through the organizational hierarchies (Party, Army, State) and develops a leadership domain. In China, it is argued that power bases are of four principal varieties: credentialist, personal, institutional and territorial. A *credentialist* power base derives from a politician's rise through the ranks. How was he recruited; how did he rise to the top of the system; what skills and credentials did he amass along the way; what were his defining socializing experiences, and what effect did they have on his subsequent elite mobility and political style? *Personal* power bases in the Chinese political system are of two principal types: patron–client and issue-based factional networks. *Institutional* power bases in China are rooted in the Party, state and military bureaucracies. Lastly, with a *territorial* power base, power derives from particular regions of the country.

The second paradigm is the "paramount leader" approach. This is a term often used to describe Deng, particularly insofar as he never held the official portfolio of President, Chairman or General Secretary of the Communist Party, or Premier of the State Council, although he did serve as General Secretary of the Central Committee, Chairman of the Central Military Commission, and Vice-Premier of the State Council. This approach seeks to understand Deng's style as supreme leader of the nation, even though he did not hold the paramount official positions. It is perhaps more appropriate to describe Deng's role as a patriarch, not unlike a Mafia godfather ruling from behind the scenes through a network of loyal lieutenants.[8] But the question here is not so much whether Deng was a paramount leader or patriarch, but how he exercised supreme authority.

7. For studies of Mao's political style see Richard Solomon, *Mao's Revolution and the Chinese Political Culture* (Berkeley: University of California Press, 1971); Lucian W. Pye, *Mao Tse-tung: The Man in the Leader* (New York: Basic Books, 1976); Michel Oksenberg, "Mao's policy commitments, 1921–1976," *Problems of Communism* (November–December 1976), pp. 1–26; Michel Oksenberg, "The political leader," in Dick Wilson (ed.), *Mao Tse-tung in the Scales of History* (Cambridge: Cambridge University Press, 1977), pp. 70–116.

8. See Lucian Pye's contribution for an extended discussion of this aspect of Deng's style of rule.

Did he have a dictatorial style – issuing commands, ruling by fiat, intervening in a variety of policy arenas when he saw fit, and brooking no opposition? Or did he act more as an arbiter – standing above the fray, reconciling competing interests, seeking conflicting opinions, and entering into the policy process in order to resolve stalemate? Did he adopt a consensual and collective decision-making style that played down conflict among subordinates, instead seeking consensus and the most rational choice of policy alternatives? Or did he utilize a combination of these methods at different times? These questions are examined in contra-distinction to China's other paramount leader, Mao Zedong.

The third paradigm focuses on agenda-setting. It is an approach that examines the national political agenda, and looks both at its content and at the degree to which a given leader sets that agenda. How did Deng seek to set the national agenda, what were his methods for doing so and how successful was he? If rival elites "captured" the agenda or moved in a direction not to Deng's liking, how did he respond? How did he seek to regain the initiative? Did he work through bureaucratic channels? Did he call a Politburo meeting to make his case? Did he, as Mao often did, appeal directly to the masses when he encountered resistance at the top? In general, did Deng favour an institutionalist, populist, or machiavellian approach, or some combination thereof? This paradigm also explores ways in which a leader manipulates the agenda to pursue specific political goals. For example, can issues and policies be used to bolster political allies or undermine enemies?

An integral part of the agenda-setting paradigm is how a leader bargains and builds a coalition to adopt and implement a given policy or package of policies. Only in the most totalitarian of political systems is policy decided by the complete dominance of the supreme leader and implemented by a subservient bureaucracy. In most political systems – including authoritarian socialist ones – leaders must lobby their colleagues and subordinates to support their policy initiatives. They must build, in William Riker's phrase, "winning coalitions."[9] Bargaining is necessary to build elite coalitions to adopt policy, but also to implement it at national, regional and local levels. A recent emphasis in studying Chinese politics adopts this approach and argues that in a system characterized by "fragmented authoritarianism" bargaining is *the* defining characteristic of political life and takes place at every level of the system.[10]

To what degree does Deng Xiaoping fit this bargaining paradigm? What trade-offs did he make at key junctures to have his policies adopted and implemented? Who did he bargain with and what was the quid pro quo? Of importance in this context are the channels of policy implementation that Deng preferred. Did Deng prefer to work through traditional

9. William H. Riker, *The Theory of Political Coalitions* (New Haven: Yale University Press, 1962).
10. See, for example, Kenneth G. Lieberthal and David M. Lampton (eds.), *Bureaucracy, Politics, and Decision Making in Post-Mao China* (Berkeley: University of California Press, 1992).

bureaucratic hierarchies (*xitong*); did he adopt the campaign (*yundong*) style of his predecessor Mao; did he use a "test point" (*shi dian*) approach; did he discharge responsibility to a cluster of key advisers; or did he even concern himself with issues of implementation?

These three paradigms and their constituent parts offer a framework to dissect and analyse Deng Xiaoping's career in the Chinese political system. By examining them sequentially it will be possible to ascertain which have the greatest explanatory value, and in what combination Deng employed different stratagems and tactics, drew upon different sets of political resources and established patterns of interaction with other elites.

Deng Xiaoping's Power Bases

The Right Revolutionary Credentials

Deng Xiaoping belonged to the first generation of Chinese Communist revolutionary elites (*lao yidai de gemingjia*). This fact alone may be the most important of all power bases as it confers a legitimacy that other more objective measures cannot match. Mere participation in the epic events of the Chinese revolutionary struggle and the personal ties Deng forged with other leading CCP figures in the process guaranteed him a place among the elite once political power had been attained.

Deng Xiaoping[11] joined the Chinese Communist Party in 1924[12] at the age of 20 while working in a Renault factory in Billancourt, France. While in France Deng established one working partnership that would help shape his entire career – with Zhou Enlai. Zhou helped recruit Deng into the CCP and became a life-long patron, although Mao proved more central to Deng's political ascent. Zhou was quick to recognize Deng's organizational abilities. When Zhou returned to Guangzhou from Paris in 1924, he entrusted the publication of the French cell of the General European Branch of the CCP, *Red Light*, to Deng. Deng had no experience as an editor or writer, but was well-versed in the mechanics of early "desk top" publishing. *Red Light* was printed in mimeograph form, and Deng acquired the *nom de plume* "Docteur du Duplication." Another colleague of Deng's Parisian days was Li Weihan, a notable CCP figure who later worked closely with Deng on united front matters, and upon

11. Deng's given name at birth was Deng Bin. In France he went by Deng Xixian. There is some discrepancy as to when he changed it to Xiaoping. In many of his Western biographies (e.g. Goodman) it is dated from 1925, but one chronological biography dates it specifically as June 1927 in Wuhan so that he could maintain a false identity and hide from local Kuomintang police; see Li Xinzhi and Wang Yuezong, *Weidade shixian*, p. 6. For a discussion of Deng's Hakka origins and early life in Sichuan see Benjamin Yang's contribution to this volume and Mary Erbaugh, "The secret history of the Hakkas: the Chinese revolution as a Hakka enterprise," *The China Quarterly*, No. 132 (December 1992), pp. 937–968.

12. Deng had previously been a member of the Chinese Communist Youth Party in Europe as well as the French Communist Party; Li Xinzhi and Wang Yuezong, *Weidade shixian*, pp. 3–4. Also see Nora Wong, "Deng Xiaoping: the years in France," *The China Quarterly*, No. 92 (December 1982), pp. 698–705. Wong's is the most complete account of this period in Deng's life, and is based on French archival sources.

whom Deng called to direct this sphere when he reorganized the Central Committee Secretariat in 1956.[13]

Deng left Paris for Moscow in January 1926, travelling via Berlin. He stayed nearly a year studying Marxism–Leninism at the University of the Toilers of the East and Sun Yat-sen University.[14] However he was never really fond of the classroom or Marxist theory, and after eight years abroad was anxious to return to make a more practical contribution to the revolution in his native land. In his absence the Republic had been further fractured by rival warlords and a sense of crisis gripped the nation.

Deng returned to China in early 1927, apparently accompanying the warlord Feng Yuxiang (the "Christian General").[15] Feng was at that time co-operating with the KMT–CCP united front, and he headed the Sun Yat-sen Military Academy in Xi'an. He was in Moscow in search of Comintern funding for the Academy. Deng returned to Feng's Academy and was put in charge of political training. He organized political training for officers, thus beginning a long involvement with commissar work in the armed forces, and was also appointed resident Communist Party secretary at the Academy. Following the April 1927 Shanghai massacre and abrogation of the first CCP–KMT united front, Feng Yuxiang purged his forces of known and suspected Communists in an effort to show his support for Chiang Kai-shek. Deng was one of over 50 CCP members expelled from the Academy, but whose lives were spared (one can speculate that it was Feng's Christianity that prevented him from following Chiang Kai-shek's 1927 reign of white terror).

Deng then made his way south to Hankou. Thus began his inclusion in the inner circle of CCP leaders. At first, he was appointed as a lowly secretary of the Central Committee, but his rank and stature grew rapidly. By the end of the summer of 1927, following the secret relocation of the Party headquarters to Shanghai, Deng was appointed chief secretary (*zong mishu*) for the Central Committee. This was a plum assignment for Deng as he was responsible for handling all inner-party "documents, orders, communications and assignments."[16] It also gave him the opportunity to renew acquaintance with Zhou Enlai and other comrades from his Parisian days as well as to meet other key CCP leaders for the first time.

13. Deng and Li also had their differences, including the fact that Li apparently persuaded Deng's first wife to leave him. Having divorced, Jin Weiying (A Jin) and Li Weihan (Lo Man) had Li Tieying – whom Deng has promoted in high Party councils in recent years.

14. Both "universities" were established by the Comintern for the purpose of training would-be revolutionaries. The former was intended for those from the Middle East and Asia, while the latter was headed by Comintern agent Pavel Mif and established with Comintern funds in 1925 specifically to train young Chinese radicals (both Communists and Nationalists) in the theoretical and practical tools of revolution. Many of the so-called "28 Bolsheviks" who returned to China to constitute the "internationalist" wing of the Party studied there, but it is unclear what – if any – relations Deng had with them. One key "returned Bolshevik" was Yang Shangkun, with whom Deng would subsequently forge close ties, who arrived at the university a year after Deng's departure.

15. Not coincidentally, Deng had befriended Feng's daughter when classmates in Moscow. Li Xinzhi and Wang Yuezong date Deng's return as March 1927.

16. Li Xinzhi and Wang Yuezong, *Weidade shixian*, p. 6.

Deng's sensitive work quickly brought him to the attention of Mao Zedong.

Following the "white terror" of 1927 and split in the CCP leadership in 1928 the Party went underground, but Mao's faction fled Shanghai to establish the Jingganshan base area (*genjudi*) in the central mountains of Jiangxi province. Deng arrived in Jingganshan in October 1930 after spending much of 1929 in Guangxi trying to organize peasant uprisings. On the way he joined the guerrilla forces of Peng Dehuai and participated in the August 1930 Changsha Uprising. Perhaps as a reward for his role in the Changsha seizure, Deng was appointed Party secretary of Ruijin district in 1931, and subsequently secretary of the Jiangxi provincial committee. This brought him into close contact with Mao. Deng chose to support Mao at the stormy Ruijin meeting of 1932 when the latter came under sharp attack by Comintern agents and the urban-oriented, internationalist wing of the Party. Deng's support at this juncture was of key importance to his subsequent career. Deng was censured along with Mao following the meeting and again in 1933 after the Luo Ming affair. As a result of both, in January 1934 at the Fifth Plenum of the Sixth Central Committee, Deng endured the first of three purges in his career as he was denounced together with Lu Dingyi for engaging in "anti-Party factionalism" and was relieved of his post as Ruijin Party secretary. There are conflicting accounts of Deng's actual fate in the wake of Ruijin, but he apparently spent some time incarcerated.[17] Mao was not to forget Deng's allegiance at these crucial junctures, and his subsequent patronage of Deng can clearly be traced to Ruijin.

When the Communist forces embarked on the Long March in 1934 Deng was designated secretary-general of the General Political Department (GPD) of the First Front Army. In this capacity he served as editor of the Party journal *Red Star* and oversaw propaganda work among the troops. Little is known about Deng's activities on the Long March beyond the fact that he served in the GPD of the First Army Corps (under Lin Biao and Nie Rongzhen) and then the reorganized Eighth Route Army (under Ren Bishi). Deng was one of the 4,000 weary soldiers to reach Yan'an in early 1937. En route he participated in the important Zunyi meeting in his new capacity as secretary of the Central Committee (*Zhonggong zhongyang mishuzhang*). He dutifully sat in the corner as designated note-taker at this pivotal meeting.[18] After Zunyi, the remainder of the march was unremarkable for Deng (who rode rather than walked), except that he fell ill with typhoid fever in Shaanxi.[19]

The Japanese invasion of China in 1937 occasioned an important period in Deng's career, *the* pivotal phase according to David Goodman.[20]

17. For interesting, if not necessarily accurate, accounts of the Ruijin affair and Deng's fate, based on participants' reminiscences (including Yang Shangkun), see Harrison Salisbury, *The Long March: The Untold Story* (New York: Harper & Row, 1985), pp. 139–142; and *The New Emperors*, pp. 40–43.

18. *Ibid.*; and interview with Mao's former secretary Li Rui, 1 June 1993.

19. *Ibid.*. p. 143.

20. Goodman, *Deng Xiaoping*, pp. 47–53.

Deng's experience in the Taihang base area in the Shanxi-Hebei region was important, Goodman argues, because it brought him into close association with other key elites (notably Liu Bocheng), and also because of his economic programme of putting "production first."[21] Deng's ties to Liu Bocheng would last a lifetime, and the "Liu–Deng forces" would become an important part of CCP and PLA lore. Liu and Deng subsequently commanded the famous 129th division which defeated Nationalist troops in the decisive Huai-Hai campaign of the civil war. Thereafter, known as the Second Field Army, they pushed southward to rout Chiang Kai-shek's forces along the middle and upper reaches of the Yangzi River, and then together with forces commanded by He Long "liberated" all of south-western China – Sichuan, Guizhou, Sikang and Yunnan.

Thus by the time the CCP came to power in 1949 Deng Xiaoping had already experienced a varied career in Party and military affairs, and had built up an important network of colleagues and patrons among the CCP senior elite.[22] His revolutionary credentials were impeccable: working in the CCP underground at home and abroad, especially in organizational and propaganda affairs, and commanding Red Army forces.

Deng's Personal Power Base: Patrons, Clients and Colleagues

Many of the personal ties Deng forged during the revolutionary struggle endured after 1949 and generally served him well in subsequent years. Both Mao and Zhou Enlai promoted Deng at different times, but his ties to other first-generation revolutionary elites also proved important.

Mao Zedong and Zhou Enlai. Mao was Deng's principal patron throughout his career. He was primarily responsible for Deng's ascent from Ruijin until the early 1970s. Mao saw to it that Deng was given important military commands during the civil war, and put him in charge of the sensitive South-west Administrative Region (*Xi-Nan Xingzheng Qu*) in 1950. Mao also sanctioned Deng's transfer to the Centre in July 1952, after which he was appointed successively as Vice-Premier, Vice-Chairman of the Finance and Economic Commission, and member of the State Planning Commission (all in 1952), Minister of Finance (1953), Secretary-General of the Central Committee Secretariat and Director of the CCP Organization Department (1954).

Following the debacle of the Great Leap, Zhou and Deng began to work more closely together in fashioning the economic recovery programme. Deng's working relations with Chen Yun, Liu Shaoqi and Peng Zhen also became closer during this period, although they had worked

21. See the excellent analysis in David S. G. Goodman, "The construction of the party-state in Jin-Ji-Lu-Yu, 1937–1945," paper presented at the conference on "Construction of the Party-State and State Socialism in China, 1936–1965," Colorado College, June 1993.
22. Also see Benjamin Yang's and June Teufel Dreyer's contributions for more detail of Deng's military exploits during the Sino-Japanese and civil wars.

together on the Secretariat during the mid-1950s. Liu and Zhou both supported Deng's appointment as acting Premier of the State Council (1963–64). Liu and Deng were purged together in 1967 as the Number 1 and 2 "capitalist roaders," but were treated very differently and suffered different fates. Zhou intervened on Deng's behalf as he did many other cadres, although Mao also sought to protect Deng.

When Lin Biao issued Order No. 1 in October 1969, both Liu and Deng were transferred out of Beijing, Liu to Kaifeng (where he subsequently died an ignominious death) and Deng to a May Seventh Cadre School in Jiangxi province. During this period Mao kept track of Deng. In 1971 he reportedly asked Wang Zhen to pass a message to Deng that Mao would consider his rehabilitation if Deng appealed by letter and confessed his "revisionist" errors.[23] Deng sent Mao two letters from internal exile, the first in November 1971 and the second in August 1972.[24] Mao then personally approved Deng's rehabilitation and recall to Beijing on 2 March 1973.

Deng's rehabilitation no doubt came with Zhou Enlai's blessing, as Zhou was at this time overseeing the rehabilitation of cadres and reconstitution of the party-state apparatus. Deng's return must therefore be seen as part of a broader pattern of rehabilitations engineered by Zhou at this time, even though Deng was the most senior victim of the Cultural Revolution to be returned to power and the Chairman's imprimateur was necessary.[25]

Knowing that he had cancer, Zhou groomed Deng to succeed him as Premier, turning over the daily management of the State Council to him in 1974. While undergoing cobalt radiation treatment for his cancer, Zhou relied on Deng to manage affairs of state. Zhou dispatched Deng to the United Nations in October to deliver a major policy address on world affairs (in which Deng outlined Mao's "theory of the three worlds") and Deng stood in for Zhou on a number of occasions. One of Zhou's last public acts was to announce the "Four Modernizations" programme at the

23. Interview, Central Committee Party History Research Office, 25 May 1991, Beijing. Little is known about this period in Deng's life. The best source is Lin Qingshan, *Fengyun shinian yu Deng Xiaoping, neibu*. Also see the reminiscences of Deng's daughter Mao Mao (Deng Rong), "My father's days in Jiangxi," *Beijing Review*, No. 36 (3 September 1984), pp. 17–18. Like Liu Shaoqi, Deng and his wife Zhuo Lin were evacuated from Beijing (where they had been under house arrest for the previous two years) under Lin Biao's Order No. 1. They spent the next three years in a former infantry academy turned May Seventh Cadre School in Xinjian county near Nanchang. Deng worked in a tractor factory under armed guard. Deng and his wife were permitted to maintain a garden and raise chickens, in which they invested much time. According to his daughter's account, Deng read books on Marxist theory and Chinese history late into the night. This account informs many of the other secondary biographies. See, for example, Han Shanbi, *Deng Xiaoping pingzhuan*, ch. 16.

24. Lin Qingshan, *ibid.* p. 267. The first letter commented on the relationship between the Party and the masses; in the second Deng admitted that he had made mistakes but remained loyal to "Mao Zedong Thought." This brought him reinstatement. Similarly, in March 1977 Deng wrote to Hua Guofeng pledging his allegiance and admitting past mistakes.

25. For further on the rehabilitation process at this time see Earl Anthony Wayne, "The politics of restaffing China's provinces," *Contemporary China* (Spring 1978), pp. 116–165; and Jürgen Domes, *China After the Cultural Revolution* (Berkeley: University of California Press, 1977).

Fourth National People's Congress in January 1975; Deng drafted the speech and crafted the programme. Fittingly, it was Deng who read the eulogy at Zhou's memorial service on 15 January 1976. In a macabre turn of Politburo politics Deng's oration was to spell his own political death and would be his last public appearance until 1977. Within six weeks Zhou's arrangements for the succession were overturned by the Gang of Four (with Mao's acquiesence) and Deng was purged for the third time in his career.

Mao's support was thus crucial to Deng's career during the 1950s and early 1960s, although it seems that the Chairman had misgivings about Deng during the commune movement of 1958 and again during the Socialist Education Movement in 1964.[26] However, it was Deng's power base in the Secretariat, and the policy programme to emerge from that body during the early 1960s, that gave the Chairman primary cause for concern. As early as November 1956 Mao began to take note of Deng's dominance of the Secretariat, referring to it as his "nest."[27] As the alarming reports of famine in the countryside began to reach the leadership in early 1960 Deng audaciously began to distance himself from Mao and the Great Leap (which he had earlier supported) by giving several speeches around the country to criticize "problems in Mao's thinking" (*Mao Zedong sixiang de wenti*).[28] When Mao withdrew to the "second line" after 1960 the Secretariat under Deng became a key locus of decision-making and target of the Chairman's ire. Mao reportedly chastised Deng in 1964 for not keeping him informed of state policy and building an "independent kingdom" (*duli wangguo*) in the Party Secretariat.[29] Mao was particularly upset with the "60 Articles on Promoting Higher Education," which Deng had taken charge of drafting but apparently had not shown to him. "Who was the emperor making such a decision?" queried the Chairman.[30] It is not surprising that those who worked closely with Deng on the Secretariat became early targets of Mao's Cultural Revolution purges and the institution itself was disbanded.

Mao clearly had serious ideological differences with Deng and other Politburo members during this time as he perceived them to be instituting revisionist capitalist restoration in several policy spheres (particularly in rural policy and education) under the guise of economic recovery from the Great Leap.[31] Deng was singled out by Mao during the Cultural

26. Deng's opposition to the pace of communization at this time is noted in Zhong Hao, *Deng Xiaoping de lilun yu shixian, 1938–1965*, pp. 42–44.

27. Mao Zedong, "Speech at the Second Plenum of the Eighth Central Committee," in John K. Leung and Michael Y. M. Kau (eds.), *The Writings of Mao Zedong, 1949–1976: Volume II* (Armonk, NY: M. E. Sharpe, 1992), p. 169.

28. Zhong Hao, *Deng Xiaoping de lilun yu shixian*, p. 83.

29. "The major accusations against Deng Xiaoping," *Ba-er-wu zhanbao* (*August 25 Battle Report*), 14 February 1967, *Selections from China Mainland Magazines*, No. 574 (1 May 1967), p. 15.

30. *Ibid.*

31. It was during a series of Politburo meetings in December 1964–January 1965 on management of the Socialist Education Movement that Mao's distrust of Deng and Liu

Revolution as the "number 2 person in authority taking the capitalist road," and encountered the Chairman's wrath again in 1976, when he was purged following the Tiananmen Incident.[32]

But in the pre-1949 period and throughout the 1950s Mao was primarily responsible for Deng's rapid rise through the higher Party ranks. In 1954 when Nikita Khrushchev visited Beijing Mao pointed to Deng and said: "See that little man there? He is highly intelligent and has a great future ahead of him."[33] Coincidentally it was Deng whom Mao dispatched to the Soviet 20th Party Congress in 1956, only to hear Khrushchev's tirade against Stalin. Mao subsequently called upon Deng to help manage Sino-Soviet relations during the disagreements of 1960–63.[34] Mao also entrusted Deng with administering the Anti-Rightist campaign in 1957 (for which Deng never showed contrition).

Liu Shaoqi. Deng's ties to Liu Shaoqi were never as close as it has been assumed from their common fate in 1967. They were more contemporaries than in a hierarchical patron–client relationship, although they worked in a mutually supportive fashion. Deng's opposition to Gao Gang's power play to usurp Liu's position as Party Vice-Chairman in 1953 was important in foiling the plot, and it was Deng who issued the full indictment on the "Gao Gang–Rao Shushi anti-Party clique" at the March 1955 National Party Conference. Liu and Deng together drafted and delivered two of the key speeches at the 1956 Eighth Party Congress.[35] They also collaborated in 1961–62 to "reverse the verdicts" on improperly-labelled rightists in the Party and to accelerate their rehabilitation,[36] and worked closely during the 1962–65 period on Party rectification, rural policy, educational reform, and generally formulating the post-Great Leap recovery programme. It was largely for this collabo-

---

footnote continued

Shaoqi crystallized. For analysis of this period see the discussion in Frederick C. Teiwes, *Politics and Purges in China* (Armonk, NY: M. E. Sharpe, 1979), ch. 11; and Richard Baum, *Prelude to Revolution: Mao, the Party, and the Peasant Question* (New York: Columbia University Press, 1975).

32. Despite the fact that Mao was largely incapacitated at this time, having reportedly suffered two strokes and the effects of Parkinson's disease, knowledgeable sources claim that he approved the Gang of Four's initiative to remove Deng from power.

33. Strobe Talbott (trans. and ed.), *Khrushchev Remembers* (Boston: Little, Brown, 1974), pp. 252–53.

34. See Michael Yahuda's contribution in this volume; and Steven M. Goldstein, "Nationalism and internationalism: Sino-Soviet relations," in Thomas W. Robinson and David Shambaugh (eds.), *Chinese Foreign Policy: Theory and Practice* (Oxford: Oxford University Press, 1993), pp. 224–265.

35. Deng delivered the "Report on Revision of the Party Constitution" and Liu the "Political Report of the Central Committee," and together they took charge of the drafting of these key documents. See Editing Group, *Mianhuai Liu Shaoqi* (*Cherish the Memory of Liu Shaoqi*) (Beijing: Zhongyang wenzhai chubanshe, 1988), p. 12.

36. At the time Deng believed that the purge of non-Party intellectuals and soldiers was warranted, but in the 1980s confessed that the scope of the movement had been too broad although he refused to repudiate the campaign itself. See "Talk with some leading comrades of the Central Committee, 19 March 1980," *Selected Works*, p. 279.

ration that they drew Mao's wrath during the Cultural Revolution, although their joint "mismanagement" of the work teams in the early phase of the Cultural Revolution also contributed to their downfall.

None the less, Liu Shaoqi's and Deng's collaboration was more by virtue of position and proximity than patronage. They had complementary expertise, as Liu was more the theorist and Deng the organization man, but their relationship was never as conspiratorial as the Red Guard materials suggest.

Peng Zhen. In contrast, Deng and Peng Zhen had a longer and closer relationship. They worked closely together on the Secretariat during the mid-1950s. Peng was appointed Deng's second in command at the First Plenum of the Eighth Party Congress, and they were the only two Politburo members serving on the Secretariat at the time. Deng frequently discharged important responsibilities to Peng, particularly in the legal and public security spheres.[37] They made inspection tours together,[38] were bridge partners and their families were close friends.[39] Together with Kang Sheng, Deng and Peng were centrally involved in managing the deteriorating relationship with the Soviet Union in the late 1950s and early 1960s.[40]

Deng's relationship with Peng apparently came under strain in 1964 during the Four Clean-ups campaign when work teams dispatched to Beijing University by Liu Shaoqi attacked the university Party secretary Lu Ping, a close ally of Peng Zhen. This situation briefly pitted Liu against Peng, with Deng siding with Liu, but earned Peng the support of Mao who was increasingly dissatisfied with Liu and Deng. Liu, Deng and Peng soon found themselves allied again in 1965–66 over the Luo Ruiqing affair. Together they tried (unsuccessfully) to defend Luo against the Chairman and Lin Biao during a series of Central Committee "working group" sessions in March 1966. When Peng Zhen came under attack and became the first major casualty of the Cultural Revolution in April–May 1966, Deng abandoned his old ally. He joined in criticizing the "February Outline Report" (a document largely drafted by Peng but disseminated with Deng's explicit approval) and presided over the crucial 9–12 April 1966 Secretariat meeting that accused Peng and opened the way to his subsequent purge. Liu Shaoqi did not attend this decisive meeting (as he was in Burma on a state visit), but Deng voted with others

---

37. Peng Zhen was put in charge of overseeing the *su-fan* campaign and public security policy more generally. See *Peng Zhen wenxuan* (*Peng Zhen's Selected Works*) (Beijing: Renmin chubanshe, 1991), pp. 240–317. Also see Frederick C. Teiwes, "Mao and his lieutenants," *The Australian Journal of Chinese Affairs*, No. 19/20 (1988), pp. 68–69.

38. For example Deng and Peng made five inspections together in Hebei province during April and May 1960, in order to ascertain the seriousness of the situation in the countryside in the aftermath of the Great Leap. See Chen Xuewei, *Lishi de qishi – shinian jiansheshi yanjiu* (*Historical Revelations – Research on Ten Years (1957–1966) of Historical Construction*) (Beijing: Qiushi chubanshe, 1989), p. 132.

39. "Drag out Deng Xiaoping from the black den as a warning to others," *Xin Beida* (*New Beida*), 25 February 1967, *Survey of Mainland China Magazines*, No. 177 (19 April 1967), p. 4.

40. See Goldstein, "Nationalism and internationalism."

in favour of criticizing Peng for "opposing Chairman Mao" and dissolving Peng's initial five-man "Cultural Revolution Group." Thus Deng abandoned Peng at the time of his greatest need, although given the tenor of the times it would have been most difficult to do otherwise. Deng atoned by helping to rehabilitate Peng in 1979.

Once back in power Deng drew important support from Peng Zhen. Peng backed Deng's bid to oust Hua Guofeng and promote Hu Yaobang and Zhao Ziyang and proved a crucial supporter of Deng's reform programme via his position as Chairman of the National People's Congress (an appointment that Deng also arranged). During the decade Deng also entrusted oversight of the legal and public security systems to Peng, at least until Peng's protégé Qiao Shi took control of these spheres in the late 1980s. Peng Zhen was also one of the key Party elders to support Deng's proposal for martial law and the crackdown in June 1989.

Peng Dehuai. Deng's relationship with Peng Dehuai was a largely professional one confined to military affairs. Their contact during the revolutionary war was limited to the 1930 Changsha Uprising and "Hundred Regiments campaign" in 1940.[41] During Deng's time as Vice-Chairman of the Central Military Commission from 1954 to 1966, Deng and Peng Dehuai worked together until Peng's purge in 1959. In fact, Deng absented himself from the Lushan Conference in 1959 where Peng Dehuai confronted Mao,[42] apparently because he had broken his leg playing billiards.[43] Deng maintained a low profile throughout the year, but his public appearances began to pick up again with the National Literature and Art Work Conference in December 1959. No doubt Deng shared many of Peng Dehuai's views on the catastrophe of the Great Leap, although he was not present to witness the Mao–Peng clash.[44] Commenting in 1980 on the Lushan Plenum Deng asserted that "Comrade Peng's views were correct" and "the way his case was handled was totally wrong."[45]

Chen Yun. Deng and Chen Yun have had a long and ambiguous relationship. Both abhorred the Maoist approach to economic development with its voluntarist emphasis on moral incentives and the "big-push"

41. See Peng Dehuai, *Memoirs of a Chinese Marshal* (Beijing: Foreign Languages Press, 1984), pp. 434–447.

42. See Jiang Huaxuan *et al.*, *Zhongguo gongchangdang huiyi zhaiyao* (Shenyang chubanshe, 1991); and Kenneth Lieberthal and Bruce Dickson, *A Research Guide to Central Party and Government Meetings in China, 1949–1986* (Armonk, NY: M. E. Sharpe, 1989). Harrison Salisbury claims that Mao ordered Deng to remain in Beijing to run the government during Lushan, but then changed his mind and required Deng to attend. Salisbury, *The Last Emperors*, p. 176. This is not corroborated by other sources, including Li Rui's account. See Li Rui, *Lushan huiyi shilu* (Henan jiaoyu chubanshe, 1988), p. 26.

43. Interview with Li Rui, 2 June 1993.

44. A Hong Kong biography of Deng asserts that Deng knew in advance of Peng's plans, as Peng had informed Huang Kecheng of his intention during June 1959 and Huang had told Deng. See Han Shanbi, *Deng Xiaoping pingzhuan*, Vol. 2, pp. 114–15.

45. Deng Xiaoping, "Talk with some leading comrades of the Central Committee, 1 April 1980," *Selected Works*, p. 280.

strategy, instead generally favouring material incentives and incremental development. Yet they have held different views on the pace and modality of economic reform. Their differences were apparent during the post-Leap recovery,[46] but became particularly manifest in the mid to late 1980s when Chen Yun's moderate economic reform programme did not embrace the bolder proposals of Deng, Zhao Ziyang and the economic think tanks and advisers to Zhao.[47] While it is important to recall that Chen supported Deng's reform push during the early 1980s, he headed a faction within the leadership that increasingly sought to blunt the more radical reforms of 1986–88 and 1992–93. After the death of Ye Jianying and the illness of Li Xiannian in the late 1980s, Chen Yun was the only leader of enough stature to challenge Deng and the two increasingly became rivals in their later years.

Yang Shangkun. Another senior leader with whom Deng was particularly close was Yang Shangkun – at least until 1992–93 when Deng forced Yang to relinquish the state presidency and all military posts. Deng and Yang first met in 1932 in Ruijin, the capital of the Jiangxi soviet, and thereafter their careers closely paralleled one another. Both are Sichuan natives; both studied in Moscow (although Deng preceded Yang by a year); both served as political commissars in the Red Army during the Long March; both worked together on the Central Committee Secretariat during the 1950s (Yang was one of Deng's key deputies); both were purged in the early stages of the Cultural Revolution; and the two men have been bridge partners for many years. One of Yang's sons reportedly married one of Deng's daughters.

In 1979, with Ye Jianying's backing, Deng was responsible for Yang's rehabilitation and reinstatement to leading positions. Yang became a key ally of Deng's throughout the 1980s. They served as the two senior ranking members on the Central Military Commission (CMC) and together oversaw the restructuring of the PLA during the decade. With Deng's support, Yang succeeded Li Xiannian as President of the republic. The Deng–Yang combination was particularly vital in mobilizing the military to suppress the Tiananmen demonstrations in 1989. Yang played a central part in overcoming opposition from other retired generals and senior commanders[48] and managing the logistical aspects of the crackdown.

Yang and his younger half-brother Yang Baibing subsequently capitalized on the Beijing massacre to build their own personal network of support in the armed forces. Yang Baibing oversaw the "cleansing of the

46. See David Bachman, *Chen Yun and the Chinese Political System* (Berkeley: Institute of East Asian Studies, China Research Monograph No. 29, 1985); Nicholas Lardy and Kenneth Lieberthal (eds.), *Chen Yun's Strategy for China's Development: A Non-Maoist Alternative* (Armonk, NY: M. E. Sharpe, 1983).

47. For a comparison and analysis of these differences see Harry Harding, *China's Second Revolution: Reform After Mao* (Washington, D. C.: Brookings, 1987), particularly chs. 4–5.

48. See the 21 May 1989 letter addressed to Deng and the CMC and signed by Nie Rongzhen, Xu Xiangqian, Zhang Aiping, Ye Fei, Chen Zaidao, Yang Dezhi and others.

ranks," court martials and intense indoctrination campaign following 4 June.[49] In the process, he moved many commanders and commissars into key central and regional military positions. Yang Baibing was reported to have convened several secret meetings of loyal commanders during the summer of 1992 to plan for the aftermath of Deng's death, including (according to Hong Kong sources) a plot to "reverse the verdict" on the Tiananmen massacre by blaming it on Deng (which, of course, would be a correct interpretation). Sensing a power play, at the 14th Party Congress in October 1992 Deng stripped both Yangs of all their positions on the CMC and at the Eighth National People's Congress in March 1993 Yang Shangkun was relieved of his post as state President. Thus, Deng turned on his old comrade when he sensed that Yang Shangkun was attempting to build a rival base of power in order to position himself to emerge as paramount leader in the post-Deng era. By stripping the Yangs of their commands and power, Deng played to a powerful constituency among military modernizers in the PLA, centred around Generals Zhang Aiping, Zhang Zhen and Yang Dezhi, and Admiral Liu Huaqing. Yet it remains to be seen whether the purge of the Yangs will be effective, as Yang Shangkun controls a powerful patronage network in the armed forces – and the Army will prove central in the succession struggle after Deng.[50]

Tao Zhu. Another elite with whom Deng maintained close ties was Tao Zhu. They maintained good working relations during the 1950s and 1960s when Deng ran the Secretariat and Tao Zhu was Guangdong Party chief. During this time Deng also became well acquainted with Tao's deputy Zhao Ziyang, and he put him in charge of the province when Tao Zhu was promoted to the Centre in 1965.[51]

Zhao Ziyang. Deng turned to Zhao Ziyang as Party leader following his ouster of Hu Yaobang in 1987, but their relationship goes back much earlier; in fact some circumstantial evidence dates it from the 1940s.[52] Deng supported Zhao during the 1960s and has cultivated him as a potential successor at least since 1974 when he arranged Zhao's transfer from Guangdong to Sichuan as provincial Party chief. Zhao used Sichuan as a laboratory to experiment with heretical agricultural and industrial reform policies. Some – such as the "three freedoms, one contract" (*sanzi yibao*) agricultural responsibility system – had been favoured by both

49. For an analysis of Yang Baibing's post-Tiananmen manoeuvrings see David Shambaugh, "The soldier and the state in China," *The China Quarterly*, No. 127 (September 1991), pp. 527–568.

50. For an analysis of the post-14th Party Congress political equation and the impact of the Yangs' purge, see David Shambaugh, "Losing control: the erosion of state authority in China," *Current History* (September 1993), pp. 252–58.

51. For discussion of Deng's and Zhao's relationship see Shambaugh, *The Making of a Premier*, pp. 105–106, 118, 122. Some sources indicate that Deng was responsible for Tao's elevation to the Centre in order to facilitate Zhao's promotion. See Han Shanbi, *Deng Xiaoping zhuan*, Vol. II, pp. 256–57; and "Drag out Deng Xiaoping from the black den," pp. 5–7.

52. Zhao Wei, *Zhao Ziyang zhuan (Biography of Zhao Ziyang)* (Hong Kong: Wenhua jiaoyu chubanshe, 1988), ch. 4.

Deng and Zhao during the early 1960s, but others – particularly industrial incentive systems – were new. Deng gave Zhao permission and political protection to experiment boldly at a time when neo-Maoist policies were still in vogue in Beijing. During Zhao's tenure in Sichuan Deng frequently visited to monitor the reforms and consult him.[53] Zhao's "production first" policies paralleled Deng's *laissez-faire* economic philosophy. The reforms were so successful they were dubbed "the Sichuan miracle"[54] and helped propel Zhao Ziyang to national prominence and appointment as Vice-Premier in 1979. This promotion could not have occurred without Deng's backing, although the success of Zhao's Sichuan policies helped overcome any resistance. A year later Zhao replaced Hua Guofeng as Premier of the State Council.

With this appointment it became clear that Zhao was one of Deng's two hand-picked successors. Deng's patronage of Zhao lasted until 1989 when the two clashed over the implementation of martial law. Zhao also made the tactical mistake of criticizing Deng in a public session with Mikhail Gorbachev, claiming that a secret Politburo ruling referred all major decisions to Deng – thus in effect passing the blame for economic overheating to his mentor. Zhao also opposed the harsh 26 April editorial that condemned the student demonstrations as "unpatriotic," which was specifically ordered and approved by Deng.[55] Zhao's real mistake, though, was to have been in power when open demands for democracy were made.

This is where Deng consistently drew the line throughout his career. With the exception of the 1978 Democracy Wall Movement when it temporarily served his political objectives, Deng never tolerated open advocacy of political liberalism, democracy or criticism of CCP political hegemony. Thus, for the second time in as many years Deng aborted his well-laid succession plans and sacked Zhao. Having done so, however, it is clear that Deng went to great lengths to protect Zhao from hardliners in the leadership who wished to punish him more severely.

Hu Yaobang. Deng's other hand-picked successor, Hu Yaobang, fell from power in early 1987 following the pro-democracy student demonstrations in December 1986. Deng had groomed Hu Yaobang considerably longer than Zhao Ziyang. Their relationship dated from 1937 when both were affiliated with the Resistance University (*Kang Da*) in Yan'an – Hu as a student and Deng as a young lecturer.[56] This teacher–student/patron–client relationship endured until 1987, and even then Deng ensured that Hu Yaobang's political career was not terminated by permitting him to retain his Politburo status. It was unusual in Chinese

53. Shambaugh, *The Making of a Premier*, ch. 6.
54. See "Zhao Ziyang's 'Sichuan Experience': blueprint for a nation," *Chinese Law & Government* (Spring 1982).
55. See "The making of the big lie: content and process in the Chinese propaganda system during 1989," *Chinese Law & Government* (Spring 1992), pp. 31–37.
56. See Yang Zhongmei, *Hu Yaobang: A Chinese Biography* (Armonk, NY: M. E. Sharpe, 1988), p. 113.

Communist history for a purge not to consign an individual to political oblivion.[57]

Deng's and Hu's careers intersected at several points after Yan'an. Hu served with Deng as political commissar in the Second Field Army that "liberated" south-western China. In fact, Hu Yaobang was personally responsible for northern Sichuan and oversaw the conquest of Deng's native village of Guang'an. Hu subsequently served in Sichuan under Deng's and Liu Bocheng's command until 1952 when he and Deng were transferred to Beijing at the same time.[58] Hu went on to a lengthy career as head of the Communist Youth League before being purged in 1967. Perhaps coincidentally, perhaps not, Deng and Hu were both rehabilitated in March 1973. As Deng set about structuring the "Four Modernizations" programme in 1975, he called upon Hu Yaobang to reconstitute the Academy of Sciences. Hu's September 1975 "Summary Report" on the Academy was the basis for the subsequent rehabilitation of thousands of researchers purged during previous campaigns and the assertion of "expertise" over "redness." A close working alliance for reform was forged. They shared a common purpose of rolling back the Cultural Revolution. Unfortunately, their work was abruptly interrupted by Zhou Enlai's death and Deng's subsequent dismissal. With Deng's return in 1977 Hu stood ready to assist him, and a decade-long partnership ensued.

Patrons, clients, colleagues and enemies. Thus, throughout his career Deng had two principal patrons – Mao and Zhou, with Mao by far the more longstanding and important one. Liu Bocheng also served as a patron of sorts during the civil war, which was important to Deng's cultivation of a career and power base in the armed forces.

Liu Shaoqi, Peng Zhen, Yang Shangkun, Peng Dehuai and Chen Yun must all be considered close colleagues of Deng's, though without the attributes of patronage. Later in their careers Chen Yun turned from colleague to competitor, but in retrospect their disagreements were more a matter of degree than substance. Similarly Deng's long-time ally Yang Shangkun also turned into a competitor of sorts, although much of the overt scheming against Deng must be credited to his half-brother Yang Baibing.

Throughout Deng's long career he also worked closely with numerous other central, provincial and military leaders. His position as Secretary-General of the Central Secretariat (and later General Secretary) during the 1950s and 1960s, and his position in the State Council and on the PLA General Staff and Central Military Commission during the 1970s and 1980s brought him into contact with virtually all senior state and Party leaders, provincial and military officials.

It is interesting to note that Deng had few real enemies during his

---

57. There are a few precedents for purged leaders retaining their Central Committee seats (e.g. Wang Ming, Peng Dehuai and Hua Guofeng), but only in pro forma fashion.

58. It is possible that Deng brought Hu to Zhou Enlai's attention at the time and arranged for his transfer to the capital.

career. This is not to say that he was not ruthless, as he did purge many and was responsible for numerous ruined careers from the 1942 Yan'an rectification to the 14th Party Congress and Eighth National People's Congress in 1992–93. But rivals, adversaries and enemies must be distinguished. Certainly Deng had many adversarial relationships, including at times with Mao, Lin Biao and Hua Guofeng, and he even had rather formidable disagreements with Chen Yun, Hu Yaobang, Zhao Ziyang, Li Peng and Jiang Zemin, but none can really be considered a political enemy. Certainly none approached the contempt he felt for Jiang Qing and her erstwhile ally Zhang Chunqiao.

Deng's true clients in the Party were Hu Yaobang and Zhao Ziyang. In the military Deng had a broad network of ties stemming from his Second Field Army connections. Xu Shiyou and Wei Guoqing were two of the most prominent, apart from Yang Shangkun, as they protected Deng in internal exile in the south during 1975–77. Jiang Zemin, Li Tieying, Zhu Rongji and Wang Zhaoguo must all be considered latter-day clients. Deng personally promoted them all. Indeed, individuals such as Qiao Shi and Li Ruihuan could not have risen to the top (nor could Li Peng have stayed there) without Deng's approval. But none of these was a client of Deng's in a true sense of the term. He did not cultivate them over time and each owed as much, if not more, personal loyalty to other senior elites. In a sense they all benefited from Deng's reform programme more than from Deng himself. Yet, as was the case under Mao, it is difficult to rise to the pinnacle of power without the blessing of the patriarch.

Deng's Institutional Power Bases

Deng did not rule through intimidation or coercion, terrorizing the populace with draconian security services (the 1989 Beijing massacre being the obvious exception). Nor did he lead the nation by great personal charisma, although he certainly possessed prestige and commanded respect. Nor did ideology serve as a tool of his leadership – his disdain for it was barely concealed. Deng's preferred *modus operandi* was to manoeuvre behind the scenes but, having taken a decision, to implement policy through established bureaucratic channels. In other words, he was a backroom politician who depended on Party institutions and Leninist norms to implement decisions. This was true throughout most of his career.

Unlike Mao, Deng was an organization man. For most of his career he worked in, and believed in working through, bureaucratic structures. Later in life, however, like Mao, he became frustrated with an organizational approach to rule and began to rely on the voluntarist impulses of the citizenry.

In 1991–92 Deng experienced the frustrations of being a retired patriarch. He encountered entrenched bureaucratic interests and designated successors who pursued their own agendas. Unable to kick-start economic reform through normal bureaucratic channels and seemingly surrounded by disloyal lieutenants, Deng adopted the Maoist approach of taking his case straight to the people during his famous February 1992 Southern Sojourn (*nan xun*). By bringing pressure from below and reinjecting himself into the limelight, Deng trapped his opponents and seized back the political initiative. This leap-frogging technique was employed repeatedly by Mao in similar circumstances.

Despite his preference for institutional rule, like any leader Deng exhibited intolerance of bureaucratic inertia and incompetence. As Martin King Whyte's contribution to this volume makes clear, Deng championed meritocracy and streamlining of bloated bureaucracy. Deng's concept of "political reform" (*zhengzhi gaige*) was really one of *administrative* reform (*xingzheng gaige*). The devolution of decision-making power and removal of the state and Party bureaucracy from guiding economic activity was a centre-piece of his reform package. Deng was very supportive of Zhao Ziyang's 1984 and 1988 overhaul of the State Council apparatus, as well as Zhu Rongji's 1993 reforms. But it is important to keep in mind that these streamlining efforts were actually aimed at *strengthening* the bureaucracy, thereby enhancing the party-state's capacities, rather than dismantling the Leninist *apparat*.

Since Deng believed in leadership via organization, it must also be asked whether he used certain organizations to build a personal power base. Deng never worked in a functional ministerial system or in a mass organization like the Communist Youth League, but he did build power bases in the Party Secretariat and PLA for lengthy periods.

To head the Secretariat was an extraordinarily sensitive and powerful position. Information is an important source of power in a bureaucratic environment – and Deng had a near-monopoly on it. He had ultimate control over the ten functional departments of the Central Committee: propaganda, organization, united front work, finance and economics, industry and communications, rural work, foreign trade, investigation (i.e. intelligence), military affairs and international liaison (external Communist Party relations). This was a very powerful cluster of institutions. Deng had overall responsibility, assisted by the other members of the Secretariat[59] and the head of the staff office (Yang Shangkun). These were powerful individuals in their own right as each was responsible for a department and its constituent ministerial system (*xitong*), and each department functioned quite independently.[60] Each member thereby served as the "opening" (*kou*) in his assigned issue area to the Central Committee, Politburo and its Standing Committee. Still, from the Eighth Party Congress to the aftermath of the Great Leap the Secretariat was primarily a body for policy implementation (not formulation) and staffing. During these years (1956–62) its principal purpose was to process documents and disseminate policy decisions taken by Mao, the

59. After the Secretariat was reorganized at the First Plenum of the Eighth Central Committee and Deng was appointed General Secretary, the other secretaries were as follows: Peng Zhen, Wang Jiaxiang, Tan Zhenlin, Tan Zheng, Huang Kecheng, Li Xuefeng, Li Fuchun, Li Xiannian, Lu Dingyi, Kang Sheng and Luo Ruiqing. Alternate secretaries were Liu Lantao, Yang Shangkun and Hu Qiaomu.

60. Interview with Li Rui of the CCP Organization Department, 2 June 1993.

Politburo, its Standing Committee or the entire Central Committee via these departments, and to monitor implementation. The Secretariat liaised in particular with Party authorities and counterpart functional organs at the provincial level. In fact, Deng probably dealt as much with provincial Party secretaries as he did with other members of the Central elite. However, before the Eighth Party Congress and after the Great Leap, the Secretariat enjoyed a status equal to the Politburo Standing Committee; it was very much a policy-making organ.[61]

In the wake of the Great Leap debacle and Mao's "retirement to the second line" Deng began to assert himself as CCP General Secretary and the power of the Secretariat grew significantly. Deng supervised, via the Secretariat, the drafting of a comprehensive national development programme.[62] These included the 60 Articles on People's Communes; 70 Articles on Industry; 14 Articles on Science; 35 Articles on Handicraft Trades; Six Articles on Finance; Eight Articles on Literature and Art; 60 Articles on Higher Education; and 40 Articles on Commercial Work.

It is true that various leaders were involved in this process, but Deng held the power of co-ordination. He took charge of the 60 Articles on Higher Education himself and had a significant input to the documents on commerce, finance, science, industry and communes. Taken together, these programmatic documents served as the basis not only for the recovery from the Great Leap but, more importantly, the relative exclusion of Mao from the policy process.

Deng, Liu, Zhou, Chen Yun, Bo Yibo, Peng Zhen, Li Fuchun, Li Xiannian, Zhou Yang and Lu Dingyi collectively took control of the Party and government. Deng's power and prestige definitely grew, but not disproportionate to others'. With Mao in the "second line" the leadership was remarkably collectivist. Deng worked well with his colleagues.

This is certainly not the picture of Deng's Secretariat portrayed by Red Guards during the Cultural Revolution. One diatribe claimed: "During the period Deng Xiaoping was in charge of work at the Secretariat of the Central Committee, he consistently monopolized power, made arbitrary decisions, and met Chairman Mao on equal terms without ceremony."[63] As noted above, Mao was particularly distressed about Deng's education programme. The 60 Articles on Higher Education proposed the restoration of academic degrees, titles, and salaries; the abolition of "absolute leadership of the Party" (*dang de juedui lingdao*) over institutions of higher learning; an end to class struggle in universities; and curtailment of Mao's work-study programme (*shixi*) for university faculty and students. The Chairman was also angry with the draft 60 Articles on People's Communes which sought to introduce the *sanzi yibao* ("three

61. I am indebted to Fred Teiwes on this point.
62. This discussion draws upon Kenneth Lieberthal, "The Great Leap Forward and the split in the Yan'an leadership," in Roderick MacFarquhar and John King Fairbank (eds.), *The Cambridge History of China*, Vol. 14 (Cambridge: Cambridge University Press, 1987), pp. 323–24.
63. "Ten major accusations against Deng Xiaoping," *Ba-er-wu zhanbao*, p. 15. This document is drawn from a speech given by Jiang Qing.

freedoms, one contract") policy, change the basic accounting unit to the production brigade, and alter the size of communal mess halls. Mao countered with the "First Ten Points," to which Deng and Liu Shaoqi responded with the "Second Ten Points."

Indeed, the entire series of policy documents drafted under Deng's aegis eventually drew Mao's ire during the Cultural Revolution. Mao was troubled not only by the content of the documents, but by the fact that Deng, allegedly, did not consult him throughout the drafting process.[64] Deng evidently took the Chairman's "retirement to the second line" too seriously.

When Deng was returned to power in the early 1970s he tended to work through the State Council and its constituent ministries and commissions. As ranking "first Vice-Premier" he set about reorganizing the State Council and promulgating a series of programmatic documents to guide national construction. In so doing he encountered stiff resistance from Jiang Qing and her minions.[65]

Deng also used his positions as chief of PLA General Staff and Vice-Chairman of the Central Military Commission to use these bodies to overturn Lin Biao's influence in the military. Indeed, as June Teufel Dreyer's contribution illustrates, he had a strong constituency in the PLA. This was based on a network of personal ties growing out of the Second Field Army, as well as institutionally in the military–industrial complex.[66]

After Deng outmanoeuvred Hua Guofeng and became paramount leader during the 1980s he came to rely more on individuals than institutions. During this time Deng tended to rule in traditional imperial fashion by making broad policy pronouncements, monitoring the overall progress of policy, but restricting his interventions to moments when his policies or political allies were flagging.

Territorial Power Bases

While Deng had bases of power among individuals and institutions, he did not possess a territorial power base during his career. Of course, he took great interest in his native Sichuan,[67] often making inspection tours of the province, and together with Liu Bocheng ruled the south-west from

---

64. Deng refutes this and states that prior to the Beidaihe meeting of July–August 1962 Mao expressed approval of these documents. Deng Xiaoping, "Talk with some leading comrades of the Central Committee, 1 April 1980," *Selected Works*, pp. 280–81.

65. A detailed description of the Gang of Four's manoeuvring and sabotage at this time (albeit a historically revisionist and, in places, inaccurate, account) can be found in Gao Gao and Yan Jiaqi, *"Wenhua da geming" shinian shi, 1966–76 (A Ten-Year History of the Cultural Revolution, 1966–76)* (Tianjin: Renmin chubanshe, 1986), ch. 8.

66. Also see the excellent study by Michael Swaine, *The Military and Political Succession in China: Leadership, Institutions, Beliefs* (Santa Monica, CA: RAND Corporation Report R-4254-AF, 1992).

67. Deng did have close ties with Li Jingquan (who ruled Sichuan prior to the Cultural Revolution and held Politburo status) and to some extent served as Li's patron during these years, but Li owed his position more to Marshal He Long, under whom he served in the First Field Army.

1949 to 1952,[68] but it cannot really be said that Deng derived power from this region. Similarly, when he was sent into internal exile in Guangdong and Guangxi from 1975 to 1977 he enjoyed the protection of regional military barons Xu Shiyou and Wei Guoqing, as well as Ye Jianying, but never developed a territorial base of power. Deng's power always derived from institutions and personalities at the Centre.

Deng as Paramount Leader

Deng's position as paramount leader never rivalled Mao's. Deng never sought the absolute authority that Mao possessed and wielded, as he was convinced that Mao's dictatorial style and cult of personality (*geren chongbai*) were the principal reasons China endured economic and political crisis for much of the period after 1957. "Generally speaking, Comrade Mao Zedong's leadership was correct before 1957, but he made more and more mistakes after the anti-rightist struggle of that year," Deng opined in 1980.[69] Much of Mao's workstyle troubled Deng deeply, and upon ousting Hua Guofeng and becoming China's paramount leader himself in 1982 he was committed to ruling differently.

The major difference between Mao and Deng as paramount leader was the manner in which they dealt with other leaders and subordinates. Deng's style was far more consensus-oriented and decisions were taken more collectively. This is partly because Deng tended to approach problems methodically and delved more deeply into the specifics of a case (induction), whereas Mao often sought to form policy from ideological doctrine in an arbitrary and dialectical fashion (deduction). "Seek truth from facts," was Deng's watchword. Another reason is that Deng was not afraid to delegate authority; that is what he had done throughout his career. Deng himself reflected on how he ran the Secretariat from 1956 to 1966, in a speech to the Fifth Plenum of the 11th Central Committee in 1980 (which resurrected the Secretariat): "I think it is fair to say that the former Secretariat of the Central Committee was quite efficient, partly because once the relevant decisions were made, specific tasks were assigned to particular persons, who were given broad powers and allowed to handle matters independently."[70] Mao, on the other hand, avoided delegating authority and always sought to retain key decisions in his own hands.[71] To some extent Deng sought to make the key decisions –

68. For an excellent study of the south-west during this period see Dorothy J. Solinger, *Regional Government and Political Integration in Southwest China, 1949–1954* (Berkeley: University of California Press, 1977).

69. Deng Xiaoping, "Talk with some leading comrades of the Central Committee, 1 April 1980," *Selected Works*, p. 280.

70. Deng Xiaoping, "Adhere to the Party line and improve methods of work," *Selected Works*, p. 267.

71. See the description of this trait in Michel Oksenberg, "The political leader," in Wilson, *Mao Tse-tung in the Scales of History*, pp. 95–98.

particularly on foreign policy – but, on the whole, he broadly delegated authority.[72]

Nor did Deng foster tensions among subordinates to test their loyalties as did Mao, and while Deng had to remove two groomed successors he did not have to fear that Hu Yaobang or Zhao Ziyang were trying to usurp his own power.[73] Deng knew who his enemies were and who opposed his policies, and he manoeuvred effectively to isolate and then overcome them. Deng's manoeuvring against Hua Guofeng, the "whateverists" and "Small Gang of Four" between 1977 and 1983 illustrated his methodical manner of overwhelming opposition. Sometimes more concerted action was called for, as in the cases of Hu Yaobang and Zhao Ziyang. No doubt Deng fully concurred with Ye Jianying's forthright handling of the arrest of the Gang of Four, as he despised the Gang.[74]

Thus, Deng learned much from Mao by negative example. Until his "retirement" in 1990 Deng remained engaged, whereas Mao was more detached and withdrawn from active participation in decision-making. Deng regularly read and commented on documents and met Party leaders (Mao did as well, but to a lesser extent). Deng insisted on being informed, sought and listened to conflicting opinions, and pressed briefers on details. In contrast, Mao's subordinates often remained silent in the Chairman's presence for fear of the consequences of speaking out. Deng insisted on precision and substance from his advisers, and Deng himself was not one to waste words.[75] Mao stopped attending regular Politburo meetings after 1959,[76] while Deng attended on occasion even into retirement. The Politburo and its Standing Committee were important institutions of rule to Deng, whereas Mao held disdain for them, considering them to be packed with enemies. Deng tried to ensure that they contained his allies. The Central Military Commission was also of great importance to Deng. He retained the chairmanship of the CMC until 1989, having served as a member since 1954.

There was, therefore, a certain collegiality, decisiveness and activeness

72. Zhao Ziyang's statement to Gorbachev that all major decisions were *referred* to Deng may have been correct, but that does not mean that Deng actually *made* the decisions.

73. Again, see Oksenberg's discussion of this propensity of Mao's, n. 71. In 1992 Deng reflected on the reasons for having to sack Hu Yaobang and Zhao Ziyang, "Two men failed, and they failed not because of problems in the economy but because they stumbled on the issue of opposing bourgeois liberalization." *CCP Central Committee Circular on Transmitting and Studying Comrade Deng Xiaoping's Important Remarks* (Central Document No. 2, 1992), Foreign Broadcast Information Service, *Daily Report – China: Supplement* (hereafter *FBIS-CHI*), 1 April 1992, p. 6.

74. For an intriguing insider's account of Ye's arrest of the Gang of Four see Fan Shuo, *Ye Jianying zai 1976* (*Ye Jianying in 1976*) (Beijing: Zhonggong zhongyang dangxiao chubanshe, 1990).

75. Here Deng and Mao are not dissimilar. Reflecting in 1992, Deng said: "When you turn on the television, the programmes are full of meetings. There are too many meetings, too many long articles, and too many long speeches.... We should speak less and do more. Chairman Mao did not like to hold long meetings, his articles were concise, and his speeches were to the point. Chairman Mao [once] instructed me to draft Premier Zhou's report to the Fourth National People's Congress. He set a word limit at under 5,000. I did it, 5,000 words. Was that not useful?" *FBIS-CHI*, 1 April 1992, p. 6.

76. Interview with CCP historian Liao Gailong, 25 June 1991, Beijing.

in Deng's workstyle that was absent in Mao's. Deng sought consensus when possible and was certainly more tolerant of dissenting opinions. In general Deng purged but protected his men; Mao attacked them. This was one of Deng's most enduring lessons from the Cultural Revolution. No colleague of Deng's met the fate that befell Gao Gang, Peng Dehuai, Luo Ruiqing, Tao Zhu or Liu Shaoqi. There was an intolerance of opposition in Mao that Deng did not share.[77] When Deng toppled Hua Guofeng, Hua was not pilloried in the press and there was no national campaign of criticism. When Hu Yaobang fell from power Deng insisted that he be permitted to retain his Politburo seat and voting rights. After Zhao Ziyang's fall Deng intervened to protect him from the hardliners who sought stiff punishment, and ensured that Zhao was not expelled from the Party. Indeed, Deng stood behind Zhao at several critical junctures during 1987–89 when Zhao and the radical reform programme came under attack from conservatives.

There were further differences between Mao and Deng. Mao never travelled abroad (except the two trips to the Soviet Union); Deng did so more frequently. Deng enjoyed talking to the foreign press; Mao did not. Mao made no effort to learn a foreign language; Deng knew French and apparently spent many years trying to learn English. Deng also received many more foreign visitors in Beijing. Deng had a far better grasp of the intricacies of world affairs and was much more tolerant of a foreign presence in China. Mao was suspicious of the West; Deng held a certain envy of it. Deng was no less nationalistic than Mao, as both were socialized with similar views of the need for a strong and dignified China, but Deng sought the West as an ally in this quest while Mao was more distrustful.

In their personal lives, Mao sought the symbolic trappings of power; Deng lived more frugally. Mao lived in the Zhongnanhai; Deng moved out. Abuse of official privilege was of concern to both Mao and Deng,[78] but it must be said that Deng tolerated degrees of corruption unimaginable during the Maoist era. Deng abhorred the Maoist personality cult (*geren chongbai*) and was determined not to start one of his own (although he assented to the publication of his own *Selected Works* and those of Zhou Enlai, Liu Shaoqi, Zhu De, Chen Yun and Peng Zhen as well).[79] Mao kept concubines and ceased living with Jiang Qing in the 1950s, while Deng truly enjoyed family life with his numerous grandchildren. Deng played bridge and fraternized with his colleagues; Mao was a loner. Both enjoyed reading, and apparently both were devotees of the *Shi Ji* (*Records of the Historian*) and other classical Chinese writings.

---

77. Deng's philosophy of dealing with opposition and criticism is evident in "Strengthen Party leadership and rectify the Party's style of work," *Selected Works*, pp. 23–26.

78. See Deng's lecture on abuse of privilege in section 1 of "Senior cadres should take the lead in maintaining and enriching the Party's fine traditions," *Selected Works*, pp. 208–213.

79. With or without Deng's blessing, an outpouring of sycophantic works praising his achievements appeared after his 1992 Southern Sojourn, and his "thought" was officially proclaimed a "magic weapon" at the 14th Party Congress and enshrined in the CCP Constitution.

Thus there were numerous differences in leadership style between Mao and Deng. In comparing the two, differing modes of leadership have been examined out of the context of the national policy agenda. But no leaders – even paramount ones – operate in a vacuum. Leaders are, after all, chief executives and as such they shape the agenda of the nation.

Deng the Agenda Setter

There are different keys to power for politicians.[80] The importance of various power bases has been noted above. Controlling the substantive agenda of the nation is another source. To do this politicians must first have an agenda of their own. Deng certainly had one. It was centred on enhancing economic productivity and social vitality, and maximizing China's national security. However, Deng was no liberal. He sought to make China strong, but not democratic. He defined strength in demonstrable terms – economic productivity, technological prowess and military muscle. He believed that creative, entrepreneurial and productive forces could be unleashed (the Promethean impulse) without the concomitant loosening of political hegemony. On the contrary, Deng believed tight political control to be vital to achieve his economic goals. In this sense, he shares a view of modernization drawn from the experience of South Korea, Taiwan, Singapore and other newly industrialized countries (NICs).

The operative research question is not so much the *content* of Deng's agenda, which numerous studies have examined,[81] but the manner in which he went about pursuing it. In substantive terms, the origins of Deng's reformist agenda in the 1980s and 1990s can be traced to the Liu–Deng–Chen Yun programme of the early 1960s. It was the series of

80. Power is one of the most extensively analysed yet elusive concepts in social science. In the Chinese context, we have examined several sources of power bases above; also see Lowell Dittmer, "Bases of power in Chinese politics: a theory and analysis of the fall of the Gang of Four," *World Politics* (October 1978), pp. 26–60. In international politics the Realist paradigm holds that power is the ability to *influence*. See, in particular, Hans Morgenthau, *Politics Among Nations* (many editions). In comparative politics, elite power has been defined in a number of ways. In a classic study Arthur Bentley also adopted an influence-based definition. See his *The Process of Government* (Chicago: University of Chicago Press, 1908). Another classic view is that of Harold Lasswell and Abraham Kaplan, who define power as "participation in decision-making": *Power and Society* (New Haven: Yale University Press, 1950). This view gave rise to the bureaucratic politics paradigm of the 1960s which continues to hold some currency and is particularly pertinent to the study of Chinese politics. See, for example, Kenneth Lieberthal and Michel Oksenberg, *Policy Making in China* (Princeton: Princeton University Press, 1988). Robert Dahl introduced a more pluralistic definition in which considerable competition exists over the control of the political agenda. See his *Dilemmas of Pluralist Democracy* (New Haven: Yale University Press, 1982). Many scholars, particularly in the field of American legislative politics, have adopted and refined Dahl's approach, and it seems that an agenda-setting approach has unexplored utility for studying Chinese leaders' distribution of power.

81. Among the numerous studies on the Deng reforms see Harry Harding, *China's Second Revolution: Reform After Mao* (Washington, D. C.: Brookings, 1987); Carol Lee Hamrin, *China and the Challenge of the Future* (Boulder: Westview Press, 1990); Gordon White, *Riding the Tiger: The Politics of Economic Reform in Post-Mao China* (London: Macmillan, 1993).

documents promulgated under Deng's aegis – the 60 Articles, 70 Articles, 14 Articles, and so on – that served as the point of departure. Similarly, the three major policy documents produced under Deng's instruction in 1975 – which Jiang Qing labelled the "three poisonous weeds" – also helped to constitute the overall programme.[82]

Of importance to this analysis is the fact that when he returned to power in 1977 Deng had a preliminary agenda for change. Much more needed to be fleshed out in due course, but the essentials were in place. So was Deng's mandate for change. Like a newly-elected President or Prime Minister, Deng enjoyed a popular mandate for sweeping reform. Many in China recognized that Hua Guofeng was not up to the task, and only Deng had the requisite combination of skills, vision and experience to move the nation.[83] There was an acute leadership vacuum in the wake of the death of Mao and arrest of the Gang of Four, and the Communist Party faced a severe crisis of legitimacy. The society was numbed by years of campaign politics, and permeated by a deep sense of alienation. The economy remained stagnant, frozen at 1957 levels of production, and was falling further behind the rapid growth of China's East Asian neighbours. In foreign affairs, China had opened a relationship with the United States but it was not consummated, lacking full diplomatic relations and the benefits that normalization would bring.[84] China continued to face a pressing military threat of conventional and nuclear proportions from the Soviet Union, and remained locked in hostilities with India and Vietnam.

Benefiting from this kind of implicit mandate, it was not difficult for Deng to seize, set and control the national agenda – particularly once he had disposed of Hua Guofeng, the "whateverists" and "Small Gang of Four." Deng's aim of demolishing the Maoist edifice was essentially accomplished in three years, between 1979 and 1982. During this time Deng moved on many fronts to discredit the Cultural Revolution era and the beneficiaries of it.

Deng first set his sights on Hua Guofeng, Mao's chosen successor. At the Tenth Party Congress in August 1977 and National People's Congress of March 1978, Deng was more than pleased for Hua to reveal his unabashed loyalty to Maoism and naivety about economic growth (ironically Hua's target growth rates were very similar to Deng's own in 1992). Having exposed Hua, Deng then manoeuvred to outflank him on personnel and policy issues at the key Third Plenum of December 1978 and the preceding work conference. Several Deng allies were added to the

82. "Some Problems in Accelerating Industrial Development," prepared by the State Planning Commission; "Outline Report on the Work of the Academy of Sciences," prepared under the direction of Hu Yaobang and Hu Qiaomu; and "On the General Programme of Work for the Whole Party and Nation," prepared by Deng Liqun and others.
83. On this point see the discussion in Roderick MacFarquhar, "The Succession to Mao and the End to Maoism," in MacFarquhar and John King Fairbank (eds.), *The Cambridge History of China*, Vol. 15 (Cambridge: Cambridge University Press, 1992), pp. 388–393.
84. Deng closely monitored and personally engaged in the final round of negotiations in 1978 that led to Sino-American normalization. Interviews with knowledgeable officials in the U.S. and Chinese governments.

Politburo and Dengist ideas dominated the policy agenda to emerge from the Plenum. The agricultural responsibility system – already being successfully tested by Deng protégés Wan Li and Zhao Ziyang in Anhui and Sichuan provinces respectively[85] – was adopted as national policy and the decollectivization of agriculture was endorsed. "Class struggle" was replaced by "economic modernization" as the principal national goal. Deng also moved to take command of the armed forces (although Hua technically remained Chairman of the Central Military Commission) and began the process of comprehensive reorganization at a CMC meeting in December 1977. He also took the initiative to reassure intellectuals with an assertive speech to the National Science Conference in March 1978. It was in this speech that Deng served notice there would be no more Maoist-style political campaigns, that theoretical research should be unfettered by politics, and scientific exchanges with foreign countries would be a high priority – all at direct variance with Hua's preferences.

Secondly, during 1979 Deng set about revamping the ideological legacy of Maoism and extracting retribution for Cultural Revolution excesses. The "two whatevers"[86] were denounced and replaced by Deng's campaigns for "practice is the sole criterion of truth" and "Four Cardinal Principles."[87] Deng's attack on the "two whatevers" brought further pressure on Hua and his associates the "Small Gang of Four" (Wang Dongxing, Ji Denggui, Chen Xilian, Wu De). The Small Gang were removed from the Politburo at the Fifth Plenum. Hua now lacked any support among the leadership. Under Deng's new principle of "the separation of Party and government" (*dang-zheng fenkai*), Deng forced Hua to give up his post of Premier of the State Council to Deng's protégé Zhao Ziyang, and then the Party chairmanship to Deng's other protégé Hu Yaobang (whom Deng had already moved on to the reconstituted Secretariat). Deng himself took Hua's third post as Chairman of the Military Affairs Commission.

Thirdly, and simultaneous with the campaign to unseat Hua, Deng called to account the Gang of Four and vestiges of Lin Biao's military clique by arranging a well-publicized show trial from November 1980 to January 1981. Although no doubt of some consolation to victims of the Gang, the trial more importantly represented a symbolic cleansing for the national body politic. Deng continued this process by rehabilitating – often posthumously – leading victims of the Cultural Revolution, and compensating those in society who had suffered so severely. Similarly, Deng and Hu Yaobang arranged for victims of the 1957 anti-rightist campaign to be "uncapped" more than 20 years after the event and permitted them to resume work. Deng also permitted Democracy Wall to

85. The use of experimental "test points" (*shi dian*) was a favoured method of Deng's dating to the 1950s.

86. This was a slogan put forward by Hua that whatever Mao did or said should be adhered to.

87. Adherence to the socialist road, dictatorship of the proletariat, the leadership of the Communist Party, and Marxism–Leninism–Mao Zedong Thought. By relegating the latter to only one (and the last) of four elements, Deng dealt Maoist ideology a severe blow.

flourish in 1978–79, as it served his purposes in his struggle against Hua because the content of wall posters, publications and speeches all sharply criticized the Maoist era (from which Hua sought to draw legitimacy).

The last step in this cleansing process was the issuing of the *Resolution on Certain Questions in the History of Our Party Since the Founding of the People's Republic of China* at the Sixth Plenum of the Tenth Party Congress in July 1981. Deng personally oversaw the drafting of this document and several times expressed his dissatisfaction with the content of early drafts.[88] His goal was to strike a balance between preserving a positive legacy for "Comrade Mao Zedong" prior to 1957 and a negative one thereafter, without jettisoning the Great Helmsman altogether as Khrushchev had done to Stalin. As Deng told Italian journalist Oriana Fallaci in a 1980 interview: "We will not do to Chairman Mao what Khrushchev did to Stalin."[89] The attempt to strike a balance was evident in the way the *Resolution* dealt with the Anti-Rightist campaign – in which Deng played no small part and specifically ordered its essential correctness affirmed.[90] The *Resolution* stated that "It was ... entirely correct and necessary to launch a resolute counter-attack. But the scope of this struggle was made far too broad and a number of intellectuals, patriotic people and Party cadres were unjustifiably labelled 'rightists,' with unfortunate consequences."[91]

From late 1982 Deng then proceeded to roll back the core norms and policies of the Maoist era, together with fashioning new programmes in virtually all policy spheres. There were many hiccups along the way, and the reform programme demonstrated a distinct start-stop quality that paralleled a boom-bust cycle in the economy.[92] There was resistance from entrenched bureaucratic interests as well as Politburo adversaries who disagreed about the pace and modalities of reform, but on the whole Deng and his principal allies dominated the national agenda throughout the remainder of the decade. At no time did Deng really lose control, and on occasions, such as in January 1987 and October 1988 to May 1989, he withdrew support from individuals (Hu Yaobang and Zhao Ziyang respectively[93]) in order to retain it.

88. See "Remarks on successive drafts of the 'Resolution on Certain Questions in the History of our Party Since the Founding of the People's Republic of China'," *Selected Works*, pp. 276–296.

89. *Selected Works*, p. 329.

90. *Deng Xiaoping wenxuan (1975–82)* (Beijing: Renmin chubanshe, 1983), p. 258. I am indebted to Keith Forster for bringing this to my attention.

91. *Resolution on CPC History, (1949–81)* (Beijing: Foreign Languages Press, 1981), p. 27.

92. The economic cycle was more one of expansion–retrenchment, with the latter phase being intentionally induced to cool off overheating, rather than a real business cycle.

93. In point of fact, Deng began to withdraw his support for both these successors nearly a year before their fall from power. In Hu's case, by the middle of 1986 it became clear that he had offended Deng over his desire to accelerate the retirement *en masse* of the remaining elders on the Central Committee. Hu was also distrusted by the military high command. Deng apparently confronted Hu at an August 1986 Beidaihe work conference and at the subsequent Sixth Plenum in September. By the time student demonstrations erupted in December Hu's fate was sealed. Similarly, in the case of Zhao Ziyang, Deng began to withdraw active support at the August 1988 Beidaihe work conference that led to the

When Deng sensed that the agenda had been captured or was being unduly influenced by others he adopted various tactics – some straightforward, some surreptitious – to regain control. Like Mao in similar circumstances, Deng knew that his best weapon was his personal prestige. He would venture into the public arena, make remarks that would become the new *tifa* of the time, have them published in the newspaper, aired on television and disseminated as Central Documents for study by all cadres.

Perhaps the best example of this tactic was in early 1992. Deng was discontented with the slow pace of economic reform and political dominance of what he termed "leftists," and decided to try and recapture the agenda by visiting the Shenzhen and Zhuhai Special Economic Zones in January and February.[94] This was his first public appearance in over a year and, after initial blockage by his opponents (who controlled the propaganda apparatus) his trip was widely publicized in China and his comments made mandatory study for all. Deng's foray into the south launched a fierce intra-leadership struggle leading up to the 14th Party Congress, but he succeeded in reorienting the national agenda and leadership more to his liking. It put pressure on Li Peng and other leaders who favoured a much more controlled approach to economic reform. It also put pressure on the PLA, a conservative institution not particularly in favour of accelerated reform. Deng knew that the PLA was the key player in his succession, and for good measure he took several leading active and retired military officials to the south with him.

Sometimes Deng would try to influence the agenda more indirectly via the media. In February 1990, in an effort to reignite reform in the midst of the post-Tiananmen crackdown, he arranged to have several reformist articles published in the Shanghai newspaper *Liberation Daily*. His intervention was short-lived however, as the conservative-controlled CCP Propaganda Department refused to replay them nationally. Deng had lost control of both the national agenda and his designated successors. Under such circumstances he was left with no alternative but to invest his personal prestige in his heralded Southern Sojourn.

At other times Deng would support individuals to regain control of the political agenda. In the spring of 1987 he intervened personally to shore up Zhao Ziyang and his programme for accelerated economic and political reform in the run-up to the 13th Party Congress. He knew Zhao lacked the personal clout to push a radical agenda through the Congress,

---

footnote continued

economic retrenchment programme. Despite his lack of open support for Zhao I do not think Deng was convinced that Zhao had to go until the spring of 1989. Zhao's contradiction of the 26 April *People's Daily* editorial, which Deng had explicitly authorized, in his speech to the Asian Development Bank and his wait-and-see attitude toward the student demonstrations was bad enough, but his statements to Gorbachev was the *coup de grâce* as far as Deng was concerned.

94. See Zhonggong Shenzhen shiwei xuanchuanbu (ed.), *Yijiuernian chun: Deng Xiaoping yu Shenzhen* (*The Spring of 1992: Deng Xiaoping and Shenzhen*) (Shenzhen: Haitian chubanshe, 1992); and David Shambaugh, "Regaining political momentum: Deng strikes back," *Current History* (September 1992). pp. 257–261.

particularly at a time when the conservatives were in the ascent, and so lent his authority to Zhao.

Deng was, to some extent, vulnerable to his ideological critics – Wang Zhen, Deng Liqun, Hu Qiaomu – who repeatedly railed against the "erroneous tendencies" that had cropped up as a result of reforms, such as crime, corruption and dissent. Deng never failed to endorse their campaigns. This shows some tactical manoeuvre on his part, but is more indicative of his own intolerance of political liberalism.

Early on Deng established his limits for political and ideological expression in his 1979 speech "Uphold the Four Cardinal Principles."[95] Yet he personally put political reform on the national agenda in 1980 with his speech "On the Reform of the System of Party and State Leadership" (which he essentially defined as *administrative* reform).[96] Less than a year later Deng ordered the closing of Democracy Wall after posters began to call for Western-style democracy, and he ensured that Wei Jingsheng received a stiff 15-year sentence for advocating a "fifth modernization." In 1983 Deng launched the inner-Party rectification campaign against Cultural Revolution beneficiaries (the "three kinds of people" or *san zhong ren*[97]) Simultaneously (at the Sixth Plenum), Deng endorsed the campaign against "spiritual pollution." Within two months he had quietly withdrawn his endorsement of the campaign, but still endorsed Hu Qiaomu's attack on the proponents of "humanism" and "alienation" in 1984.

In 1986 Deng thought it a propitious time to push for further political reform.[98] He again began calling for "political structural reform" – the separation of Party and government (*dang-zheng fenkai*).[99] But with the outbreak of student demonstrations in December Deng once more shifted his position, sacking Hu Yaobang as CCP General Secretary and expelling dissident intellectuals Fang Lizhi, Wang Ruowang, Liu Binyan, Wu Zuguang and others from the Communist Party. By late spring 1987 Deng was again speaking of political reform, and he supported Zhao Ziyang and Hu Qili in reviving the *dang-zhang fenkai* discussions. The separation of Party and government was subsequently placed as a top

95. *Selected Works*, pp. 166–191.
96. *Selected Works*, pp. 302–325.
97. "Beaters, smashers, and looters" during the Cultural Revolution.
98. At a meeting of provincial governors in April Deng called for renewed attention to "reform of the political structure." In June he instructed the Central Committee Secretariat to formulate concrete political reform proposals. See Deng Xiaoping, "Reform the political structure and strengthen the people's sense of legality," *Fundamental Issues in Present Day China*, pp. 145–48. This endorsement of Deng's led to a summer-long series of political reform seminars and formation of a leadership small group under the direction of Hu Qili, until the conservatives counter-attacked at the August Beidaihe work conference. For details of the debate see Cheng Hsiang, "News From Beidaihe," *Wen Wei Po*, 8 August 1986, in *Summary of World Broadcasts: Far East*, 12 August 1986, pp. B2–4. In the wake of the Beidaihe meeting it is unclear whether Deng backed Zhao Ziyang's formation of the Political Structure Reform Office under the Central Committee in October 1986 or whether he began to withdraw his support.
99. On Deng's support for a new round of political structural reform, see Hou Dongtai, "Deng Xiaoping he zhengzhi tizhi gaige," *Da Gong Bao* (Hong Kong), 16 July 1986, pp. 5–7.

priority in Zhao Ziyang's report to the 13th Party Congress in October 1987.[100]

Deng's views of the Tiananmen demonstrations of 1989 are clear enough. From his meeting with Yang Shangkun and Li Peng on 25 April to his 6 June speech, he took decisive and drastic action.[101] For Deng, the demonstrations represented a direct threat to the survival of the CCP and PRC. No doubt memories of Cultural Revolution anarchy were also present in his mind. To save the party-state required firm and intimidating action. At first Deng watched as his designated successors factionalized and proved indecisive. Then he took matters into his own hands. He rallied the remnants of the Old Guard, mobilized the main force units of the PLA (with the assistance of Yang Shangkun), and called in the tanks.

Following Tiananmen Deng initially acquiesced to the ideologies and hardliners, yet by 1991 showed signs of frustration with the conservative leadership.[102] This was expressed in various ways, but ultimately in his Southern Tour. Deng's decision to emerge from retirement to re-energize the reform process had much to do with the lessons he drew from the collapse of Soviet and East European Communism. Deng apparently concluded that Communist rule crumbled in these countries because it had failed to deliver the goods, because political reform advanced ahead of economic reform, and because the regimes concerned did not have adequate control over their militaries and security services. Deng decided that for the CCP to survive, the material well-being of the populace must be rapidly improved; political reform must be postponed and the formation of any groups that could challenge the hegemony of the Communist Party must be suppressed; and the absolute loyalty of the military to the Party must be ensured.

Thus, in terms of agenda-setting, Deng Xiaoping demonstrated different strategies and tactics throughout his career. At times – during the 1950s and 1960s – he tended to work within and through central Party and state institutions, although he became quite assertive in 1963–64. In the mid-1970s, with the blessing of Premier Zhou and Chairman Mao, he gained an authority and independence he did not possess before the Cultural Revolution. During the 1980s and 1990s Deng employed a combination of these and other tactics. Generally speaking, though, Deng controlled the national agenda through classic balancing tactics.[103] Deng bargained through balancing, and vice versa. His proclivity was to

100. Zhao Ziyang, "Advance along the road of socialism with Chinese characteristics," *Documents of the Thirteenth National Congress of the Communist Party of China* (Beijing: Foreign Languages Press, 1987), pp. 42–60. I am indebted to Fan Cheuk Wan's analysis of this period; Fan Cheuk Wan, "Reform to separate Party and government: an abortive attempt to undermine Party domination over the state between 1986 and 1989," M. A. seminar paper, School of Oriental and African Studies, 1992.

101. *Cf.* n. 55.

102. For an analysis of this period see Shambaugh, "Regaining political momentum: Deng strikes back"; and David Shambaugh, "China in 1991: living cautiously," *Asian Survey* (January 1992), pp. 19–31.

103. For a useful discussion of this propensity see Harding, *China's Second Revolution*, pp. 90–93.

support radical reform, and he would push it when he could, but Deng's pragmatism more often made him occupy the middle ground.

By adopting varying leadership styles Deng has acted not unlike other politicians. Compromise and coalition building are necessary parts of the political process. So is bureaucracy; bureaucracies implement policies, but they also sabotage them. A leader needs to work through institutions, but also needs to circumvent them at times. Institutions create paperwork, and much of the governmental process is consumed with drafting and promulgating documents. Making speeches, using the power of the press and making forays into public to take one's message to the masses are standard devices for political agenda-setting in most countries. Deng has proved Chinese politics not very different in these respects.

Conclusion

In summarizing the political style of Deng Xiaoping, it may be instructive to recall the typology of leadership offered in 1978 by American political scientist James MacGregor Burns.[104] Burns elaborated nine distinct leadership styles, but argued that they clustered into two principal types: transformational and transactional. Transformational leaders, Burns argued, seek to transform society through ideas. They are generally intellectuals who pursue an ideological agenda of comprehensive social reform. Revolutionaries are one sub-type of transformational leader, and Burns – writing before Deng's ascendance – was quick to note the inclusion of Maoist China in this category. He observed that leaders of developing countries were often of the transformational type.

Burns found transactional leadership, on the other hand, to be more rooted in developed polities. Transactional leaders fit within a structural–functionalist interest aggregation model where public opinion is mobilized, interest groups act as a two-way channel for communicating political interest, and political parties aggregate diverse public interests and convey them to government for conversion into public policy.

Just as with Mao Zedong, the transformational leadership model helps to describe and understand Deng Xiaoping's leadership style and political behaviour. This probably says more, however, about the nature of the Chinese political system than it does about Deng. While opinion clusters, interest groups, and intra-governmental bargaining certainly exist in China, and Deng Xiaoping's reforms have done much to stimulate the rise of rudimentary civil society (and hence the public sphere approach to studying Chinese politics), China remains a developing country. China is an unparalleled political mass, excepting perhaps India. To "move a nation" (to quote John F. Kennedy) transformational leadership is required. As the East Asian experience has shown, the state can be a powerful force for socio-economic change if its leadership has a strong mandate, clear agenda and motivated working class. Deng had all three.

By initiating economic reform, however, Deng Xiaoping unleashed

104. James MacGregor Burns, *Leadership* (New York: Harper & Row, 1978).

powerful centrifugal forces that threaten to overwhelm the Communist party-state he sought to preserve. Deng studied the East Asian developmental model carefully, but learned incomplete lessons. He did not, or refused to, recognize the inevitable political pressures that well up from below as a result of economic growth and wealth accumulation. These inexorably breed popular demands for meaningful political participation and an improved quality of life (in, for example, environment, education, health care). To accommodate these demands devolution of political power is necessary, leading in time to an erosion of the hegemony of the party-state and the beginnings of democracy. Deng failed to recognize this linkage, and failed to create the institutional mechanisms for improved political participation. It is the most vexing problem he will bequeath to his successors. In the end, Deng failed to grasp the most fundamental of all Marxist precepts – the influence of the economic base on the political superstructure – and his successors may have to pay dearly for this obstinacy.

Deng Xiaoping: The Economist

Barry Naughton

Deng Xiaoping's economic legacy is overwhelmingly positive and quite secure – in this, it stands in contrast to his troubled and ambiguous political legacy. Of all of Deng's achievements, the transformation of China's economic system is the only one that is currently judged to have succeeded, and to have benefited large numbers of people. Deng presided over the Chinese government during a period of enormous economic change. Under his leadership, the government extricated itself from a legacy of massive economic problems and began a sustained programme of economic reform. Reforms transformed the economic system and initiated a period of explosive economic growth, bringing the country out of isolation and into the modern world economy.

Yet it is deeply paradoxical to credit Deng Xiaoping primarily with economic success, for he has never said anything original about economics or economic policy, and rarely displays any particular insight into the functioning of the economy. The relatively infrequent discussions of economic matters in Deng's speeches are usually either very broad generalities, or simple restatement of points made by others.[1] There is no Deng Xiaoping *vision* of the economy or the economic system. Thus, while he has intervened repeatedly and forcefully to keep the economic reform process moving forward, these interventions have always been precisely calculated for political effect, and extremely vague on economic content. Deng was a politician, a manager and a generalist whose most successful role was as the political godfather of economic reform.

Though Deng lacks vision, there are nevertheless certain areas where he is extremely clear-sighted. The most striking example is his insistence on the need for real incentives and delegation of authority in order to motivate individual effort. More broadly, there are several consistent themes that have marked Deng's career in economics. These make it possible to sketch out some aspects of the economic world according to Deng Xiaoping. Moreover, because the Chinese political system is so hierarchical, the themes of the person at the top inevitably shape long-term policy outcomes. This is true of China's economic reform process after 1978: it bears the stamp of Deng's personality. Like Deng himself, China's economic reforms have consistent themes, but no over-arching design or vision.

To a remarkable degree, the apparent failings of the reform process have turned out to be advantages. Lacking a clear objective, reforms unfolded in a gradual, evolutionary fashion, avoiding much of the economic trauma that characterized economic reforms in Eastern Europe and

---

1. David Bachman notes that "there is remarkably little discussion in Deng's [1975–1982] *Selected Works* on economic affairs." *Chen Yun and the Chinese Political System* (Berkeley: Institute of East Asian Studies, China Research Monograph No. 29, 1985), p. 156.

the former Soviet Union.[2] Similarly, absence of vision can be seen as Deng Xiaoping's personal strong point. Without a vision of his own to impose on society, Deng has been willing to adopt policies of non-intervention. He has allowed economic (but not political) developments to unfold without constant interference from the Party or government. Deng was willing to delegate economic decision-making, and he used capable subordinates effectively. He has expressed admiration for foreign economic accomplishments without defensiveness. Deng has displayed a personal talent for *laissez-faire*: he has mastered the ruler's art of non-acting.

The following takes Deng Xiaoping's career in roughly chronological order, while looking for patterns that extend across that career. The first section covers his activities in 1957–66 when he was an important, but junior, member of the small group of top leaders. The second section discusses his first brush with absolute power in 1975. The bulk of the article covers the post-1978 "era of Deng Xiaoping." Five consistent themes are seen to mark Deng's attitudes toward economic issues. These are the paramount importance accorded to economic development; the need for rapid growth; the importance of clear delegation of authority in order to utilize human resources; the importance of non-intervention; and the need to open to the outside world.[3] These simple themes do not add up to much of a theory of economic reform, but as general guidelines or reference points in rapidly changing situations, they are probably adequate. The final sections consider the overall legacy of economic reform, and Deng's role in shaping the reform process. Since Deng may be said to have provided the basic orientation for a generally successful programme of economic reform, we may give him some of the credit for China's recent string of economic successes.

Deng the Organization Man: 1952–67

Deng Xiaoping has been a member of the small group of top Communist Party leaders during most of the post-1949 period. He was the first of the major regional leaders to be brought to Beijing, in July 1952, and he rose rapidly to a position of great influence under the overall command of Mao Zedong. By mid-1953, at the latest, Deng was supervising crucial aspects of economic decision-making. As Vice-Premier, he was assigned to oversee the transport sector. Moreover, in September 1953 he was

2. On this aspect of the reforms, see Cyril Lin, "Open-ended economic reform in China," in Victor Nee and David Stark (eds.), *Remaking the Economic Institutions of Socialism: China and Eastern Europe* (Stanford: Stanford University Press, 1989); and John McMillan and Barry Naughton, "How to reform a planned economy: lessons from China," *Oxford Review of Economic Policy*, Vol. 8, No. 1 (spring 1992).
3. We should note that our list is not too different from the official Chinese list of Deng's accomplishments. The hagiographic literature credits Deng with four economic innovations: legitimizing economic development as the main task of government; setting effective long-run economic objectives; initiating economic reform; and supporting the open door policy. See Yao Ping (ed.), *Xin shiqi Deng Xiaoping zhanlue sixiang yanjiu* (*Studies in the Strategic Thought of Deng Xiaoping during the New Era*) (Xi'an: Shaanxi renmin chubanshe, 1989).

appointed to serve concurrently as Minister of Finance, replacing Bo Yibo, who was under fire for political errors. During late 1953, Deng worked with Chen Yun to implement the monopoly purchase of grain and cotton in the countryside, a key element of state control over the economy. Important as these responsibilities were, they were only one part of Deng's steady rise to a key position as political generalist at Mao's right hand. In April 1954, Deng was appointed Secretary General (*mishuzhang*) of the CCP Central Committee and head of the organization department, directly controlling the Party personnel function. Finally, in September 1956, following the Eighth Party Congress, he became General Secretary (*zong shuji*) of the Central Committee, a position he maintained until 1967, when he was deposed during the Cultural Revolution. With these positions at the core of the Party organization, Deng had responsibility for hands-on management of an extremely broad range of issues, including economic issues. As General Secretary, he routinely controlled the assignment of responsibility over important tasks, as well as presiding over promotions and demotions through the Party personnel system. Deng was thus a generalist whose responsibility for aspects of economic policy was but one part of his broad portfolio.[4]

Given Deng's positions, all important economic decisions flowed through his management system, and there is evidence that he participated in virtually every important economic decision made between 1957 and 1966. Yet the nature of his position was such that he rarely had sole authority over any area of economic policy. Like all central officials, Deng had to ascertain Mao Zedong's position on important issues, and fall in line when the Chairman expressed his views. Deng's senior colleague Chen Yun had far greater expertise on economic issues, and there is considerable evidence that Deng routinely deferred to Chen's views on important matters.[5] In addition, authority over ordinary management of economic affairs was shared with Premier Zhou Enlai, who presided over the government bureaucracy and outranked Deng within the Party. Deng was able to maintain remarkably good relations with these three individuals. Zhou and Deng co-operated particularly well, and after December 1963 Deng was formally designated to serve as Acting Premier in Zhou's absence.[6]

4. Li Xinzhi and Wang Yuezong, *Weida de shijian, guanghui de sixiang: Deng Xiaoping geming huodong dashiji* (*Great Practice and Glorious Thought: A Chronology of Deng Xiaoping's Revolutionary Activity*) (Beijing: Hualing chubanshe, 1990), pp. 102, 104, 109. Han Shanbi, *Deng Xiaoping pingzhuan (A Critical Biography of Deng Xiaoping)* (Hong Kong: Dongxi wenhua shiye gongsi, 2nd ed., 1988), p. 283. An interesting perspective on Deng's role and ascent during the early years is provided by Frederick C. Teiwes, *Politics at Mao's Court: Gao Gang and Party Factionalism in the Early 1950s* (Armonk: M. E. Sharpe, 1990), esp. pp. 21, 70, 87–88, 117, 134, 145, 286.

5. See, for example, Deng Liqun, *Xiang Chen Yun tongzhi xuexi zuo jingji gongzuo* (*Study Economic Work from Comrade Chen Yun*) (Beijing: Zhonggong zhongyang dangxiao, 1981), p. 9.

6. Li Xinzhi and Wang Yuezong, *Great Practice and Glorious Thought*, p. 132. The association between Zhou Enlai and Deng Xiaoping dates back to their time in France in the 1920s. Deng Xiaoping had in effect served as Acting Premier on occasion in the late 1950s as well. Han Shanbi, *A Critical Biography*, pp. 258–59.

To the extent that an individual Deng Xiaoping contribution to economic policy can be discerned during this period, it has to do with the design of incentive systems. During his brief tenure as Minister of Finance, Deng supported the introduction of incentive measures into the fiscal system. He supported having lower levels of government guarantee (*baogan*) revenues and expenditures, and allowing local governments to retain surpluses of planned revenues over expenditures for use in the following year. This last provision in particular represented a modest but significant departure from the standard Soviet practice of highly centralized control of the budget.[7] Another case of Deng's individual input occurred during the immediate post-Great Leap Forward crisis, during 1960–62. At that time, the top leaders divided among themselves responsibility for overseeing different aspects of the economic rehabilitation. Deng's responsibility was the reform and rectification of enterprise management and the rehabilitation of the labour union system. As part of this process, Deng personally supervised the drafting during 1961 of a document on enterprise management that emphasized clear definition of tasks and responsibility within industrial enterprises. This document, the 70 Articles on State Industrial Enterprise Work, stressed the need for regularization of management systems (for which it was denounced during the Cultural Revolution as a conservative and bureaucratic document).[8] The need for regular systems of responsibility and authority, along with appropriate motivational devices, is thus a consistent feature of Deng's approach to economic problems. Such an emphasis was certainly related to his position in the Communist Party system. As General Secretary, Deng presided over the Party's day-to-day operations, of which arguably the most important was running the Party's personnel system. The Party controls all important jobs in society, most of them in government or urban enterprises, with industry a particular focus. By at least 1961, Deng had staked out special expertise in the operation of personnel systems, and began thinking about ways to improve systems of authority and responsibility.

Yet apart from this modest area of specialization, and in spite of Deng's active involvement with the *process* of economic decision-making, there is remarkably little evidence of an economic viewpoint that can be specifically attributed to him. It is worth emphasizing how surprising this is. During this period of over a decade, the Chinese leadership grappled with economic issues of tremendous importance and great complexity. The prevailing policy shifted several times, and created great successes and enormous disasters. Yet in all these issues, there is virtually no case where there can be seen an independent position advocated by Deng Xiaoping. A short list of the most crucial economic policies developed during this period – the policies toward capitalist business

7. Deng Xiaoping, "Six directions for fiscal work" (12 January 1954), in *Deng Xiaoping Wenxuan (1938–1965)* (*Selected Works of Deng Xiaoping, 1938–1965*) (Beijing: Renmin chubanshe, 1989), pp. 182–83.

8. Yu Guangyuan, "Develop economic sciences," *Jingji yanjiu*, No. 10 (1981), p. 4; Li Xinzhi and Wang Yuezong, *Great Practice and Glorious Thought*, p. 121.

established during 1953, the acceleration of collectivization and national-
ization in 1955–56, the economic readjustment and liberal policies of
1956–57, the formation of communes and beginning of the Great Leap
Forward in 1958, drastic rehabilitation of the economy following the
catastrophic Great Leap collapse, and then renewed radicalization first of
rural policy in late 1962 and subsequently of growth policy with a new
Five-Year Plan in 1964 – shows in each case Deng participating in the
implementation of policy, but nowhere influencing the making of policy.
In none of these important issues can we discern a viewpoint specifically
attributable to Deng Xiaoping.

Deng always carried out the established policy, vigorously and effectively, whatever that policy was. This was notoriously true in the case of
the Great Leap, which Deng supported from the beginning, as he himself
has repeatedly acknowledged.[9] Subsequently, after the Leap collapsed,
Deng played an active role in carrying out the effective policies that
began China's economic recovery; and Deng's Secretariat produced a
draft Third Five-Year Plan in 1964 that stressed continued priority to
restoring agriculture and recovering pre-Leap levels of consumption. But
in late 1964, in response to Mao's intervention, this Plan was abandoned
and the emphasis shifted sharply toward militarization and accelerated
heavy industrial investment, and the drafting of the radically revised
Third Five-Year Plan was also supervised by Deng's Secretariat.[10] It is
not unusual to find Deng on both sides of a single issue at different times;
however, he is always following the prevailing line, without regard to his
previous position. His record was one of unprincipled but effective
implementation of whatever policies were adopted by the Centre.

Deng's approach to economic problems should be clearly distinguished
from what we might term "principled pragmatism." Deng was pragmatic
and effective in carrying out whatever policy was set by the central
government (in most cases, ultimately by Mao Zedong). But this pragmatism did not apply to the definition of economic problems themselves.
Rather, Deng let other top leaders define the economic problems, and
then confined his skills to the implementation of policies they had
established. The contrast here is especially great with Chen Yun. Chen,
like Deng, never overtly opposed any of Mao Zedong's policies, but
Chen's activity and visibility among the elite fluctuated dramatically.
When policies congenial to Chen's consistently-expressed ideas were
being implemented, he played a major role; when policies conflicted with
his views, he tended to become invisible. As a result, Chen's consistent

9. Deng Xiaoping, "Adhere to the Party line and improve methods of work," *Selected
Works (1975–1982)*, pp. 262–63; "Remarks on successive drafts of the 'Resolution on
Certain Questions in the History of Our Party'," *ibid.* p. 281. For more on Deng Xiaoping
during the Great Leap Forward, see Roderick MacFarquhar, *The Origins of the Cultural
Revolution, 2: The Great Leap Forward, 1958–1960* (New York: Columbia University
Press, 1983), pp. 60–61, 121, 166, 176, 323.

10. According to Li Yue, cited in *Jingjixue dongtai*, No. 2 (1981), p. 14, the original plan
was drafted "according to the ideas of Chen Yun and Deng Xiaoping." Yan Mingfang, "The
compilation and fulfilment of the Third Five-Year Plan," *Dangshi yanjiu*, No. 6 (1986), pp.
38–39; Li Xinzhi and Wang Yuezong, *Great Practice and Glorious Thought*, pp. 136, 140.

views on economic affairs could be fairly readily deduced, even if he had not written extensively on a wide range of economic issues.[11] No such patterns are discernible in the case of Deng. He played a major role as manager, fixer and enforcer under a wide variety of policy orientations.[12]

The view of Deng Xiaoping as above all a pragmatist has been crucially bolstered by his statement, "it doesn't matter if a cat is black or white, so long as it catches mice." This statement was indeed made by Deng, and moreover made in the context of a crucial economic issue with explosive political connotations. It was said in July 1962 in the course of a speech in which he supported the experimental policy of contracting farmland to individual peasant households.[13] Subsequently, this policy was condemned by Mao Zedong as a serious deviation from the correct Party line, and during the Cultural Revolution an entire public relations offensive against Deng was drummed up on the basis of this one quotation.

In fact, in this speech Deng was simply echoing statements that Mao Zedong had been making over the previous year and a half. Mao had explicitly supported contracting land to individual households in Anhui province on an experimental basis, and he called for a flexible and experimental approach to rural policy in general. In March 1961, referring to an explicit request for guidance on contracting land to households, Mao told the Party secretary of Anhui, "Try it out! If it doesn't work, you'll do a self-criticism, and that'll be the end of it. If it works, and you can produce an extra 500,000 tons of grain, that will be a great thing."[14] Mao's commitment to open-minded experimentation was doubtless be-

11. As a result of Chen's consistence and importance, we have two excellent English language studies of his life. Bachman, *Chen Yun and the Chinese Political System*; Nicholas Lardy and Kenneth Lieberthal, "Introduction" in *Chen Yun's Strategy for China's Development* (Armonk: M. E. Sharpe, 1983).

12. One commonly-held view is that after 1962 there was increasing divergence of views between Mao and other leaders, including Deng. See Wang Nianyi, "A tentative discussion of the origins of the Cultural Revolution," *Dangshi yanjiu*, No. 1 (1982) pp. 24–31. That may indeed be true, but there is no real evidence to substantiate it with the evidence currently available. In fact, it is still difficult to make any confident assertion about Deng's views during this period given the current state of our knowledge. Because Deng was not the top person in the hierarchy, his speeches have been less abundantly published and studied until very recently. Nearly all his important statements currently available have been subjected to high selective editing. See Michael Schoenhals, "Edited records: comparing two versions of Deng Xiaoping's '7,000 Cadres Conference Speech'," *CCP Research Newsletter*, No. 1 (1988), pp. 5–9, and below on factory manager systems. The selection of documents available is systematically biased to project certain images of Deng – for example, the official *Selected Works* contains no speeches between May 1957 and March 1960, in spite of Deng's intense activity during this period. Finally, since the most characteristic feature of Mao's proclamations during this period was *inconsistency*, and the most characteristic feature of most other Party leaders (including Deng) was *slavish subordination* to Mao's proclamations, it follows that selective compilation can produce almost any kind of historic record. All we can say is that there is currently no reliable evidence to support the view that Deng independently advocated *any* significant policy position before 1967.

13. Deng Xiaoping, "How to revive agricultural production," *Selected Works (1938–1965)*, p. 305.

14. Liu Yishun, "Ceng Xisheng and the responsibility fields in Anhui," *Dangshi yanjiu*, No. 3 (1987), pp. 26–27; Liu Yishun and Zhou Duoli, "The question of 'responsibility fields' in Anhui in 1961," *Dangshi yanjiu*, No. 5, (1983), pp. 35–40.

ginning to fade somewhat by the following year when Deng spoke, but it was still official Maoist policy. Only in the following months did Mao reverse himself.[15] Similar conclusions follow whenever Deng's statements are carefully matched with the policy lines prevailing at the time the statements are made. For example, Deng as General Secretary supervised the drafting of a programmatic document on rural policy in September 1963, which came to be known as the "Second Ten Points." Denounced during the Cultural Revolution as a revisionist document, it seems clear that it was routinely drafted under Deng Xiaoping's general supervision, and was seen as a refinement and polishing of existing policies, rather than a new departure.[16]

Thus, in the period before 1967, Deng operated as the consummate organization man. With a crucial position in the organization, he exemplified the effective bureaucrat, accepting a delegation of authority from above and carrying out tasks with great responsibility. Meanwhile, he gave attention to extending effective bureaucratic mechanisms into the state-run industrial economy, seeking to expand the scope for delegation of authority and responsibility. At the same time, Deng was the organization man in another sense: responding to the needs of the organization, he seems to be without a personal vision, and possibly without personal principles.

Deng's Interlude: Power, Purge and Return, 1975–78

Deng was recalled to Beijing in February 1973 to work in foreign affairs.[17] His role gradually expanded, and in December 1974 Mao – after reportedly concluding that Wang Hongwen was not sufficiently competent to run the country – designated Deng Vice-Chairman of the

15. In fact, in this speech, Deng is very careful to specify that the policy of open experimentation is in effect only until a scheduled August Party meeting, which will develop more specific (and restrictive) rural work methods. Deng Xiaoping, "How to revive agricultural production," p. 305. Much later, Deng specifically noted that at that time "it seemed that Comrade Mao Zedong was then earnestly correcting 'Left' mistakes .... At the Beidaihe Meeting of July–August [1962], however, he reversed direction again, laying renewed and even greater stress on class struggle." "Remarks on successive drafts of the 'Resolution on Certain Questions in the History of Our Party'," *Selected Works of Deng Xiaoping (1975–1982)*, (Beijing: Foreign Languages Press, 1984), p. 281.

16. Indeed, the document served as the basis of policy for over a year without significant controversy, until it was swamped by the intensifying tensions between Mao and Liu Shaoqi, with their contrasting "experiences" and approaches to rural policy formulation. It may be, as some have argued, that the document represents a subtle shift towards greater acceptance of rural commercial activities than might have been envisaged by Mao, and argued for some safeguards to protect cadres. Even if true, such subtle shifts of emphasis were well within the general policy framework. Richard Baum, *Prelude to Revolution: Mao, the Party and the Peasant Question, 1962–66* (New York: Columbia University Press, 1975), pp. 43–59. Baum's summary of Deng's position on p. 165 still seems right: "Above all, Deng seems to have been concerned with establishing routinized bureaucratic norms and procedures and with regularizing the channels of communication between higher and lower levels within the Party – in short, with perfecting the instruments of 'rational' public administration."

17. The fact that Mao was willing to recall Deng in early 1973 may also serve as indirect evidence that Deng played "by the rules" before 1967. If Mao seriously believed Deng had ignored Mao and pushed his own agenda, as charged by Cultural Revolution radicals, he surely would not have advanced him to positions of great power during the 1970s.

Communist Party, Vice-Premier, and vice-head of the Military Commission. Deng was effectively replacing Zhou Enlai, who was already incapacitated by the cancer that would prove fatal a year later. Throughout 1975, Deng possessed enormous power, second only to that of Mao; no longer was there any presumption that Deng would implement the policies of others. He was undoubtedly constrained by what was acceptable to an increasingly erratic Mao, and by the need to pay lip-service to Cultural Revolution principles. But overall he was primarily responsible for the policies adopted during 1975 and, in sharp contrast to the past, the policies adopted bear the unmistakable stamp of Deng Xiaoping.

In the economic sphere, policy was dominated throughout 1975 by two consistent themes: rectification and accelerated growth. Rectification was not just an economic policy – it began with the military and extended into nearly every part of society as part of "overall rectification." Part of it was reshuffling personnel: firing incompetents and political opponents and promoting capable individuals and loyal supporters. But it was also an important economic policy, in that it involved rebuilding clear systems of command, responsibility and incentives. The focus of rectification in this sense was the industry and transport complex, and it began with the railways. Deng's programme for the railways rested on explicit centralization of authority, combined with clear rules governing responsibilities and power. He turned to his old friend Wan Li, making him Minister of Railways and head of the rectification work group. A Central Document "Decision on Strengthening Railway Work" (*zhongfa* No. 9) gave additional authority to Wan Li and was also used as a model for extending rectification to other sectors. It was applied in succession to steel, petroleum and military industries during the first half of the year.[18]

After mid-year, Deng sought to expand the ongoing rectification with a programmatic document that would cover all industrial sectors. He had the State Planning Commission begin drafting "On Several Questions of Accelerating Industrial Development." Deng took a direct personal interest in the revision of this document, and pointed out that it should be based on the 70 Articles of 1961.[19] This document stresses centralization of authority and comprehensive planning of economic activity. Above all, though, it can be seen as a return to principles of personnel management that call for clearly delineated responsibility and authority.[20] The stress is on rules and regulation, and on central control, rather than delegation of

18. Wang Nianyi, *1949–1989 nian de Zhongguo 3: da dongluan de niandai* (*China from 1949–1989, III: The Period of Great Chaos*) (Zhengzhou: Henan renmin chubanshe, 1989), pp. 516–523. I am grateful to Kam Wing Chan for providing a copy of this source. Li Xinzhi and Wang Yuezong, *Great Practice and Glorious Thought*, pp. 178–183, 187.

19. Wang Nianyi, *China from 1949–1989*, p. 526.

20. A draft version of the document is reprinted in Chi Hsin, *The Case of the Gang of Four* (Hong Kong: Cosmos Books, 1977), pp. 239–272. See also Deng Xiaoping, *Selected Works, 1975–1982*, pp. 45, 8–11, 28–31. As Bachman points out, "Beginning in 1975, Deng has consistently advocated rectification of leading bodies in factories." Bachman, *Chen Yun*, p. 156. As we have seen, this advocacy can be traced back to 1961. See also Kenneth Lieberthal, with James Tong and Sai-cheung Yeung, *Central Documents and Politburo Politics in China* (Ann Arbor: Michigan Papers in Chinese Studies, No. 33, 1978), esp. pp. 27, 44–49.

authority and decentralization. This can be seen as the outcome of an attempt to establish clear, well-functioning authority systems in the wake of Cultural Revolution chaos.

The other consistent theme was the desire to accelerate economic growth. In order to provide a broader legitimacy to the growth objective, Deng reaffirmed the goal of the "four modernizations." The four modernizations were a visionary programme introduced by Zhou Enlai in 1965, designed to be the second stage of a two-stage, long-term development strategy. During the first stage (1965–80), China would build a self-sufficient industrial base and be relatively autarkic – out of necessity, since it had few export products and little hope of aid from the superpowers. Zhou then envisaged China emerging from isolation around 1980, and beginning a period of accelerated growth and a renewed opening: this he called the four modernizations. He had thus tried to build into the long-term development strategy the idea that economic growth and opening to the outside world would return to the top of the agenda. Shunted aside during the Cultural Revolution, the idea was revived by Zhou himself during the Fourth NPC in January 1975, in what was virtually his last major personal initiative. Deng immediately seized on the theme, and made the idea of the transition to the second-stage "four modernizations" one of his major themes from February 1975.[21]

Yet the specific strategy that Deng pushed to accelerate economic growth was deeply flawed. Planners under Deng in the autumn of 1975 drew up a "Ten-Year Plan" for development of the economy from 1976 to 1985. This was a terrible plan: it was unrealistic and inconsistent, and it reflected a single-minded concentration on the heavy industrial sectors that had been top priority under the Stalinist (and Maoist) development strategy of the past. Very high targets were set for steel and petroleum, and planners were unable to reconcile supplies and demands for key commodities even in 1975, the first year of implementation.[22] In any case, significant improvement in the economy became impossible as, in 1976, Deng was purged again and open struggle raged over the succession to Mao.

Deng returned to positions of significant power from July 1977. Between then and December 1978 he exerted substantial influence, although he was formally outranked by Hua Guofeng.[23] One of the most distinctive characteristics of this period was the revival of the Ten-Year Plan drawn up under Deng in 1975, which was dusted off and declared operational again. A few targets were raised to even more unrealistic levels, and the export of petroleum in exchange for imports of Western machinery, present in the original plan, was given greater prominence. But this was essentially Deng's plan brought back to life. It was finally

---

21. Li Xinzhi and Wang Yuezong, *Great Practice and Glorious Thought*, pp. 177, 179–180.

22. Barry Naughton, "China's experience with guidance planning," *Journal of Comparative Economics*, No. 14 (1990), pp. 746–48.

23. On this period, see Kenneth Lieberthal, "The politics of modernization in the PRC," *Problems of Communism*, May–June 1978, pp. 1–17.

abandoned at the end of 1978, more or less collapsing under the weight of its own contradictions. It was quickly forgotten, and those who thought of it tended to pin responsibility on the hapless Hua Guofeng. By this time, Deng was leading the way toward economic reform, and it would have been unnecessarily backward-looking to burden him with responsibility for a failed economic plan.

After 1978: The Era of Deng Xiaoping

At the end of 1978, during the Third Plenum of the 11th Central Committee, Deng emerged as the paramount leader. From that point until the present (1993), no major policies were adopted of which Deng did not approve, and Deng himself was the initiator of many important policies. In that sense, the entire reform period is legitimately seen as the era of Deng Xiaoping. Yet Deng has not managed economic policy on a day-to-day basis. In spite of occasional interventions into economic policy, he must be thought of as presiding over policy-making, rather than controlling it directly. In this sense, Deng's role after 1978 is something of a mirror image of his role before 1967. Before 1967 he was a hands-on administrator with little ability actually to make policy, while after 1978 he was a hands-off leader who established a general orientation for policy, but left the details to others.

While Deng's direct interventions in economic policy-making were rare, they were always crucial. This was particularly so at the very beginning, when, at the end of 1978 and beginning of 1979, he allied with Chen Yun and Li Xiannian to initiate the twin policies of economic readjustment and reform. Chen Yun in particular was advocating ideas with which he had long been associated, and which he had been vocally upholding since mid-1978. Deng, on the other hand, clearly moved to distance himself from a faulty economic plan with which he was closely associated, and embraced economic ideas with which he had no past association. Deng's change of heart began the economic reform era. Shortly thereafter, he was able to promote Zhao Ziyang to Premier, placing an effective administrator in the key economic policy-making role. With a capable subordinate in charge of daily affairs, Deng resumed his preferred role as presider over the policy process. He intervened forcefully again in 1984, laying the groundwork for the crucial October 1984 Party decision on urban reform and jump-starting the stalled reform process. Again, during 1987–88, Deng repeatedly made comments designed to give added momentum to the reform process. Finally, immediately after the Tiananmen massacre, he began trying to repair the damage to the economic reform process. By December 1990, he was actively meeting top leaders, trying to get the economic reform programme going again, and at the beginning of 1992 he made his famous trip to the Shenzhen Special Economic Zone in order to re-ignite the economic reform process. Thus, over a 15-year period, Deng personally shaped economic policy in only four or five instances, but each instance was crucial.

Given this general pattern, it makes no sense to survey Deng's activities over those 15 years in chronological fashion. Instead, it is more appropriate to identify several consistent themes that have characterized the general policy environment that Deng has created. Five stand out.

The central importance of economic development. One of Deng Xiaoping's greatest accomplishments was to shift the focus of the Communist Party to economic construction. This new goal was enshrined in the declaration of the Third Plenum in December 1978, and in various permutations has been included in all successive programmatic documents. Deng was not the first, nor the most articulate, advocate of economic development within the Chinese Communist Party. If any individual deserves that credit, it is Zhou Enlai.[24] But in any case, giving it priority is a practical accomplishment, rather than an intellectual one. In the highly politicized atmosphere of the immediate post-Cultural Revolution, Deng succeeded in making Zhou's objective into Party policy. Central to that accomplishment was the effective neutralization of competing Party objectives. Initially there were three competing goals: political mobilization and transformation, equity of income distribution and military strength. Deng was able to push each of them to the margins of the political agenda.

The Third Plenum ushered in an era of political relaxation, at least until the June 1989 Tiananmen incident. Deng described this pretty well in 1992: "Not to engage in debates – this was an invention of mine. Not to debate – this is in order to get more time to accomplish things."[25] Distributional considerations were effectively sidelined after Deng began proclaiming the necessity to "let some people get rich first." He never abandoned the idea that equity was a fundamental characteristic of socialism and one that showed the fundamental superiority of socialism to capitalism: this became a recurrent theme of his in 1985–86. But he redefined the notion of equity, moving it away from simple egalitarianism towards less politically constricting notions. He described the superiority of socialism in terms of avoiding polarization, achieving common prosperity and eliminating poverty.[26] Each of these formulations allowed Deng to maintain a long-run commitment to broad-based income growth, while insisting that in the short run equity should be subordinate to economic construction. Finally, he shifted the focus of Party and governmental activity away from the military. Deng's successive declarations during the early 1980s that a period of extended peace was possible – backed by his prestige with the military – were essential in obtaining a

---

24. Deng's 1957 speech was, however, an articulate expression of the importance of economic development: "From now on, the main responsibility is to carry out economic construction" (8 April 1957) in *Selected Works (1938–1956)*, pp. 249–257.

25. Deng Xiaoping, "1992 nian 1 yue 18 hao zhi 2 yue 20 hao Wuchang, Shenzhen, Zhuhai he Shanghai shi de jianghua" ("Speeches given from 18 January to 20 February 1992 while visiting Wuchang, Shenzhen, Zhuhai and Shanghai"). Internally circulated study materials, p. 9.

26. Deng Xiaoping, *Fundamental Issues in Present-Day China* (Speeches, 1985–1986) (Beijing: Foreign Languages Press, 1987), pp. 124, 127, 178.

substantial reduction in the flow of resources to the military and military industry.

The central importance of economic construction is stressed by Deng not only in opposition to political mobilization by the left, but also in opposition to active democratization of society. Political activity outside strictly controlled bureaucratic channels is seen merely as a diversion of energy from economic construction: it can create chaos but cannot make a positive economic contribution. Deng told former United States President George Bush on 26 February 1989:

There are so many Chinese people, and each has his own viewpoint. If there's a demonstration by this one today, and that one tomorrow, there'd be a demonstration every day, 365 days a year. In that case, economic construction would be entirely out of the question.[27]

In a sense, Deng's stress on economic construction can be seen as another sign of his lack of an affirmative vision of the good society. Economic development is a good thing, but, unusually for a political leader, Deng has never even hinted at his ideas about what kind of society ought to emerge as its product.

Authority and responsibility should be clearly delegated. The importance Deng gave to issues of authority and responsibility in 1961 and 1975 have already been seen. This focus re-emerged as soon as he returned in 1977. Again, in one of the few instances in which there is evidence of a distinct personal contribution by Deng, it is related to the clarification of authority and responsibility. His important March 1978 speech on science and technology was drafted by aides, but he personally added two points to the draft: the need to rely on science and technology to develop production, and the need to adopt a research institute director responsibility system.[28] This was the first of the various "responsibility systems" that so strongly characterized the reform decade of the 1980s. Clearly delineated authority, reinforced by increasingly significant material incentives as the reform process went on, is the most characteristic "Dengist" element of reform.

Of the various "responsibility systems," the most important was the "factory manager responsibility system." Its importance lay in the fact that the alternative to factory manager responsibility was authority held by the Party secretary, or diffused among the various contenders for power in the factory.[29] In a major speech on leadership on 18 August

27. Li Xinzhi and Wang Yuezong, *Great Practice and Glorious Thought*, p. 297. Cf. *ibid.* p. 282.

28. This is according to Lin Zixin, who wrote the original draft. Informal remarks at Meridian House workshop on economic policy-making during the 1980s. Washington, D. C., 24 October 1991; Deng Xiaoping, *Selected Works (1975–1982)*, pp. 112–13.

29. A 1980 description held that "in general, the current system is that the Party secretary is the number one man, and the factory manager is the number two man. Even when the number one man doesn't give direct orders, the number two man has to secure his agreement when managing production and doing administrative work." Yan Chongzong, "Reform of

1980, Deng proposed that the system in which managers were subordinate to Party committees (and secretaries) be replaced:

[We must] progressively and with preparation change the system of factory manager responsibility under the leadership of the Party committee and, after testing, gradually implement the system of factory manager responsibility under the leadership of the factory management committee or board of directors.... This reform will take the Party committee out of day-to-day affairs, and allow it to concentrate on political and ideological work and organizational supervision.

This is a clear case where Deng is personally setting the agenda. Indeed, he was sufficiently out in front on this issue that when the public version of his *Selected Works* was printed, this passage was omitted.[30] The idea was shelved for four years while the focus of work shifted to enterprise rectification within the existing framework: regularizing management positions and appointing a whole new group of managers. Widespread implementation of factory manager responsibility did not begin until May 1984. Again Deng was personally involved, appointing a work group under his close associate Peng Zhen to supervise gradual implementation. After some delays during 1985–86 caused by political scuffles, the factory manager responsibility system became nearly universal in 1987–88.[31]

A clear sustained pattern emerges from these incidents. Deng is consistently concerned with the personnel function, and just as consistently advocates clear delegation of authority to specified individuals. Moreover, he is primarily concerned with organizations that are directly part of the state/Party bureaucratic chain of command, that is, with urban rather than agricultural organizations. To a certain extent this is understandable in terms of Deng's political position: as the real top leader of the Communist Party, he is the only individual who can order the Communist Party out of factory management. But, significantly, Deng has seen authentic decentralization of authority as the fundamental principle of economic reform. As early as 1978 he said: "Whoever is given responsibility should be given authority as well."[32] Even retrospectively, Deng has propounded a view of responsibility for mistakes committed under Mao: "Whenever we had the right to speak, we must bear some of

---

footnote continued
the factory management system cannot be delayed," *Gongye jingji guanli congkan*, No. 2 (1980), p. 26.

30. Deng Xiaoping, *Selected Works (1978–1982)*, pp. 322–24; the original version is cited from System Reform Commission, *Zhongguo jingji tizhi gaige shinian* (*Ten Years of Economic System Reform in China*) (Beijing: Jingji guanli, 1988), p. 24.

31. System Reform Commission, Enterprise Reform Section, *Zhongguo qiye gaige shinian* (*Ten Years of Enterprise Reform in China*) (Beijing: Gaige, 1990), pp. 458–59; Zhang Zhanbin, *Xin Zhongguo qiye lingdao zhidu* (*New China's Enterprise Leadership System*) (Beijing: Chunqiu, 1988). There was some erosion of this accomplishment after 4 June 1989, which is discussed below.

32. Deng Xiaoping, *Selected Works (1975–1982)*, p. 163.

the responsibility."[33] This also became Deng's favourite explanation for the success of rural reforms: "The main idea is to delegate power to lower levels. The reason our rural reform has been so successful is that we gave the peasants more power to make decisions, and that stimulated their initiative."[34]

In the reform era, Deng's stress broadens from clear lines of authority to encompass incentives – including, but not limited to, material incentives. Deng is a manager and a leader: he is concerned with exhortation, discipline and reward. David Bachman points out that with Deng, "the CCP is a major actor ... Deng is constantly exhorting the Party ... this mobilizational view in Deng's thought can probably be traced back to his days as a political commissar ... in this sense, he is the most Maoist of China's major leaders today."[35] This is true, but there is an important difference from the Maoist view in that Deng appears to believe genuinely that real decentralization of authority is essential in order to achieve the mobilization of initiative that he seeks. It is his willingness to countenance this decentralization that separates him so sharply from Mao. Deng appears to have recognized early on that the existing system stifled creativity, and that only economic and administrative reform of a fairly radical character could ever resolve the problem.

Finally, the central importance of personnel management in Deng Xiaoping's career can be traced in his use of subordinates. Deng was able to listen to good advice, and willing to let go of control over economic matters. He has been willing to allow specialists in economic policy-making to make economic decisions without much interference on his part. In 1978–79, the crucial innovations in economic policy were made by Li Xiannian and Chen Yun, with Deng serving rather to orchestrate the overall political conditions that made these changes possible. Beginning in 1981 and extending to the end of 1988, most concrete economic policy was made by Zhao Ziyang, who enjoyed Deng's support until the end of this period. These individuals, from their very different perspectives, all had substantial economic expertise, and Deng was wise to rely upon them.[36] The stress on his direct management of personnel also draws attention to an aspect of his accomplishment that might otherwise be missed. Not only did he remove "political correctness" as the criterion guiding overall Party policy (in favour of economic construction); he also largely removed political correctness as the criterion guiding appointment and promotion within the system. During the 1980s, Deng directly or

33. Huang Kecheng, "On the question of the appropriate attitude to Chairman Mao and Mao Zedong Thought," *Dangshi yanjiu*, No. 2 (1981), pp. 2–10.

34. Deng Xiaoping, *Fundamental Issues*, p. 195.

35. Bachman, *Chen Yun*, p. 159.

36. In this respect, the most telling contrast is with Mikhail Gorbachev. Gorbachev also had a weak grasp of economics, but unlike Deng he did not have good instincts with respect to the use of subordinates in economic matters. Gorbachev jumped from one fashionable economic adviser to another, each promising a quick solution to economic problems. Nothing was done, and the Soviet economy went to pieces. By contrast, Deng allowed Zhao Ziyang to chart a consistent policy course, and the Chinese economy responded well to effective policy-making.

indirectly promoted a large group of qualified and effective managers and local officials to replace the former Party hacks. This leadership turnover contributed substantially to China's improved performance in the 1980s.

Deng's stress on authority and responsibility may also help explain his narrow interpretation of political reform. He has always supported "political reform" of a sort: "Whenever we move a step forward in economic reform, we are made keenly aware of the need to change the political structure.... So unless we modify our political structure, we shall be unable to advance the economic reform or even to preserve the gains we have made so far."[37] But this has rarely gone beyond simple clarification of authority relations – which explains why he believes it is so closely linked to economic reform. In another sense, Deng's consistent belief in clear delegation of authority may explain some of the problems he had with his subordinates Hu Yaobang and Zhao Ziyang. Because Deng was so effective carrying out policies decided by Mao, he had expected his subordinates to carry out his policies, without regard to broader principles or alternative visions of the future. With respect to economic policy, this expectation was not misplaced. As Deng commented on Zhao Ziyang and Hu Yaobang, "Both men failed, and it wasn't because of economic problems. It was on the question of opposing bourgeois liberalization that both men came a cropper."[38] Put another way, both men had visions of a more comprehensive process of social reform to which they attached more importance than unquestioning obedience to the views of Deng Xiaoping.

Rapid economic growth is best. Deng Xiaoping has a strong tendency to push for unsustainably rapid economic growth rates. There was evidence of this in his support for the Great Leap Forward in 1958, and his advocacy of the unrealistic Ten-Year Plan in 1975 and 1977–78. This was also true generally in the post-1978 period, but during one crucial instance, Deng was willing to modify his high growth advocacy. In 1979, he deferred to the views of Chen Yun and Li Xiannian, and supported the policy of economic readjustment that resulted in a period of slow growth. These policies were implemented even more strictly in 1981 – clearly with Deng's acquiescence – and resulted in a brief recession. The readjustment period was essential for China's subsequent development. As Chen Yun argued, the economy needed a "breathing space" to release resources for consumption and rebuilding of reserve capacities.

By 1982, though, Deng's eagerness for more rapid growth was becoming apparent. At the 12th Party Congress, Party Secretary Hu Yaobang formally advanced the goal of quadrupling China's output by the year 2000, which clearly reflected Deng's views. This was an ambitious but not entirely unrealistic target and thus stimulated realistic long-term thinking about the capabilities of the Chinese economy. Doubtless Deng's objective was mobilizational rather than to serve as a stimulus to long-run

37. Deng Xiaoping, *Fundamental Issues*, p. 149.
38. Deng Xiaoping, "Speeches given in 1992," p. 17.

planning, but his judgment was sufficiently practical to enable the target
to serve as a positive stimulus to realistic planning.

In the mid-1980s Deng pushed repeatedly for more rapid growth and
reform. There is at times a fundamental confusion between rapid growth
and rapid economic reform in Deng's mind. Both are seen as the outcome
that prevails when minds are liberated and individuals move boldly and
energetically toward their objectives. This confusion was particularly
evident during 1988, when Deng pushed for additional economic reforms – particularly price reform – during a period when inflationary
pressures were already building up in the economy. The price reforms
were desirable, but they could be most effectively implemented during a
period of slack economic demand. Up to at least the end of July, Deng
was repeatedly arguing that officials must be bold in attacking problems
of growth and reform – meanwhile inflation was steadily accelerating out
of control. Only after it surged to annual rates above 50 per cent and the
crisis was plain to all did Deng finally recognize, in September, that
officials were now "bold enough" and more stability was required.[39]

By 1992, Deng was willing to use the imperative of economic growth
to criticize the overly conservative policies of hardliners. Indeed, during
1992–93 the desire for growth was used to divide conservatives and
reformers, and each time the planned growth rate was increased, this was
rather bizarrely interpreted as a triumph for the reform camp. However,
at the same time, Deng's conception of growth appeared increasingly
sophisticated.

From our experience of these last years, it is entirely possible for economic
development to reach a new stage each few years…. During the 1984 to 1988 period
… our national wealth was increased by a large amount and the whole economy
reached a new stage…. While the accelerated development during these five years
could be considered a kind of "flying leap," it was different from the Great Leap
Forward because it did not harm the organism or mechanism of economic growth: the
achievement was not small…. Rectification of the economic environment also has
achievements … but if we had not leaped forward during the preceding years, if the
economy had not reached a new stage, the subsequent three year rectification could
not have been smoothly carried out…. It is important to pay attention to economic
stability and co-ordinate development, but stability and co-ordination are relative, not
absolute. Development is the only hard truth (*ying daoli*).[40]

Although the political motivation of this statement is transparent, the
more important fact is that it is true. During the 1984–88 period the
Chinese economy became much bigger, more flexible, more market-ori-
ented and more successful. Those successes have propelled the economy
through a period of necessary, but uninspired, retrenchment policies
without serious difficulties. Before 1978, Deng pushed for rapid growth
in ways that were often harmful; since the 1980s, he has moderated his
growth advocacy. More important, though, is that the economy has

39. Li Xinzhi and Wang Yuezong, *Great Practice and Glorious Thought*, pp. 287, 290,
291–92.
40. Deng Xiaoping, "Speeches given in 1992," pp. 11–12.

caught up with Deng's advocacy. It is now more diverse and capable of rapid growth. Deng's statement here is thus quite perceptive.

The importance of non-intervention. Why was Deng willing to abstain from intervening in broader economic processes? In a sense, this is merely an extension of his belief in the decentralization of authority. What is striking, however, is the surprising tolerance for not deciding things, for allowing a period of "muddling through" – even to accept the idea that there might not ever be a definitive resolution of theoretical problems. "Not to engage in debates" about unresolvable principles is in fact one of Deng's guiding principles.

At crucial junctures when economic policy was changing and uncertain, Deng had the wisdom to proclaim temporary non-intervention. This was most apparent in two episodes, both primarily involving rural economic policy. It is important to note at the outset that Deng initially did not take much interest in rural reforms. His speech before the Third Plenum never mentions markets or economic laws, and barely mentions peasants at all. In 1980, when he does discuss rural policy, he argues strongly in favour of a continuation of the collective system.[41] But subsequently, during the spread of agricultural responsibility systems – household farming – during 1980 and 1981, Deng was willing to take a hands-off attitude, in spite of his own misgivings about the process. An anecdote about his attitude at this time is revealing. In early 1980, during a discussion of rural reforms, Deng Liqun passed on to Deng Xiaoping the report that the peasants were saying "*Mao rang women shenfan; Deng rang women chifan*" ("Chairman Mao led us to stand up; but Deng Xiaoping allowed us to fill our bellies"). An obviously pleased Deng Xiaoping is reported to have nodded, and declared that it was necessary to wait and see how the rural reforms unfolded. Deng subsequently allowed the rural responsibility system to spread, even though no official document to this effect was ever promulgated. Instead, the fundamental decision was communicated through the personnel system. At the end of 1980 Zhao Ziyang was promoted to Premier and Wan Li to head of rural work. Since both men had been closely associated with the development of rural responsibility systems in their provinces (Sichuan and Anhui respectively), it was obvious that their promotion implied official acceptance of the new system.

During the mid-1980s, as private businesses spread, Deng again called for a "wait and see" attitude toward the private economy. As he himself describes it:

During the early period of rural reform, there was the question of "Blockhead Melon-seeds" (*shazi guazi*) in Anhui [a successful private business that sold dried salted melon seeds, and greatly exceeded the stipulated size for household businesses]. At that time, many people were uncomfortable – said this guy's made a million – and advocated intervention. I said, don't intervene, if you intervene people will say policy has changed and the benefits would not be worth the costs. There are

41. Bachman, *Chen Yun*, pp. 157–58.

still many problems like these and if they are not handled appropriately it would be easy to shake our direction and influence the whole reform situation.[42]

This is a pretty accurate recounting of events. Deng was instrumental in allowing relatively spontaneous changes to go ahead.

Deng's greatest contribution to rural reform was simply in allowing it to go forward. In fact, he does not seem to have ever been much interested or involved in rural reforms. Particularly telling is a remark he subsequently made about the growth of rural industries.

Our greatest success – and it is one we had by no means anticipated – has been the emergence of a large number of enterprises run by villages and townships. They were like a new force that just came into being spontaneously…. The Central Committee takes no credit for this…. If the Central Committee made any contribution, it was only by laying down the correct policy of invigorating the domestic economy. The fact that this policy has had such a favourable result shows that we made a good decision. But this result was not anything that I or any of the other comrades had foreseen; it just came out of the blue.[43]

This is a charming statement, and it is often quoted, but has one problem: it simply is not true. The idea that nobody anticipated the growth of rural industry is easily refuted if one goes back to the earlier literature. The State Council document on township and village enterprises in 1979 says clearly: "We should raise the share of commune and brigade enterprises in the total gross income in the three-level rural system from 29.7 per cent in 1978 to around 50 per cent in 1985." Clearly, policy-makers *did* anticipate the emergence of a large number of enterprises run by villages and townships, and in fact the share of commune and brigade enterprises actually fell somewhat short of this target in 1985.[44] Deng's direct policy involvement in rural reforms was modest. As usual, he was more concerned with the more formally organized and predominantly urban Party and governmental system. But he allowed rural reforms to go ahead without imposing ideological obstacles.

Opening up to outside. The fifth area in which a specific accomplishment directly linked to Deng Xiaoping can be identified is in the area of opening up to the outside world. Deng's commitment to the open door policy has been early and consistent, and more thorough than most of his colleagues. He appears to approach foreign countries without defensiveness. He is not sensitive about national sovereignty considerations

---

42. Deng Xiaoping, "Speeches given in 1992," p. 5.

43. Deng Xiaoping, *Fundamental Issues*, p. 189.

44. The share of gross income accounted for by rural enterprises was 33% of total rural income in 1985. *Zhongguo tongji nianjian* (*Statistical Yearbook of China*) 1986, p. 221. The document is "Draft regulations relating to several problems in developing commune and brigade enterprises," (Guofa (1979) No. 170) in System Reform Commission, *Jingji tizhi gaige wenjian huibian 1977–1983* (*Collected Economic System Reform Documents, 1977– 1983*) (Beijing: Zhongguo caizheng jingji, 1984), pp. 97–104. The lower proportion of rural income accounted for by rural enterprises than targeted was due primarily to the more rapid growth of household agricultural income than anticipated – but clearly rapid growth of township enterprises had been anticipated.

implied in the policy of Special Economic Zones, and he is willing to give generous and apparently heartfelt praise to advanced foreign experiences. Much of this appears to be related to his respect for science and technology. This was evident early on in a March 1978 speech:

Profound changes have taken place and new leaps have been made in almost all areas. A whole range of new sciences and technologies is continuously emerging ... we have lost a lot of time as a result of the sabotage by Lin Biao and the Gang of Four.... Backwardness must be recognized before it can be changed.[45]

Deng has no problem acknowledging outstanding foreign performance. When he visited Nissan in Japan in 1978 he said, "today I have learnt what modernization is like." When he came to write an inscription, he said, "learn from the great, diligent, valiant and intelligent Japanese people."[46] This is recognizably the same Deng Xiaoping who shortly thereafter toured the United States and was photographed in Texas wearing a cowboy hat.

This openness is apparent in the policy of Special Economic Zones (SEZs). According to one authoritative account:

It was Deng Xiaoping who proposed (*changdao*) the Special Economic Zones. During the April [1979] Central Work Conference, Xi Zhongxun and Yang Shangkun, the people in charge of Guangdong, talked about bringing Guangdong's advantages into full play. Deng brought up the question of special zones, and said, "we can carve out a patch of land and call it a special zone. Shen-gan-ning [the Communist revolutionary base area] was a special zone! The Centre doesn't have any money, though, and wants you people to do it by yourselves; squeeze out a bit of precious cash."[47]

Clearly, this account overstates Deng's originality somewhat. Deng could not have been the first to make the proposal, since various concrete steps had already been taken in Shenzhen in the first months of 1979, and Deng himself credits the leaders of Guangdong province with the idea.[48] But top policy-makers are not required actually to invent ideas – all they need do is quickly adopt and support the good ideas proposed by advisers. In this sense, the thrust of the anecdote is basically true. Deng is seen here giving strong support to his close associates Xi Zhongxun and Yang Shangkun and legitimizing the use of the honest term "special zone."

In subsequent years, Deng repeatedly gave support to the SEZs, using them as a metaphor for the economic reform and open door policies as a whole. During 1984 he responded to criticisms of the existing SEZs by travelling to Shenzhen and declaring the decision to develop them

45. Deng Xiaoping, *Selected Works (1975–1982)*, pp. 103, 106. According to Lin Zixin, Deng also said he wished to serve as "general head of logistics" for science and technology work. I have been unable to locate this remark in the published version of the speech.

46. Hua Sheng, Luo Xiaopeng and Zhang Xuejun, "Chinese reform and state socialism," unpublished book manuscript, Oxford University, 1990, ch. 2.

47. Li Zhining, *Zhonghua renmin gongheguo jingji dashidian 1959.10–1987.1 (A Dictionary of Major Economic Events in the PRC, October 1949–January 1987)* (Changchun: Jilin renmin chubanshe, 1987), p. 453.

48. Deng Xiaoping, *Fundamental Issues*, p. 190; George T. Crane, *The Political Economy of China's Special Economic Zones* (Armonk: M. E. Sharpe, 1990), pp. 26–27.

"correct," then moving to extend elements of them to an additional 14 coastal cities.[49] Again, at the beginning of 1992, he intervened directly in the political process by travelling to the Shenzhen Zone. A swing towards renewed reform had been under way since 1990, but Deng's trip was used symbolically to bolster reform and provide an appropriate platform for a pro-reform manifesto. His commitment to openness seems never to have wavered. In 1992 he said, "looking backward, one mistake I made was that when we developed the four Special Economic Zones, we didn't add on Shanghai."[50]

Deng Xiaoping and the Legacy of Economic Reform

The foregoing has outlined ways in which Deng contributed personally to the evolution of economic policy in China. In a broader sense, one might ask whether China's economic reform reflects any of the personal characteristics of Deng's approach to economic issues. Here the answer must be yes. Paradoxically, the most important characteristic is simply the lack of an over-arching vision of the reform process or its goal. China's reform has proceeded gradually and experimentally, and without a clear sense of ultimate objective. Indeed, it was not until the end of 1992 that a Communist Party Congress even endorsed the goal of a market economy. Instead, each phase of reform has been directed at solving certain limited problems and moving the economy in the general direction of greater openness and market orientation. The Chinese have called this "crossing the river by groping for stepping stones."[51] It is not unreasonable to link the process of reform without a clear blueprint to Deng's absence of vision in the economic realm.[52]

At the same time, the reform process has turned out to be remarkably resilient and constructive. The experimental aspect of reform has meant that local governments have had significant latitude to experiment with economic policies, and successful policies were then adopted on a nation-wide basis. Even more fundamental has been the growing sphere of economic activity outside the traditional state-controlled sectors. The growth first of rural enterprises and subsequently of private and foreign-invested enterprises has been one of the most dynamic and constructive aspects of the whole reform process. The Chinese government under Deng Xiaoping has been willing to accept the growth of a by now quite large sector of the economy that escapes from direct state control. This phenomenon can surely be linked to Deng's willingness to accept policies

49. Li Xinzhi and Wang Yuezong, *Great Practice and Glorious Thought*, pp. 254–56.
50. Deng Xiaoping, "Speeches made in 1992," p. 10.
51. On this aspect of the reform, see Nicholas Lardy, "Is China different? The fate of its economic reform," in Daniel Chirot (ed.), *The Crisis of Leninism and the Decline of the Left: The Revolutions of 1989* (Seattle: University of Washington Press, 1991), pp. 147–162; and Lin, "Open-ended economic reform in China."
52. The contrast is particularly acute with reformers in Poland and Czechoslovakia at the end of the 1980s, who stated clearly at the outset that the objective of the reform process was to create a market economy with mixed ownership forms, but based primarily on private ownership.

of non-intervention and his general lack of defensiveness, particularly when it is noted that there have been many opportunities to reverse the trend. Problems with corruption, growth of private businesses beyond stipulated sizes, and competition between non-state and state firms for scarce inputs could all have been used as the pretext to clamp down on the vigorous non-state sector. Indeed, China's conservatives have repeatedly suggested doing just that. But under Deng's general leadership, most experiments – provided only that they have been reasonably successful economically – have been permitted to survive.

This growing non-state sector has been crucial in creating a more competitive and dynamic environment even for the state sector. Yet it should remain clear that one of the distinctive characteristics of China's reform has been precisely that the state sector has continued to operate. While its relative share in the economy has declined, its absolute size has increased. At no point has it been cut loose, either abandoned or privatized, as in Eastern Europe. Instead, the government has made persistent efforts to restructure managerial incentives within the state sector. The government has tried to prod state enterprises to become more oriented to profit and the market, by creating incentive systems that link managerial pay to profitability and sales. Moreover, there is substantial evidence that this effort has been at least partially successful, and has produced significant improvements in state sector productivity.[53]

It is reasonable to link the persistence of a workable incentive system within the state sector to Deng's approach to economic issues. His persistent attention to personnel matters has understandably meant that the management system has been a consistent focus of attention and of attempts at reform. As a result, the chain of command within the state sector has been maintained intact. The coexistence of a large state sector with a rapidly growing non-state sector has been the most important single element of China's dual-track economic system. In turn, the dual-track economic system is the most characteristic element of the pattern of China's economic reform.[54] Some observers of the Russian reform experience argue that Russia could not follow a Chinese reform strategy precisely because Russia was unable to maintain discipline over state firms. Thus, for better and for worse, it is possible to argue that Deng's attention to workable personnel systems was an important factor allowing China to follow its more gradual reform strategy.

Another characteristic of reform in China has been its persistently outward-looking character. Bold moves to open the economy to outside forces characterized the earliest stages, and particularly since the mid-

53. On managerial incentive systems, see Theodore Groves, Yongmiao Hong, John McMillan and Barry Naughton, "China's evolving managerial labor market," University of California, San Diego, Department of Economics Discussion Paper 92–36 (September 1992). On state sector productivity, see K. Chen, G. Jefferson, T. Rawski, H. Wang and Y. Zheng, "Productivity change in Chinese industry, 1953–1985," *Journal of Comparative Economics*, No. 12 (December 1988), pp. 570–591.

54. On these characteristics, see McMillan and Naughton, "How to reform a planned economy." Barry Naughton, *Growing Out of the Plan: Chinese Economic Reform, 1978–1992* (New York: Cambridge University Press, forthcoming).

1980s, impressive progress in foreign trade reforms have paced the progress of reform overall.[55] Finally, China's reforms have taken place within the context of sustained and accelerating economic growth. While all the Eastern Europe countries and former Soviet republics experienced sharp contractions in economic activity for at least three years following the initiation of their reform programmes, China has reformed gradually with increasing economic growth. Of course, that record reflects differences in the initial economic conditions facing different countries. But it is also an artifact of China's particular approach. Indeed, within China, reform and accelerating growth have gone hand in hand, alternating with reform retrenchment and slower growth.

China's economic reform can thus be characterized as proceeding experimentally, without a blueprint. Its most distinctive characteristics have included a dual-track economic system with a resilient state sector co-existing with a vibrant growing non-state sector. Paced by growth of foreign trade, the entire economy has displayed vigorous growth throughout the reform process. Each of these characteristics can be plausibly linked to one of Deng Xiaoping's persistent themes. Perched at the top of the Chinese political system, Deng has ended up stamping the economic reform process with some of his own personal characteristics. In the process, economic reform has inevitably become one of the most important parts of his legacy. Not guided by Deng's vision, economic reform in China was nevertheless shaped by his personality and by his characteristic approach to issues.

One way that is probably less useful in understanding Deng is to think of him as a pragmatist. It is unlikely that Deng is any more pragmatic than most world leaders. However, he is a master at presenting himself as a pragmatist: nobody cultivates more ardently the image of Deng the pragmatist than Deng himself. Some examples of this self-presentation from his talks are the following: "There is no other solution for us [than economic reform]. After years of practice it turned out that the old stuff didn't work." Or alternatively: "We began with the countryside, applying the open policy there, and we achieved results very quickly. In some places it took only one or two years to get rid of poverty. After accumulating the necessary experience in the countryside, we shifted the focus of reform to the cities."[56] This "gee-whiz" attitude really amounts to a cheerful miscasting – a wilful misinterpretation – of the Chinese reform experience into a mode of progressive learning and pragmatism. No doubt it is an attractive image. But it clearly misrepresents the actual process of economic reform in China, as well as the evolution of Deng Xiaoping's personal attitudes. We should be very suspicious of an overly simple interpretation of Deng as the supreme pragmatist.

55. Nicholas Lardy, *Foreign Trade and Economic Reform in China, 1978–1990* (New York: Cambridge University Press, 1991).
56. Deng Xiaoping, *Fundamental Issues*, pp. 187, 176.

Deng Xiaoping in Contrast with Others

Deng can be usefully contrasted with three other Chinese leaders: Mao Zedong, Chen Yun and Zhao Ziyang. There are a number of important similarities between Mao and Deng. Both were superb leaders and manipulators, with an instinctive grasp of motivation. Mao was able to act as pragmatically as Deng when he chose, and Deng was almost – but not quite – Mao's equal in terms of strategic cunning. Mao however was consumed by his visions, and in the end, in spite of his understanding of human motivation, proved utterly incapable of allowing individuals or parts of society to strike off in independent ways outside the scope of his vision. He repeatedly lauded the spontaneity of the masses, but ultimately nothing displeased him more than genuine spontaneity at the "bottom." Both Mao and Deng possessed, at best, erratic insight into economics, but Mao insisted on imposing his flawed economic visions on society, while Deng did not. As a result, Mao led China into repeated economic disasters while Deng, without Mao's presumption, has presided over China's economic revival.

Deng can also be contrasted with Chen Yun. Chen Yun has had an extremely clear vision of the economy as a whole. Understanding the interactions among the various sectors of the economy, he has persistently seen the dangers of overly rapid growth, and also the importance of markets as a safety valve, co-ordinating resources when planners fail to make the right decisions. But Chen's macro vision occludes his micro vision. He pays little attention to incentives and motivation. He has a rather bleak view of human nature, stressing the need for controls to prevent selfishness from getting out of hand.[57] Deng, on the other hand, is primarily a micro-economist: he gives attention to the design of effective incentive systems. Among China's gerontocrats, only Deng emerges as an individual genuinely willing to accept spontaneous economic activity among the masses.

Finally, Deng can be contrasted with Zhao Ziyang. Deng's vision of economic reform never had much content, and as a result, it never changed or evolved very much. His hands-off attitude toward policy-making meant that he was never forced to develop a more detailed and practicable notion of what reform was to mean. He never articulated a conception of economic reform that went beyond the simple notion of decentralization of authority. By contrast, Zhao Ziyang's understanding of economic reform can be seen growing and evolving through the 1980s. By some time in the mid-1980s, Zhao Ziyang had clearly become convinced that China had to move to a true market economy. He managed repeatedly to push forward the process of marketization, opening up China's economy to the increasingly open play of economic forces. Ironically, the great merit of Zhao's policy-making was that it was

---

57. Chen's real attitude to spontaneous action is captured by his own simile, comparing plan and market to a caged bird: without a cage, the bird will fly away. Without controls, spontaneous activity will lead to degeneration into chaos. For full discussions of Chen's rich economic thought, see Bachman, *Chen Yun* and Lardy and Lieberthal, "Introduction."

completely "hands-on," continuously involved in realistic compromise and progress. As a result, Zhao's views and understanding of the economy also became increasingly sophisticated. His economic vision included both the macro and the micro level. He had insights about the interrelation of politics and economics, and understood the need for macroeconomic stability, even when he failed to achieve it. At the micro level, Zhao, like Deng, seemed to understand the need for motivation and diversity; unlike Deng, this belief led him to accept the need for substantially more open society as well as economy.

The comparison between Deng and Zhao may lead naturally to consideration of the damage to his own economic legacy that Deng did at Tiananmen in June 1989. His abandonment first of Hu Yaobang and then of Zhao Ziyang was a serious violation – even betrayal – of his own principles about delegation of authority. Moreover, after June 1989 reassertion of Communist Party control led to widespread regression in the reform of authority relations, with damage most evident within the state system. Indeed, ironically, the single reform measure most directly attributable to Deng personally – the factory manager responsibility system complete with the sidelining of Party secretaries in the factories – was reversed in 1989. For nearly two years, the government advanced the silly slogan that the factory manager should be the "centre" but the Party secretary the "core" of the factory leadership group. This ridiculous distinction was incomprehensible to most Chinese, but particularly meaningless in the context of Deng's long-term drive toward clarification of authority relations. In a broader context, there was serious regression as well in the hard-won but still tentative independence of state-run enterprises. The reassertion of political correctness and "equity" in income distribution led to a significant back-pedalling in the realm of state enterprise reform. Deng in this respect curtailed and undermined his own most positive legacy.

Yet acting against these negative effects was the undeniable fact that Deng had already fully identified his own legacy with the process of economic reform. His conception of economic reform is rather thin and abstract. Yet precisely because he was more associated with the vague abstraction "economic reform" rather than any specific reform measures, he has a strong vested interest in seeing that the *overall* programme of economic reform succeeds, whatever that may turn out to be. As a result, despite his own complicity in the post-Tiananmen crackdown, by the end of 1990 Deng was already beginning to intervene again in a positive way to reignite the general reform process. Fortunately, the massive changes set under way in China under Deng Xiaoping are not subject to the control of a single leader, and in that sense, Deng's positive economic legacy is likely to survive the limitations of any single individual. China's society and economy have become more diverse, more complicated and more resilient after 15 years of reform. As China's economy repeatedly escapes from the limits that its political handlers attempt to impose on it, the economic reform process appears increasingly well suited to serve as a positive legacy for Deng Xiaoping.

Deng Xiaoping: The Social Reformer

Martin King Whyte

Deng Xiaoping's legacy as a social reformer can be considered in the context of his ideas regarding the selection and promotion of human talent, and the implications of those ideas for the political and social order. Deng's ideas are contrasted primarily with those of Mao Zedong, even though at many times and in many of the utterances of both men there is little that can be distinguished.[1]

Approaches to Human Talent

How do you select individuals worthy of positions of power, prestige and privilege? How do you educate and guide such individuals so that they will develop and contribute their talents to the full and be worthy of the public trust? How do you supervise them to see whether they are performing properly? How do you deal with misconduct by these chosen few? How much of the effort to create a desirable social order rests on such questions of personnel management; how much instead depends upon the proper design of the social order itself? In other words, are there alternative ways of constructing the political and social system such that one structure will produce better promotion of human talent than another? Might one set of structures incline even the most noble and talented to indolence and corruption, while another induce the devious and mediocre to upright behaviour? These are some of the questions that have to be faced in considering how to promote talent in any society.

In the United States, for example, the central stress in the political system is on creating the best set of structures rather than the best set of institutions for training and promoting talent. No strong role is given to the government in overseeing the creation and promotion of talent for the political system, not to mention for businesses, voluntary associations and other sectors of society. Much of the moral instruction of the population is supposed to take place elsewhere – in homes and churches, in particular. Institutions designed to foster competition and provide limits on power accretion are assumed to provide the best setting to motivate individuals to acquire training, work hard, seek promotion, and serve honourably. At the apex of this competitive process in the American political system, things are arranged so that lawyers, generals, oilmen, engineers, peanut farmers, haberdashers, actors and even professors can win the presidency. Hope that such a varied cast of characters will return the trust placed in them depends not on some prolonged process of moral

---

1. Describing what is distinctive about Deng's approach is difficult for a variety of familiar reasons. Most of his ideas have not been recorded for scholarly scrutiny, he worked closely for decades with Mao Zedong and others from whom I want to distinguish him here, and even his recorded speeches and writings may be the product of collective authorship and have in many cases been revised for publication in light of subsequent events. For all of these reasons, some degree of oversimplification is involved in trying to describe Deng's distinctive approaches.

and political training they have undergone, but on familiar American political institutions of checks and balances, a free press, opposition parties, term limits, competitive elections, and so forth. One way to describe this situation is to say that America opted for a system of "contest mobility" rather than "sponsored mobility."[2] Rather than select a few individuals worthy of training and then sponsor their preparation for leadership, the American system encourages as many as possible to compete for elite positions, leaving it largely to each individual to acquire and sustain those qualities needed to succeed.

Mao Zedong's Approach to Cultivating Talent

Mao's approach to the initial questions about how to detect and promote talent was quite different from the American one just described. It could be regarded as almost neo-Confucian, but with an important addition of several different types of class struggle. In contrast to the American approach, Mao's emphasis was very much on developing specific mechanisms for personnel selection, training and supervision, rather than focusing primarily on perfecting the structures in which those individuals would serve. At least up until the Cultural Revolution the structures themselves were seen as relatively unproblematic. A set of Marxist–Leninist institutions was borrowed from the Soviet Union and modified, and the result was a social order that was similar to the imperial Chinese system, but more highly centralized, bureaucratic and penetrating. The CCP itself played the central role in detecting, training, supervising and disciplining talent throughout this hierarchical system.[3] To use the terminology introduced above, this was very much a system of sponsored rather than contest mobility.

Within this Party-led system, it was assumed that a central issue was how to develop and promote people with the correct ideas, and how to prevent them from developing the wrong ideas. As in the imperial Chinese system, it was assumed that a unitary set of political ideas and moral principles could be specified from above, and that if only people could be educated to absorb these ideas and live by them, society would become strong and prosperous. From this orientation came the impressive array of indoctrination instruments employed by the CCP: thought

2. These terms are discussed by Ralph Turner in his article, "Sponsored and contest mobility and the school system," *American Sociological Review*, No. 25 (1960), pp. 555–567. The discussion above concerns selecting talent for high political office. As noted, leadership in other sectors of society is chosen in a variety of ways, and generally with little input from the government. In many of these other sectors the route to leadership is more via contest than sponsored mobility, but there are exceptions, such as in the U.S. armed forces and the Roman Catholic Church hierarchy.

3. At the higher reaches of the system, the CCP's personnel management was exercised through the system of *nomenklatura* borrowed from the CPSU, under which power to appoint and approve lists of various officials in the state administrative hierarchy was vested in particular levels of the Party. See John P. Burns (ed.), *The Chinese Communist Party's Nomenklatura System* (Armonk, NY: M. E. Sharpe, 1989). However, the CCP's power over personnel extended much further than the formal *nomenklatura* lists to include all positions of any power and influence in the PRC.

cultivation for Party members, required political study and mutual criticism for all citizens, special cadre schools, thought reform institutions, and so forth. Also impressive were the many mechanisms used to try to maintain the proper conduct and thinking of elites – rectification campaigns, manual labour stints, the mass line, May Seventh cadre schools, and so on. This personnel management system involved what could be called "close tutelage": even though the CCP made the decisions about selection and promotion of talent, it still felt it had regularly and closely to monitor those selected to make sure that they were sanctioned or re-educated if they "deviated." The central stress was on monitoring thinking – even when people's behaviour was the focus of scrutiny, it was as an indicator of whether their thinking was good or bad.

All this sounds quite compatible with China's Confucian heritage. One major difference from the neo-Confucian system concerned the process of selecting talent in the first place. Rather than assuming in principle that virtually anyone was capable of learning to think and behave in proper ways and thus could be cultivated for leadership,[4] Mao-era China employed a shifting set of class struggle policies to discriminate among individuals.

Initially after 1949 a class line was adopted in order to reverse existing patterns of privilege. Preference was given to former workers, poor peasants and early recruits to the Revolution, for example, and landlords, capitalists and those who had worked closely with the KMT were barred from office or discriminated against. However, during the 1950s, with a vast expansion of the bureaucracy, rapid urbanization and robust economic growth, this class line mostly worked in a relatively benign way in regard to China's younger generation. Many individuals from disadvantaged backgrounds were promoted rapidly, but the educated offspring of former elite families mostly found their talents rewarded as well. Even though individual landlords, capitalists and others were treated harshly, if their children were old enough and far enough along in school, through a fairly superficial "drawing a class line" with their families and by pledging to support the Party, they could also take advantage of the many new opportunities being created.[5] In other words, during this period talent was still sought almost everywhere, despite the official class line of the new regime.

After 1956, with the completion of socialist transformation, there was a period of uncertainty and debate over whether class struggle would continue (see below). While initially it appeared that the regime would

4. The major exception to this universalism of the imperial system concerns the fact that leadership positions were only open to males. Minor exceptions concerned specific occupational and ethnic groups that were excluded from the imperial examination process, such as actors, boat people, soldiers, etc.

5. Highly publicized cases to the contrary, most children from former elite families did not have publicly to denounce their parents or cut off all contact with them, but only to promise not to let family loyalty interfere with obedience to the CCP. See the discussion in my chapter, "Urban life in the People's Republic," in Roderick MacFarquhar and John K. Fairbank (eds.), *The Cambridge History of China*, Vol. 15 (Cambridge: Cambridge University Press, 1991).

"phase out" class struggle, this situation changed markedly after 1962, following Mao's warning to "never forget class struggle." Not only was it maintained, but the scope of its targets broadened. This occurred in several ways. In part it involved former middle groups (such as middle peasants, those with overseas relatives), being in effect recategorized as among the suspect "bourgeois classes." It also involved the fact that the class labels which had developed were based not simply on former economic positions (such as landlord, merchant) but political behaviour (such as counter-revolutionary, bad element). Through a series of campaigns new class struggle targets were added (rightists, capitalist roaders, and so on). There were also repeated efforts to uncover hidden class enemies by investigations of personal and family history, resulting in a substantial number of "class demotions" into bad class categories in the 1960s and 1970s. In addition, since class and political labels were effectively inheritable, the stigma of bad status was passed on to millions of children and grandchildren of the (ever expanding) pool of class struggle targets. As a result of these expansions, the number of individuals and families who were subject to discrimination in employment, education, military service, Party membership and other realms was considerably broadened.

Not coincidentally, the 1960s and 1970s were characterized by retrenchment, slow growth, frozen wages and campaigns to send urbanites to the countryside. A narrower range of more reliable people was to be eligible for selection and promotion into desirable positions in the late-Mao era. What had been a "non-zero sum" form of class struggle in the 1950s became very much a "zero-sum game" subsequently, with fewer winners and many more losers.[6]

Other important changes in class struggle policy occurred in the 1960s and 1970s. Mao and others in the leadership, particularly those radicals who rose to prominence in the Cultural Revolution, were increasingly uncomfortable with the rigid, caste-like implications of the class label system developed in the 1950s.[7] Not coincidentally, Mao and the radicals were also increasingly unhappy with the ideas and behaviour of many Chinese who did not fall into the "bad class" categories. Their response to the problem of how to describe and deal with undesirable tendencies that did not fit into the established system of analysing classes was an effort to develop new class struggle rubrics. Two alternative frameworks emerged in Mao's later years, one fairly fully after 1964, and the other more hesitantly and partially, mostly during the course of the Cultural Revolution.

The system of class struggle established in the 1950s may be designated as one which focused on "old classes," since it was based on

6. On the worsening prospects for upward mobility after the Great Leap Forward, see my essay, "The politics of life chances in the People's Republic of China," in Yu-ming Shaw (ed.), *Power and Policy in the PRC* (Boulder: Westview, 1985).

7. The best account of the class label system and the debates surrounding it is Richard Curt Kraus, *Class Conflict in Chinese Socialism* (New York: Columbia University Press, 1981).

classifying people according to the property and positions their families held in the three years prior to 1949. In parallel fashion the two new class struggle frameworks might be termed systems of "thought classes" and "new classes." Both frameworks implicitly rejected the idea that the position of one's family prior to the Revolution was a good basis for judging potential for proper thought or the likelihood of bad tendencies in the 1960s and beyond. But they differed in their analysis of where bad ideas came from and who was most likely to display such ideas.

The "thought class" framework is a radically non-materialist way of dealing with issues of promoting talent. It assumes that certain correct ways of thinking and behaving can be specified, and these are labelled "proletarian." Likewise, certain incorrect ways of thinking can be outlined, labelled "bourgeois." Thought class analysis is closer than "old class" analysis to the Confucian paradigm in assuming that virtually anyone can under the proper circumstances develop proper ideas, but under unfavourable circumstances they may display bad tendencies. The task of personnel managers is then to monitor people's thinking as regularly as possible (that is, with even closer tutelage than before), in order to determine whether to reward or punish them. People manifesting good thinking and behaviour can expect favourable treatment and promotion, while those displaying bad tendencies will receive extra scrutiny, re-education, and even demotion or other penalties. This sort of tutelage may operate without giving much consideration to whatever "old class" origins the individuals involved bear.

The result of this "thought class" analysis is an effort to create what Susan Shirk has termed "virtuocracy."[8] Efforts are made to construct a system that rewards and penalizes people for their exhibited political and moral virtue. Although the rhetoric of social classes is used in thought class analysis, in fact there is no linkage required with any identifiable social positions. As noted above, everyone is considered potentially vulnerable to bourgeois tendencies.

The third and final form of class analysis to emerge in the late-Mao years may be called a "new class" framework. This term stems from the close parallels between the ideas involved and the critique of state socialism developed by the Yugoslav Marxist heretic Milovan Djilas.[9] In the Cultural Revolution and beyond, Mao and the radicals struggled to find ways to express their growing sense that holding high office and prestigious positions within the post-1949 system was a primary source of elitism, corruption and other undesirable tendencies. A variety of ideas that emerged in these years – for example, criticism of "people in power taking the capitalist road," critiques of a "new bureaucratic stratum," idealization of the Paris Commune, and the republication of Lenin's utopian *State and Revolution* – conveyed a growing conviction that the

8. Susan Shirk, "The decline of virtuocracy in China," in James Watson (ed.), *Class and Social Stratification in Post-Revolution China* (Cambridge: Cambridge University Press, 1984).

9. See Milovan Djilas, *The New Class* (New York: Praeger, 1957).

concentration of power and privilege of the socialist order itself (and not improper thinking or fallible elites) was the basic source of the problems Mao and others wanted to eliminate. For the first time, then, the structure of Leninist institutions built in China after 1949 was seen as problematic.

However, Mao Zedong was never willing to take the next logical step that a new class analysis led to by initiating a major reform of the hierarchical political order in the PRC. When Zhang Chunqiao and others came to him early in 1967 to have him approve their newly-established "Shanghai Commune," he torpedoed the idea on the grounds that this organizational form would leave no role for the Party to play.[10] Mao's attempted solution to the problem of how to pursue the implications of a new class analysis without reforming the hierarchical system was not very appealing: it involved the prospect of launching new cultural revolutions every few years to cleanse elites of the bad tendencies developed since the last cleansing. Because of the inability to reconcile new class analysis with the structures of Leninism, new class ideas remained only partially developed at the time of Mao's death and were denounced after the purge of the Gang of Four in 1976.[11]

These two alternative class struggle frameworks, of "thought classes" and "new classes," competed for influence with "old class" analysis during the final 15 years of Mao's life. The effect of this ideological confusion was, once again, to enlarge the scope of potential class struggle significantly. Now class enemies might be found not only among families who had held elite positions prior to 1949 or among groups later designated as suspect (such as rightists and counter-revolutionaries), but among all of those in positions of power and privilege (particularly cadres and intellectuals) and, under a thought class analysis, literally everywhere.

The obsession with finding new sources of hostile class tendencies was combined after the Cultural Revolution began with a dismantling of most of the incentive systems established during the 1950s (systems which existed in other socialist societies). The message conveyed was that if you want to motivate people to think and behave properly, you don't have to, and in fact you shouldn't, set up opportunity structures to reward the

10. See the discussion in Victor Nee, "Revolution and bureaucracy: Shanghai in the Cultural Revolution," in Victor Nee and James Peck (eds.), *China's Uninterrupted Revolution* (New York: Pantheon, 1975).

11. Chinese dissidents have, however, put forth more systematic ideas that have much in common with new class analysis. See, for example, Liu Binyan, *People or Monsters?* (Bloomington: Indiana University Press, 1983); Chen Erjin, *China: Crossroads Socialism* (London: Verso, 1984); Wei Jingsheng, "The fifth modernization," in James D. Seymour (ed.), *The Fifth Modernization* (Stanfordville, NY: Human Rights Publishing Group, 1980); Jonathan Unger, "Whither China? Yang Xiguang, Red Capitalists, and the social turmoil of the Cultural Revolution," *Modern China*, No. 17 (1991), pp. 3–37. For further observations on Mao's ultimate unwillingness to modify the political structure his regime had built, see my essay, "Who hates bureaucracy? A Chinese puzzle," in Victor Nee and David Stark (eds.), *Remaking the Economic Institutions of Socialism* (Stanford: Stanford University Press, 1989). There I point out that the impression that either Mao or the Cultural Revolution was anti-bureaucratic is mistaken, since the initiatives Mao took in his later years enhanced, rather than reduced, structural bureaucratization.

favoured few. To do so would only encourage people to behave properly opportunistically and temporarily in order to gain personal advantages, thus actually reinforcing a central bourgeois value. Instead you should test people's moral purity by monitoring their thinking and behaviour closely in the absence of significant chances for material advancement.[12] Virtue was not quite supposed to be its own reward, but more so than in the past.

By the time of Mao's death it was increasingly apparent that the personnel practices that resulted from these Maoist approaches were causing serious problems. The neo-Confucian/old class combination of the 1950s had had a number of favourable consequences, particularly the recruitment and promotion of large numbers of people who felt they owed everything to the Revolution. However, the changes in approaches for detecting and promoting talent introduced after 1962 had a number of undesirable results. The opportunities for significant personal advancement were much reduced, while chances for negative treatment expanded greatly. Many groups and individuals who had felt quite secure and grateful toward the Party and willing to make great sacrifices for it in the past became very angry at the new anxieties and mistreatment they had to face. The effects of these shifts on popular morale and productivity were pervasive. In addition, the competition spawned by virtuocracy led to absurd phrase-mongering and diversion from work, academic learning and other practical pursuits. The inherent subjectivity of a virtuocratic system made it very difficult to distinguish "genuine" from "sham" activists and proletarians, and as a result concentrated even greater arbitrary power in the hands of the bureaucrats who had to make the judgments involved.[13] By the time of Mao's death, China had become an overheated, inefficient and increasingly anxious society where fear and resentment replaced gratitude as the dominant source of political motivations.

Deng Xiaoping's Approach to Cultivating Talent

Already during the 1950s there were signs that Deng Xiaoping had ideas on developing and promoting talent that differed in important ways from those promoted by Mao. As noted earlier, at the time of the Eighth Congress of the CCP in 1956 there were debates about the meaningfulness of class labels and class struggle in an era in which socialism was

12. Of course, no society can operate without some rewards and promotions, and in China of the Cultural Revolution decade people received not only moral incentives but also privileges and promotion into positions of power. On the internal contradictions of this effort to create virtuocracy, see Shirk, "The decline of virtuocracy in China," and her book, *Competitive Comrades* (Berkeley: University of California Press, 1982). During these years there was the bizarre phenomenon I have termed "competitive selflessness" – individuals who wanted to get ahead had to appear to be less concerned about getting ahead than everyone else. For example, the best hope an urban youth had to avoid being sent to the countryside was to be the earliest and most fervent in "volunteering" to go.

13. These are points stressed in the work of Susan Shirk cited earlier and in Andrew Walder, *Communist Neo-Traditionalism* (Berkeley: University of California Press, 1986).

victorious and ownership of productive property by individuals was being phased out. The debate in China, as is well known, was influenced by developments in the Soviet Union, where 1956 was the year of Nikita Khrushchev's "Secret Speech" denouncing Stalin's crimes.[14] Khrushchev argued that Stalin's erroneous claim that class struggle intensified after socialist transformation had provided the rationale for the mass terror that enveloped the Soviet Union in the 1930s. Khrushchev eventually presided over the development of a new framework for describing Soviet society, which was characterized as a "state of the whole people." This odd formulation indicated a belief that hostile classes and class struggle had ceased to exist in the Soviet Union, which was composed of two main classes (state employees and collective farmers) and one "stratum" (the intelligentsia), all involved in non-antagonistic relationships with one another. This ideological shift formed the basis for the CPSU's development of a meritocratic or technocratic ethos under Khrushchev and Brezhnev.[15]

In Deng Xiaoping's speech to the Eighth CCP Congress in 1956, he struck several notes that can be described as meritocratic, and these are precursors of the policies he presided over after 1978. Deng was among the most outspoken advocates of phasing out discrimination based upon the "old class" system. Speaking specifically of the elimination of a class origin criterion for admission to the CCP, Deng stated:

The distinction previously made in the procedure of admitting new members has been removed because the former classification has lost or is losing its original meaning. Both before the Seventh Congress [in 1945] and for a considerable period after it was essential to have different procedures of admission for applicants of different social origin, and this served a very good purpose. But in recent years the situation has drastically changed. The difference between workers and office employees is now only a matter of a division of labour within the same class.... The vast majority of our intellectuals have now come over politically to the side of the working class, and a rapid change is taking place in their family background.... What is the point, then, of classifying these social strata into two different categories?[16]

Deng's argument was quite direct. Not only was the class label system losing its meaning, but continuing to discriminate on the basis of these labels would discourage those with bad class backgrounds from making a contribution to society.

14. According to one of Deng Xiaoping's biographers, Uli Franz, Deng was one of two representatives of the CCP (the other being Zhu De) who attended the CPSU's 20th Party Congress and heard the secret speech, barely eight months before China's Eighth Party Congress was convened. See his book, *Deng Xiaoping* (New York: Harcourt Brace Jovanovich, 1988), p. 142.

15. See, for example, David Lane, *The Socialist Industrial State* (London: Allen & Unwin, 1976); Jerry Hough, *How the Soviet Union is Governed* (Cambridge: Harvard University Press, 1979); Allen Kassof, "The Administered Society," *World Politics*, No. 16 (1964), pp. 558–575.

16. Deng Xiaoping, "Report on the revision of the constitution of the Communist Party of China," 16 September 1956, in Deng Xiaoping, *Speeches and Writings* (Oxford: Pergamon Press, 1984), pp. 29–30.

In the same speech, Deng also denounced excessive reliance on seniority in the promotion of talent, and in very similar terms:

... there are still serious defects in the selection and promotion of cadres. The chief of these is that even today many comrades still use "seniority" as the criterion in selecting cadres. Party members of long standing with a rich store of experience are undoubtedly a valuable asset to the Party. But we should be making a very grievous mistake if we value this asset to the exclusion of everything else, because our revolutionary cause is advancing and the number of cadres required is increasing all the time, while the number of old Party members is necessarily falling. This being so, if we don't resolutely and confidently employ carefully selected new cadres, what other outcome can there be except harm to the cause of the Party and the people?[17]

There are two elements visible in these ideas. First, as with the Confucian approach or Mao's virtuocracy, competition for advancement should be open to all or virtually all. However, unlike these approaches, the basis for evaluating and promoting individuals should be not their thinking and political virtue, but their contributions to society. Here the meritocratic aspect can be seen. What is important is how hard you work, how much special training you acquire, whether you introduce useful innovations, and whether you take on extra responsibilities. Later Deng's ideas on this issue were revealed in his less formal but more famous 1961 statement: "White cat, black cat, what does it matter as long as it catches mice?"

A large number of the changes Deng presided over after 1978 can be related to his attempt to replace the personnel policies of the Mao era with a more meritocratic system in order to restore morale and improve incentives: bonuses and piece rates banned under Mao were restored, and frozen wages were unfrozen. Competitive examinations and grade-based academic practices of the pre-Cultural Revolution schools were reinstated, with direct entry into colleges and urban jobs available to middle school graduates. Entire new categories of educational opportunities were opened up – to enrol in graduate study, earn advanced degrees and go overseas to study. A mania for testing and credentialism emerged, with candidates for large numbers of jobs and other opportunities now selected on the basis of competitive examinations. Incumbents in positions such as teaching who had started work in the late-Mao era also had to pass tests in order to hold on to their jobs. The bureaucracy was pressured to change recruitment policies so that ever-higher percentages of officials holding college degrees could be reported. Mandatory retirement for officials was pushed through, using arguments that follow directly from Deng's 1956 statement quoted above. The "iron rice bowl" provided by permanent employment in state enterprises was attacked, and efforts were made to replace it with a contract labour system, with new possibilities of demotion, termination, salary cuts and even enterprise bankruptcy. The entire Maoist ethos of selfless service and moral incentives was repudiated in favour of an emphasis that "it is good to get rich," with

17. *Ibid.* p. 34.

conspicuous consumption by the successful serving to motivate others to try to catch up.

The class label system used for 30 years was officially repudiated, and not only former class enemies and their descendants, but millions of other victims of the Mao era were rehabilitated and encouraged to contribute to the "four modernizations." The class struggle campaigns of the Mao era were characterized as a grave mistake which subjectively and arbitrarily stigmatized millions of worthy citizens. (Deng refused to repudiate the anti-rightist campaign of 1957–58, in which he had played a central role, but he did acknowledge that the scope of targets of even that campaign had been unfairly expanded.) The era of such mass campaigns was formally declared to have ended. It was also claimed that China did not possess a "new bureaucratic stratum," and that bureaucrats, intellectuals and other elites were all members of the working class. Therefore there was no valid reason to encourage class struggle against such people. In other words, after 1978 an analysis of Chinese society emerged that sounds very much like Khrushchev's "state of the whole people."

One of Deng Xiaoping's clearest statements of these views is contained in his speech at the National Conference on Science in March 1978, where he took up again the ideas he had expressed at the Eighth Party Congress 22 years earlier:

How should the mental labour involved in scientific research be regarded? … generally speaking, the overwhelming majority of [mental workers] are already intellectuals serving the working class and other working people. It can therefore be said that they are already part of the working class itself. They differ from the manual workers only insofar as they perform different roles in the social division of labour. Everyone who works, whether with his hands or with his brain, is part of the working class in a socialist society.[18]

In the same speech, Deng attacked those who argued that intellectuals were not to be trusted and required constant inspection of their political thoughts and heavy doses of political study. He argued that intellectuals needed political study and criticism and self-criticism no more than those who would impose these activities on them: cadres doing political work and long-time Party members. Moreover, Deng explicitly gave his approval for a sharp reduction in political tutelage of intellectuals:

Scientists and technicians should concentrate their energies on their professional work. When we say that at least five-sixths of their work time should be left free for professional work, this is meant as the minimum requirement. It would be better still if more time were made available. If someone works seven days and seven nights a week to meet the needs of science or production, it shows his lofty and selfless devotion to the cause of socialism. We should commend, encourage, and learn from such people…. We cannot demand that scientists and technicians, or at any rate, the

18. Deng Xiaoping, "Speech at the opening ceremony of the National Conference on Science," 18 March 1978, in Deng, *Speeches and Writings*, p. 43. It was noted at the time that the speech by Hua Guofeng at the same conference was much more "virtuocratic" and less "meritocratic" than this speech of Deng's.

overwhelming majority of them, study stacks of books on political theory, join in numerous social activities and attend many meetings not related to their work.[19]

The same speech also stressed another of Deng's favourite themes – the search for people with talent who can be promoted into scientific careers should be very broad, with no groups and strata discouraged from applying.

In other speeches during the early years of the reforms, Deng again attacked the practice of relying heavily on seniority in judging and promoting personnel:

Some comrades argue that it is better to promote cadres one step at a time.... We shall never repeat the mistake [of the Cultural Revolution period] of elevating cadres so quickly that they soar like a rocket or a helicopter.... But we can't stick to the old concept of a "staircase" forever.... In future [sic], many positions will be filled and titles granted solely on the basis of examination. Only by doing away with the outdated concept of the "staircase," or by creating new staircases suited to the new situation and tasks, can we boldly break through the conventions in promoting cadres. But whether the staircases are new or old, we must not just pay lip-service to the necessity of promoting young and middle-aged cadres. We must see to it that the really outstanding ones are indeed promoted, and promoted in good time. We must not be too hasty in this matter, but if we are too slow we will retard our modernization programme.... Exceptional candidates should be provided with a sort of light ladder so they can come up more quickly, skipping some rungs. It is to make room for the young and middle-aged cadres that we have proposed reducing concurrent posts and eliminating over-concentration of power. How can they come up the staircase if all the steps are occupied, or if they aren't allowed to occupy the empty ones?[20]

The other side of Deng's emphasis on promotions due to merit, as already indicated, was a reduced emphasis on ideological remoulding. At various points during Mao's final years official pressure for political study often reached frenetic heights. There were efforts to encourage daily political study and even to foster rituals of confessing personal failings to live up to Mao's ideals at the end of each day's activities. Mandatory political study sessions did not disappear from work units during the 1980s, but in keeping with Deng's speech at the 1978 National Science Conference, they did become notably less frequent, generally no more than once a week. Their content also shifted away from intense scrutiny of personal ideology and towards general discussions of current Party policy or even of recent work problems. The atmosphere altered as well, making superficial participation and even bored indifference more acceptable than in the past. The clear message of the times was that, while political tutelage would not be dropped entirely, what determined

19. *Ibid.* pp. 47–48. Of course, it could be debated whether Deng meant these ideas to apply to intellectuals generally, or only to "hard" scientists and technicians. Nevertheless, the comments were interpreted by Chinese as calling for a general reduction of the burden of political study activity for all intellectuals.

20. Deng Xiaoping, "On the reform of the system of Party and state leadership," 18 August 1980, in *Selected Works of Deng Xiaoping* (Beijing: Foreign Languages Press, 1984), pp. 306–307.

how people were treated and promoted was not so much their perceived ideological purity as their test scores, work records and credentials. Efforts to make sure that this new emphasis stuck required that the individuals making personnel evaluations be changed as well. This was done both by the recruitment on a more meritocratic basis of new administrative leaders and by the effort to remove Party secretaries from primary control over personnel decisions.

All the aspects of Deng's reforms mentioned so far do not involve basic changes in the structure of the political system, only in the criteria that were supposed to be used to detect and promote talent. To oversimplify somewhat, it could be said that Deng wanted "expert" criteria to be used more in personnel decisions, and "red" criteria less. Another change from the Mao era was that in the 1980s a full range of material rewards was used without apology in order to provide incentives and compensate the talented. However, the centralized hierarchical structure persisted into the reform era, with bureaucrats monopolizing the power to make most personnel decisions.

Going Beyond Meritocracy?

Other aspects of Deng's reforms did make some dent in this hierarchical system. The wide variety of market reforms introduced reduced the role of the party-state in controlling access to all rewards and opportunities. By allowing private enterprise, foreign investment, economic activity outside the plan, and particularly the household responsibility system in agriculture, the potential for fundamental changes in the structure that rewarded talent was created.

To understand the implications of these changes, the most important of these reforms, the dismantling of collectivized agriculture, is considered. Deng and his leadership group could have tried to implement meritocratic reforms in the countryside without such a fundamental change, and for a few years in the late 1970s and early 1980s this appeared to be their aim. Communes would still have operated, but with most managerial decisions decentralized to the production team. Efforts to award work points based upon political enthusiasm or community evaluations (as in the repudiated "Dazhai model") would have been scrapped in favour of piece rates and other incentive schemes designed to heighten work effort and skill enhancement. In essence this would have been an effort to return to the collective system of the "60 points" of 1962, wiping away the virtuocratic and levelling innovations introduced in the countryside during the Socialist Education Campaign and the Cultural Revolution.[21] Such changes would have preserved bureaucratic control. Peasants still would have passively waited to be assigned to particular farming chores by local cadres, and the rewards they would have received for those chores would

21. See the discussion of the 60 points in William L. Parish and Martin King Whyte, *Village and Family in Contemporary China* (Chicago: University of Chicago Press, 1978), p. 34.

have depended on the evaluations of their work by those cadres. But the criteria and rewards would have been more meritocratic than under Mao, and perhaps more work effort would have been stimulated. The point is that one can imagine a system that is both meritocratic and bureaucratic – the prototype effort to create such a system, as noted earlier, was Brezhnev's Soviet Union.

Of course, that is not how things worked out in the Chinese countryside. Within a brief time span the collectivized system was swept aside in favour of the household responsibility system. The reformed rural system differed from the communes in many ways, but one distinction is central: the main rewards did not require any evaluation and decision by bureaucratic superiors. After meeting basic agricultural production and delivery quotas (areas in which cadre oversight persisted), peasants could cultivate other crops, engage in non-agricultural jobs, market their own produce, and sell their services to willing buyers. Whether they prospered or not depended much more on their own efforts and on market conditions, and less on cadre decisions, than during the commune era.[22] In substantial ways, then, the incentives for people to behave in the desired ways were built into the very structure of the reformed system, rather than depending upon indoctrination, supervision and evaluation by bureaucrats. The success of the Chinese rural reforms illustrates the potential of the alternative to "close tutelage" via system design which was discussed at the outset of this article. If a social system can be organized in such a way that it provides an attractive range of realizable opportunities for those who display desirable behaviour, then there is less need for the heavy hand of bureaucrats.

The most successful parts of Deng's reforms involved not simply substituting meritocratic for political criteria and adding material rewards within the existing bureaucratic structure, but some modification of that structure, as described above. The messages conveyed by this success were, however, complex. Much of the dynamism and productivity lost in the late-Mao era could be restored. However, to do so the basic features of the system would have to be modified or undermined. The central implication of this success is that leaving power in the hands of bureaucrats to tell people how to behave always leads to problems, even if the bureaucrats are telling them to behave meritocratically.

There are several things that China's Leninist leaders fear from any effort to change the structure and not just the rewards and reward criteria. In a less structurally bureaucratized system people have much more unsupervised time, resources and activity which they may use in ways that officials feel are undesirable. For example, peasants who prosper as a result of the reforms often spend their new wealth on fancy houses, elaborate tombs and expensive weddings, rather than on soil improve-

---

22. The extent of this change should not be exaggerated, however. Rural cadres still held considerable power, and they could often affect peasant livelihood in ways that were both positive (e.g. granting contracts and concessions for use of village resources) and negative (e.g. demanding payoffs, imposing new "taxes").

ments or new tools. People can also decide to leave their present organizations and either switch to other organizations or go off on their own. In either case their behaviour gives rise to the ominous (to a Leninist) possibility of individuals escaping from official tutelage and exercising personal choices that may not match official preferences. Additionally, weak tutelage means that some people get ahead for the "wrong" reasons – not because they work harder or are more entrepreneurial, but because they can use connections and trick their way into easy profits, for example. But as already noted, the main lesson the success of the market reforms conveys is that many bureaucrats and bureaucratic structures left over from the Mao era are not only superfluous, but actually harmful. Obviously this is not a lesson devoted Leninists are anxious to learn.

This is not to claim that the sensible alternative to China's current system of dealing with talent promotion is some sort of totally non-bureaucratic or purely market system. Obviously no such system exists anywhere in the world, and no modern society can function without extensive bureaucracies and numerous bureaucrats. The problem arises in the way in which various individuals and organizations are knitted together to make up the overall system. In non-Leninist systems there is a wide variety of competing and fairly autonomous bureaucratic structures. Within any one organization there may be bureaucrats who make decisions about whom to hire, promote and dismiss. However, they devise their own rules and procedures for managing personnel, rather than having the central government or some political or religious authority monitor everything. Furthermore, the members of these organizations generally have the option to leave and start again elsewhere, and the organization itself may operate in a competitive environment in which keeping members satisfied and motivated, and also remaining efficient and meeting the needs of clients or customers, can affect its very survival. In this sort of institutional setting there is at least some likelihood that bureaucratic excesses and arbitrariness will be held in check. In China's Leninist system, in contrast, very serious constraints on the "exit" option for staff members and dominance over personnel decisions by the *nomenklatura* produce an institutional setting ready-made for bureaucratic arbitrariness and the undermining of meritocratic principles.[23]

During the heady days of the early 1980s, it seemed as if Deng and his advisers were willing to confront normal Leninist fears and consider more basic structural changes. They advocated attacks against concentrated bureaucratic power in political as well as economic institutions. At

---

23. In his perceptive work, *Exit, Voice and Loyalty* (Cambridge: Harvard University Press, 1970), Albert Hirschman discusses exit (i.e. leaving the organization) as well as voice (internal dissent) and loyalty (currying favour) as mechanisms subordinates within organizations use to gain some autonomy and influence vis-à-vis their superiors. The virtual impossibility of exercising either exit or voice in most contemporary Chinese organizations leaves loyalty as the only real possibility. Reliance on that option leads to the sort of subordinate dependency and superior arbitrariness detailed by Andrew Walder in his book, *Communist Neo-Traditionalism*.

this time Deng Xiaoping was one of the most forceful critics of the over-concentration of power in the political system, as shown particularly by his August 1980 speech on reform of the system of Party and state leadership:

Many places and units have patriarchal personages with unlimited power. Everyone has to be absolutely obedient and even personally attached to them.... The patriarchal ways I have described are partly responsible for the grave mistakes some cadres make.... It is true that the errors we made in the past were partly attributable to the way of thinking and style of work of some leaders. But they were even more attributable to the problems in our organizational and working systems. If these systems are sound, they can place restraints on the actions of bad people; if they are unsound, they may hamper the efforts of good people or indeed, in certain cases, may push them in the wrong direction. Even so great a man as Comrade Mao Zedong was influenced to a serious degree by certain unsound systems and institutions, which resulted in grave misfortunes for the Party, the state and himself.... I do not mean that the individuals concerned should not bear their share of responsibility, but rather that the problems in the leadership and organizational systems are more fundamental, widespread, and long-lasting, and that they have a greater effect on the overall interests of our country.[24]

Deng Xiaoping followed this sociologically astute (and very un-Confucian) statement in subsequent years with more calls for political reform. As late as 1986 he stressed the critical importance of the effort to reduce power concentrations:

The last time I talked with some comrades about economic work I called their attention to the necessity of reforming the political structure, including the need to solve this problem of Party interference.... While we are demanding that powers be transferred to lower levels, they are taking them back. I am told that some comrades think there were also man-made causes for the lower economic growth rate in the first half of this year, and that this tendency of higher levels to take powers back was one of them. Our policy is to continue the devolution of powers, but many institutions are resisting it. As a result, the enterprises are deprived of their powers and their initiative withers. So this is one of the reasons why the growth rate has gone down.... In the final analysis, all our other reforms depend on the success of the political reforms, because it is human beings who will – or will not – carry them out.... Without political reform, economic reform cannot succeed, because the first obstacle to be overcome is people's resistance.[25]

Despite such sentiments, Deng ended up repeating Mao's failure to make fundamental alterations to the over-concentration of power in the political system. Deng appears to have recognized the need to make such changes more clearly than Mao ever did, but whenever the debate over political reforms led to discussion of modifying core elements of the

24. Deng Xiaoping, "On the reform of the system of Party and State Leadership," pp. 313–16. At about the same time, some of Deng's advisers were making even more pointed critiques of their Leninist legacy. See Liao Gailong, "Historical experiences and our road to development," translated in *Issues and Studies*, No. 17 (1981), especially pp. 89–90.

25. Deng Xiaoping, "Reform the political structure and strengthen the people's sense of legality," 28 June 1986, in Deng Xiaoping, *Fundamental Issues in Present-Day China* (Beijing: Foreign Languages Press, 1987), pp. 147–48.

Leninist system, Deng and those around him recoiled and shut off discussion. In response to the student demonstrations of 1986–87 and then the much larger ones of 1989, China's conservative leadership re-emphasized the need for strict hierarchical control, and any talk of "political reform" was reduced to superficialities.

Unanticipated Consequences of Deng's Reforms

Deng Xiaoping's failure to follow through with the effort to introduce major political reforms is related to a larger blind spot. Throughout his career Deng has shown talent for dealing with the pressing problems of China's political economy. However, he has been quite inept at anticipating the social consequences of the reforms he has presided over. At times it has seemed that Deng was trying to outwit his Marxist heritage by ignoring the changes in the superstructure that were being unleashed by transformations of the material base of China (through economic reforms).

Some of the unanticipated consequences of the reforms, of course, posed no great threat to Party control. For example, market reforms fostered a reluctance of many work units to employ women and a tendency of rural parents to withdraw their daughters from school early, thus jeopardizing the fragile gains for women that had been achieved in earlier years.[26] Decollectivization of agriculture brought with it the collapse of most rural co-operative medical insurance systems, contributing to growing inequality in this area and endangering the impressive gains in health care and life spans made after 1949.[27] Market reforms and the relaxation of migration restrictions led to the mushrooming of the "floating population" as millions cascaded into China's large cities and across provincial boundaries looking for greater opportunities. This increased mobility made it more difficult for the authorities to keep track of people and enforce regulations such as the official "one child" policy.[28] Social trends such as these produced anxious commentary and criticism in the official media, but no major efforts to reverse reform.

The reforms designed to alter the system of selecting and promoting talent were quite another matter. They inevitably brought in their wake consequences that directly threatened the Party's control over Chinese society. Promotion more by "expert" than "red" criteria produces individuals in influential positions who feel they have some basis for making independent judgments about their society's problems, rather than people willing to rely entirely on Party and leader dictates. Market reforms produce more individuals and families whose livelihood depends in

26. See the rich discussion in Emily Honig and Gail Hershatter, *Personal Voices* (Stanford: Stanford University Press, 1988).

27. Gail Henderson, "Increased inequality in health care in China," in D. Davis and E. Vogel (eds.), *Chinese Society on the Eve of Tiananmen* (Cambridge: Harvard University Press, 1990).

28. See the discussion in Dorothy Solinger, *China's Transients and the State: A Form of Civil Society?* (Hong Kong: Chinese University of Hong Kong, 1991).

whole or in part on their own efforts, rather than solely on the resources monopolized by their *danwei* and bureaucratic superiors. The attempted shift in the basis for legitimizing the system from pursuit of socialist goals and class struggle to the quest for modernization and raised living standards carries related perils for the Party. Ordinary citizens have no basis for independently judging whether their leaders are successfully pursuing lofty political goals. However, economic trends can be judged by all, and any citizen is competent to form an opinion about whether his or her life is improving materially.

The 1980s reforms thus contributed to growing possibilities that Chinese would have enough autonomy to form critical judgments about economic and other trends. The reforms also provided new ideas and contexts within which such critical judgments could be framed. The various aspects of the "open door" policy showed that there were alternatives to the system of rule in China and suggested that Party dominance might be an obstacle to economic improvement. The flood of information and ideas from the outside world also created an awareness that Leninist political institutions in places like Taiwan and the Soviet Union were in the process of being dismantled. The reforms helped to break down China's isolation not only from the outside world, but also from its own recent past. The mass rehabilitations and restoration to prominent positions of many victims of the Mao era resulted in some of China's best critical minds once again finding a voice and an audience in the 1980s.[29] The critical views raised by these older, rehabilitated intellectuals and the many young protégés they inspired had a dramatic effect on popular thinking during the 1980s. To these developments was added the Party's own self-imposed restraint (prior to 1989), which expanded the "zone of indifference" for ordinary citizens.[30] Although the reasons for this restraint were once again primarily economic – to allow expertise and innovation to flower without excessive interference and tutelage – one consequence was that the risk of sharing independent ideas and critical opinions was dramatically reduced in comparison with the Mao era.

As a consequence of the reforms designed to foster meritocracy, then, a set of changes occurred which fundamentally altered the Party's ability to dominate opinion formation within Chinese society. During the Mao era, the Party's overwhelming control produced a situation in which individuals who felt abused by, and alienated from, the system perceived themselves as isolated – surrounded by activists and intensely loyal supporters of the regime. They were unable to voice critical views beyond a very narrow circle of family members and intimate friends. Many victims

29. Of course, how rehabilitated rightists, victims of the Cultural Revolution and others reacted to their new opportunities varied. Some, such as the writer Ding Ling, seemed so grateful that they became ardent defenders of Deng Xiaoping's rule. However, many others, in an almost Rip Van Winkle fashion, resumed critical commentary broken off more than two decades earlier. The prototypical case is Liu Binyan, but there are many similar examples.

30. See the discussion in Tang Tsou, "Back from the brink of revolutionary-'feudal' totalitarianism," in David Mozingo and Victor Nee (eds.), *State and Society in Contemporary China* (Ithaca: Cornell University Press, 1983).

of the system, given this setting, ended up blaming themselves for being out of step with the masses who were marching triumphantly toward socialism.[31]

By the mid-1980s, the situation had changed fundamentally. Individuals with critical views perceived that they were no longer alone. Voicing complaints to whomever would listen became a common part of everyday life. Even the official media carried increasingly searching critical examinations of what was wrong with the system. Now it was the dwindling number of activists, many of them true believers who had come of age in the 1950s, who felt isolated. As the decade wore on, a variety of informal grassroots associations arose that were at least to some extent removed from the Party's "transmission belt" control system. Some of these were completely apolitical, but many were intensely concerned with debating China's fate. Within the context of an increasingly autonomous public opinion and the rudiments of a "civil society," the most free-wheeling discussion that had occurred since the May Fourth era was nurtured.[32]

The Party leadership reacted to these developments with a variety of efforts to proclaim limits, with Deng Xiaoping taking the lead. The elimination from the constitution in 1980 of the right to display wall posters and freely engage in public demonstrations, the similar elimination in 1982 of the right of workers to strike, the proclamation of the Four Cardinal Principles that were supposed to be beyond any criticism, the launching of campaigns against "spiritual pollution" and "bourgeois liberalization" – these and similar efforts were intended to enable the Party to maintain control over popular attitudes. They failed miserably in their aim to bottle up discontent, as the recurrent waves of demonstrations, culminating in the events of 1989, demonstrate. Here again we see in Deng an ironic reflection of Mao's efforts earlier. Both leaders criticized bureaucratic rigidity and launched reforms that checked bureaucratic control and promoted greater autonomy at the grass roots, but both were unable to countenance the fact that many would use their increased autonomy to form and exchange "unacceptable" opinions.

These observations point to the misleading nature of the claim that

---

31. Accounts of former rightists are filled with descriptions of the self-doubt that gripped them as a result of the attacks they received in 1957–58. See, for example, Yue Daiyun and Carolyn Wakeman, *To the Storm* (Berkeley: University of California Press, 1985).

32. See the discussion in my article, "Urban China: a civil society in the making?" in Arthur Rosenbaum (ed.), *State and Society in China* (Boulder: Westview, 1992); Clemen S. Ostergaard, "Citizens, groups and a nascent civil society in China: towards an understanding of the 1989 student demonstrations," *China Information*, No. 4 (1989), pp. 32–36; Solinger, *China's Transients and the State*. These developments were most visible in China's urban areas. Similar changes took place in rural areas, but there the new personal and intellectual autonomy often took other forms besides direct criticism of the system – for example, revivals of traditional religious practices and enthusiasms for new religions and charismatic cult figures. It should be noted that some of this new autonomy to think and share critical opinions began even during the Mao era, fostered by the disorder and suffering of the Cultural Revolution. That earlier trend helps to explain the 1976 Tiananmen demonstrations. See comments in my article "Urban China."

Deng's reforms produced qualitative changes in the economic system while preventing anything but minor changes in China's political system. Of course, the strategy of Deng and others was precisely that, his occasionally more exuberant calls for political reform notwithstanding. However, what such claims about the disjunction between economic and political reform overlook is the unintended consequences of Deng's programme. The changes implemented in order to create a more merito-cratic social order have steadily and pervasively undermined the ability of the CCP to dominate society and prevent critical views from circulating. As a result, the system has been psychologically undermined, even though the Leninist structures still stand and proclaim their dominance. This undermining of the Party's totalistic control and the rise of more autonomous social life and public opinion is a qualitative transformation of the political system, albeit an unintended one. Even though the post-1989 crackdown has raised fears and increased caution among critics of the system, there seems to be little evidence that it has been able to reverse the situation and enable the Party to regain its former dominance over society.

Conclusions

Analysts debate whether a reformed socialism is a viable system or an oxymoron, a temporary stop on the way toward more fundamental changes. Whatever the merits of each side of this theoretical debate, the current system for handling talent in the PRC does not appear to be workable in the long run. Preserving centralized bureaucratic allocation via a *nomenklatura* system at the core of the social order and trying to install meritocratic criteria for bureaucrats to use in promoting talent has a number of fairly obvious drawbacks. Bureaucrats with close to unlimi-ted authority to make personnel decisions are not disinterested industrial engineers, willing to appoint and promote the most talented. They are political animals who will inevitably want to do what is necessary to preserve and enhance their own power. While at times such consider-ations may lead them to promote experts and the entrepreneurial, at other times they may want to select sycophants, children of high officials, those willing to make payoffs, or simply individuals much like themselves.

Those who possess merit and have made contributions are not likely to display maximum initiative and creativity when their careers continue to depend upon the whims of bureaucratic superiors rather than on any sort of external or professional validation. They are not likely to show much enthusiasm for their organizations and their jobs if they continue to operate under something like indentured servitude (through the *danwei* "ownership" system). The precedent of Brezhnev's USSR can hardly be encouraging to China's would-be designers of technocracy. Even though theoretically it may seem possible to combine centralized bureaucratic control with a meritocratic personnel system, in practice in the USSR the result was declining efficiency and morale and increasing corruption. The *perestroika* programme launched by Gorbachev after 1985 was designed to counteract such problems, but in retrospect it was too little and too late.[33]

In China's partially reformed and marketized society there are new routes to rewards that are not fully dependent upon bureaucratic approval (such as in new private entrepreneurial firms, in foreign joint ventures). These alternative mobility channels make the continued need of the majority who labour in the less reformed parts of the system to curry favour with their superiors all the more obvious and onerous. The competition for advancement and the very real increase in material rewards unleashed by the reforms generate suspicion and resentment wherever control remains in the hands of bureaucratic gate-keepers. Perceptions that individuals are getting ahead not because of competence and merit, but because of connections, favouritism or outright corruption are inevitable in such a partially reformed system. The result is that the reformed system is seen in the public's eyes not as genuinely meritocratic, but as hypocritical and corrupt. Given the qualitative change in the political system noted above, such critical views can now be shared fairly widely, resulting in a growing conviction that further changes in the political system are called for. As this conviction spreads, the likelihood of social unrest and protest activity grows.[34]

Deng Xiaoping has tried to use reforms to preserve the political system to which he has devoted his life. He hoped that by introducing meritocratic reforms within that system it could regain legitimacy and be preserved. However, like Mao Zedong before him, his effort to confront the problems of Leninism has failed. Indeed, his reforms have unintentionally accelerated the process of undermining the Party's rule. In the wake of Tiananmen, Deng and his fellow gerontocrats have presided over a temporary and enforced stability. However, under the surface the trends his reforms unleashed continue to create fertile ground for future challenges to the system. Given the failure of both Mao and Deng to deal

33. A generation ago Soviet specialists debated whether the increasing reliance on experts and managers in the post-Stalin USSR would undermine the Party's control and lead to "convergence" toward the democratic West. At the time the dominant view was that hope for such convergence was misguided, and that the Party would be able to dominate the technocrats and prevent pluralistic trends from emerging. See, for example, Jeremy Azrael, *Managerial Power and Soviet Politics* (Cambridge, MA: Harvard University Press, 1966). In retrospect this conclusion was premature. The system of Party control was being undermined in the USSR from the 1950s onward, although it took longer for the process to be completed than some champions of "convergence" hoped. Given the demise of the system in the Soviet Union and Eastern Europe, the task of preventing the undermining of Leninism in China becomes even more difficult. For further thoughts on this issue, see my article, "Prospects for democratization in China," *Problems of Communism*, Vol. 41, No. 3 (1992), pp. 58–70.

34. As noted earlier, these observations on the popular mood primarily apply to China's urban areas, and particularly her large cities. Conditions of life in the countryside produce their own discontents, but these are not as likely to accumulate into a "pressure cooker" of demands for change as is the case in urban areas.

effectively with the problems of China's Leninist system, it seems unlikely that any successor will be able to do much better. If this conclusion is borne out, then history's verdict on Deng Xiaoping's personnel reforms will be that they were intended to save the system but instead hastened its collapse.

Deng Xiaoping: The Soldier

June Teufel Dreyer

Deng Xiaoping's attempt to modernize and professionalize the People's Liberation Army (PLA) will surely be remembered as one of the most important components of his historical legacy. Yet, ironically, Deng's military activities formed a decidedly minor part of his career. Deng received no formal military training, and Chinese Communist sources have very little to say about his military contributions before 1980; most of what was reported comes from his enemies[1] and is difficult to corroborate. What has been written after 1980 has a suspiciously hagiographic ring[2] and is also difficult to confirm.

Deng was born to a prosperous family and received a traditional education in his native Sichuan. One of his classmates was Nie Rongzhen, who would later become one of the ten military men honoured by the People's Republic of China (PRC) with the title of Marshal.[3] In 1920, at the age of 16, Deng was sent to France to complete middle school. Pursuing a course of general studies there, he met Zhou Enlai who was instrumental in persuading him to join the Chinese Communist Party (CCP). In 1926, Deng left for Moscow where he studied Marxism–Leninism and the theory and practice of revolution rather than military affairs. One of his fellow students was the daughter of Feng Yuxiang, best known in the West as "the Christian warlord." It may have been through her that Deng received his first "military" position, as Deputy Director of the political department and Director of Education at the Sun Yat-sen Military Academy Feng had recently founded in Xi'an. As is implied by its title, Deng's job was to instil his students with loyalty to Feng and Feng's agenda rather than dealing with such matters as strategy or military training.

Even so, Deng's stay at the military academy was brief. He had arrived in Xi'an in March 1927; during the following month, Chiang Kai-shek and his Kuomintang (KMT) forces turned definitively against the CCP in the Shanghai massacre, thus ending the united front between KMT and CCP. As evidence of his loyalty to Chiang, Feng Yuxiang expelled Communists from his academy, Deng included. Leaving Xi'an to join his erstwhile mentor, Zhou Enlai, Deng participated in various organizing activities on behalf of the Party. In September 1930, he became political commissar of the Seventh Red Army in Guangxi. Beleaguered by KMT forces, the Seventh Army attempted to join the Red Army's main force in the rural soviet Mao Zedong had established at Jinggangshan in Jiangxi

---

1. See, for example, Shen Ping, "Forever adhere to Chairman Mao's line on army-building: criticize Deng Xiaoping's revisionist fallacies on army-building," *Hongqi*, August 1976, pp. 4–9.

2. For example, Yang Qunzhang, *Deng Xiaoping: Xinshiqi jianjun sixiang yanjiu* (Beijing: Liberation Army Publishing House, 1989).

3. Nie's career paralleled Deng's precisely for a time: both studied in France, worked at the Renault factory, and then left for Moscow and the University of the Toilers of the East. However, Nie then transferred to the Red Army Academy.

province. It suffered heavy losses, with Deng sharing the blame for the disaster.[4]

Shortly thereafter, Deng arrived in Jinggangshan, where his duties were primarily organizational. In 1934, he was appointed Secretary-General of the General Political Department of the First Front Army, his principal duty apparently being to edit the military journal *Red Star*. However, the Long March began shortly thereafter, precluding any publication duties. Deng, with the other Long Marchers fortunate enough to survive until its end in Yan'an, were immediately faced with yet another battle for survival, against both KMT and Japanese forces. Deng's contribution, in conjunction with Liu Bocheng, concentrated on expanding the Red Army and using it in conventional regimental and division-sized operations against Japanese supply trains, isolated bases, and small troop concentrations. Deng's position at the time was political commissar of the 129th Division of the Eighth Route Army; Liu served as commander.

The Eighth Route Army was commanded by Peng Dehuai, known as a champion of military professionalism. Thirty years later, critics of Liu and Deng (as well as Peng) argued that this gave them a different focus from the guerrilla force tactics associated with Mao Zedong's vision of People's War. Yet there is no evidence that the two methods were viewed as antagonistic to each other at the time; it is just as likely that circumstances dictated whether regular units or guerrillas would be employed in a given operation. It should also be pointed out that, until 1942, an important part of Deng's job was co-ordination of "irregulars," including local troops, guerrillas and militia – none of whom were expected to fight much beyond their native villages – with the movements of the regular forces of the 129th Division. Rather than being devoted to an abstract model of military professionalism, as he has generally been portrayed,[5] Deng appears rather as someone who was willing to use whatever means were available and efficacious to a given end. This is consonant with his image as a statesman who wished to seek truth from facts, and whose economic philosophy was to ignore the name of a system so long as it was able to produce goods and services. Whether because or in spite of his outlook, Deng apparently earned the respect of both commanders and commissars; Liu Bocheng reportedly thought so well of him that he regularly sought Deng's opinion of the military and political implications of any operation before beginning it.[6]

In later years, the growth of Communist forces would lead to major reorganizations of troops. Peng Dehuai became commander of the First

4. See Benjamin Yang's "The making of a pragmatic Communist: the early life of Deng Xiaoping, 1904–49," in this issue, for a fuller treatment of this episode.

5. For example, by William Whitson, arguing that Deng's Soviet training and time with Feng Yuxiang were formative experiences. See *The Chinese High Command* (New York: Praeger, 1973) p. 123. As noted above, Deng did not study the military during his year in the USSR and there is no evidence that he was otherwise exposed to it. His time with Feng was very brief, and spent in indoctrination of cadets.

6. *Ibid.* p. 158.

Field Army, which conquered the north-west of China and had its principal strength there. Liu and Deng's troops became the Second Field Army, which was instrumental in conquering central China and, after that, south-west China. The Second Field Army and his native Sichuan, the most populous and prosperous province in the south-west, were to provide Deng with power bases. He served as political commissar of the South-west Military and Administrative Commission from 1950 to 1952.

Through Zhou Enlai's patronage, Deng relocated to Beijing in 1952 and received a series of important positions, including head of the Party's Organization Department and Secretary-General of the Secretariat of the Party Central Committee. Only one of these, a vice-chairship of the National Defence Council, had direct responsibility for military affairs. However, many of the others had supervisory functions with regard to matters of great importance to the military, such as defence budgets and personnel appointments.

Deng was unscathed by the purge of his former commander and later Defence Minister, Peng Dehuai, in 1959. Although Peng was known, and subsequently vilified, for his efforts to modernize and professionalize the PLA, the proximate cause of his downfall was not so much dissatisfaction with his military policies, but his criticism of Mao Zedong over the failure of the Great Leap Forward. Deng's own purge during the Cultural Revolution was accompanied by the generic charge that he had followed the "capitalist road" and the specific criticism that he did not care whether an economic system was capitalist or socialist so long as it produced goods. There was no mention of military matters, and indeed a leading scholar of the PLA clearly did not even consider Deng a military figure. William Whitson, writing in the early 1970s about late 1966, noted that "key Party figures disappeared at this time, with Liu Shaoqi and Deng Xiaoping the most prominent Party members to be disgraced, but no important military figure was removed."[7]

Deng was rehabilitated in August 1973, through Zhou Enlai's efforts. His initial appointment was as first Vice-Premier of the State Council. Although again not directly tasked with military affairs, Deng must have been aware of concerns at the highest levels of leadership during this period about the PLA. The military had emerged from the Cultural Revolution with far too much power, thus threatening Mao's dictum that the Party must always control the gun rather than vice versa. Furthermore, in certain areas, several military leaders held concurrently the top Party and government jobs as well, causing worries that they would form "independent kingdoms" that could ignore central government directives. In addition, radical leaders felt that military officers were in general hostile toward both them and their cause. Realizing that Mao was in declining health and painfully aware of the role the PLA might play in any succession struggle, radicals were concerned that neither they personally nor their philosophy might survive the death of the Chairman.

Two important steps were taken in this period to allay these fears,

7. *Ibid.* p. 376.

neither of them associated with Deng. First, in October 1973, radicals associated with the Gang of Four began reorganizing militia units under urban command centres. The new units combined public security and firefighting functions along with more traditional militia duties. Working from the radicals' power base of Shanghai, they also began to supply units with more sophisticated weapons manufactured in the city's munitions factories. It would later be alleged that the Gang planned to make the militia into a counterweight to the PLA in order to decide the succession struggle, and indeed the 1975 Constitution raised the militia to a position of parity with the PLA.[8]

Secondly, on 31 December 1973, there was a major, and unprecedented, reshuffle of high-ranking PLA leaders involving eight of the PRC's eleven military regions. In several cases, these involved lateral transfers: for example, the commanders of the Guangzhou and Nanjing military regions simply exchanged places, as did the commanders of the Jinan and Wuhan military regions and the Fuzhou and Lanzhou military regions. Since the commanders' Party and government positions did not move with them, the net effect was to reduce the ability of these individuals to form independent kingdoms.

On 29 January 1975, Deng was named head of the General Staff Department (GSD) of the PLA. Although it had been rumoured for some time that Deng would receive a high-ranking military position, this particular appointment was surprising: given his previous experience as a commissar, the directorship of the General Political Department (GPD) would have seemed more appropriate. That post, however, went to a member of the Gang of Four, Zhang Chunqiao, and it is possible that Zhou Enlai wanted Deng in the GSD as a counterweight to his radical arch-enemies.

Deng's military role was publicly invisible, whatever may have been going on beneath the surface. By contrast, Deng was extremely visible in his role as Vice-Premier, making a well-publicized visit to France, greeting German Chancellor Helmut Schmidt on his arrival in Beijing, meeting American Secretary of State Henry Kissinger, and hosting banquets on behalf of his terminally ill mentor Zhou Enlai. None of the speeches made in connection with these occasions mentioned the military. At least in terms of the public record, Deng met no visiting military delegations. News of the PLA concerned its study of the works of Chairman Mao, its denunciations of empiricism – a cause dear to Deng's heart – and its vilification of Lin Biao. Military units were reported helping the peasants under various unlikely circumstances. For example, the crew of a fishing boat discovered, after putting to sea during peak season, that its refrigeration equipment had failed, and that they had brought no spare parts. A Chinese navy warship happened to have the

8. According to Article 15, "The Chinese People's Liberation Army and the people's militia are the workers' and peasants' own armed forces led by the Communist Party of China; they are the people's own armed forces." See *Beijing Review*, 24 January 1975, p. 15, for the complete text.

right spare parts. Its officers immediately interrupted the ship's duties, sent men to install the refrigeration equipment, and saved the catch.[9] Also during this period, a number of individual valiant officers were perishing in an extraordinary repetition of the same scenario: throwing themselves on hand grenades which trainees had activated and then "inadvertently dropped."[10]

Deng's silence with regard to military matters is all the more puzzling in that it would later be alleged that, four days *before* his appointment as head of the GSD, he delivered a major speech which was in effect to become the blueprint for his military reforms. It was not published at the time, nor even mentioned by the press. Study sessions of PLA units regularly dealt with other materials, and a search of those major foreign wire services with good records on reporting rumours from major Chinese cities at that time also fails to find any reference to it.[11] The speech began to be alluded to in 1978, when Jinan PLA units were reported studying "documents of the enlarged meeting of the Military Commission held in 1975," including major addresses by Defence Minister Ye Jianying and Deng.[12] The mysterious document, containing many of the same themes alluded to in 1978, was finally printed in the *Selected Works* of Deng Xiaoping published in July 1983, where it was described as a speech to a meeting of the cadres of the GSD headquarters[13] rather than an address to an enlarged meeting of the Military Commission. Ye Jianying's speech remains unavailable to this day.

If delivered in the form later published, Deng's speech must have been a bombshell, and all the more so in the context of the ritualized cant that was standard in official speeches during that period. Deng announced bluntly that a large majority of PLA members were dissatisfied with the state of affairs. The military was too large; defence expenditures took up too large a proportion of the state budget, much of it for personnel expenditures; discipline was poor; and the military was riven with factionalism. The General Staff had not acted as a staff. Since the Army had become "bloated and is not a crack outfit that would make a good showing in combat," Deng announced that Chairman Mao had proposed a reorganization. The overall size was to be reduced, and the large numbers of excess officers cut. The three General Headquarters that supervise the work of the PLA, the General Staff Department (GSD), the General Political Department (GPD) and the General Logistics Department (GLD), would also be overhauled so as to improve command and control.

Although it would later be alleged that Zhang Chunqiao, as head of the GPD, was able to block publication of various materials and documents,

9. *Xinhua* (hereafter *XH*), Beijing, 15 January 1975.
10. *Renmin ribao*, 7 March 1975, p. 4, in United States Technical Information Service, *Foreign Broadcast Information Service*, Vol. 4, China (hereafter *FBIS-CHI*), 13 March 1975, p. E7.
11. AFP (France), CNA (Taiwan), Kyodo (Japan) and Tanjug (Yugoslavia).
12. *XH*, 12 January 1978, in *FBIS-CHI*, 16 January 1978.
13. *Deng Xiaoping wenxuan* (Beijing: People's Publishing House, 1 July 1983), pp. 1–3.

one must wonder whether even the collective power of the Gang of Four would have been able to suppress the circulation of such an important speech if, first, the demobilization had, as Deng stated, been devised by Mao and had his backing, and secondly, the speech actually said in 1975 what in 1983 it was purported to have said. Moreover, the call to reduce the size of the PLA drastically does not seem to fit with the general air of anticipation at that time of a war with the Soviet Union. In August 1975, Deng himself told visiting Japanese reporters that a third world war was inevitable, and that there was a need to prepare against it.[14] Nor is there any evidence of an attempt to reduce the size of the military. The PLA regularly demobilized about a million men each year, but seemed to be conscripting at least that many at the same time. The International Institute of Strategic Studies in London estimated that in 1975 the PLA had *added* 250,000 men to its armed forces and created three new armoured divisions.[15]

Though no rumours surfaced about Deng's January 1975 speech, other rumours were current that appeared to indicate his attitude toward the Gang's re-organized militia. There were reports that militia groups were acting as foot-soldiers for the radical agenda, and also tales of clashes between rival units, particularly in the city of Hangzhou.[16] In 1976, the attacks against Deng began with wallposters in Hangzhou indicating that problems connected with workers there had been followed by a personal visit by Deng and an "energetic" solution involving central government and local military intervention.[17]

These attacks on Deng began almost immediately after the death of his mentor Zhou Enlai in January 1976. PLA units all over the country were among those denouncing him, though usually for such abstract sins as "opposing class struggle" rather than for particular crimes with regard to the military. In mid-March, an Agence France Presse (AFP) report judged that the number of PLA units involved in criticism was relatively small, and that even these units had "stayed well away from making any innovations in the campaign."[18] Deng would eventually be attacked for his attitudes toward the military, as he would for his attitudes toward virtually every other facet of Chinese society, including even sport (Deng was alleged to have "twisted Mao's words 'friendship first, competition second' in order to exclude class struggle").[19]

Some of these attacks, such as that Deng wished to separate the army from Party control, were ritualistic, and had been consistently levelled against other top leaders being purged, including Peng Dehuai, Liu Shaoqi and Lin Biao. Others involved construing Deng's words in a

14. Kyodo (Tokyo), 16 August 1975, in *FBIS-CHI*, 18 August 1975, p. A3.
15. *The Balance of Forces, 1976–77* (London: International Institute for Strategic Studies, 1976), pp. 59–60.
16. See, e.g., Edward K. Wu, "People's militia total secret, but it is everywhere in China," *Baltimore Sun*, 8 July 1975, p. 1.
17. AFP (Hong Kong), 27 February 1976, in *FBIS-CHI*, 27 February 1976, p. E1.
18. AFP (Hong Kong), 18 March 1976, in *FBIS-CHI*, 18 March 1976, p. E2.
19. *XH*, 9 May 1976, in *FBIS-CHI*, 11 May 1976, p. E3.

far-fetched manner: for example, when Deng said that the PLA must be able to "fight a war of steel," that does not necessarily mean, as charged, that he was "advocating a purely military viewpoint" or "peddling the theory that weapons decide everything."[20] And to allege that Deng "undermined militia-building" and "ordered the disbandment of militia units"[21] overlooks the fact that Deng was opposing the building of a particular *type* of militia organization created by his, and Zhou Enlai's, enemies. Moreover, to advocate purchasing some foreign weapons is not proof positive that Deng was "sacrificing China's independence" and therefore possessed a traitorous "comprador mentality."[22]

Yet other charges, such as that Deng had "written off preparations against war"[23] were plainly at variance with his published statements on the need to fight a war of steel and on concern with the Soviet threat. Finally, charges that Deng wanted to "concentrate on the training of a few 'aces' in the militia" (vis-à-vis giving everyone in it the same training)[24] and opposed Mao's concept of people's war in favour of fighting "a professional war"[25] appear to be accurate.

Deng's attempt to strike back, in the form of an April 1976 demonstration to honour the memory of Zhou Enlai, became the proximate cause for his dismissal and disgrace. In light of later charges that it was the militia, acting on orders from the Gang of Four, that put down this demonstration, it is interesting to note that the official press at the time was careful to point out that the suppression had been carried out jointly by militia, PLA and the Public Security Bureau. *Renmin ribao*[26] carried a follow-up piece devoting an entire page headlined "Salute to the Heroic Capital Worker-Militiamen, People's Police and PLA Guards" to stories and pictures depicting the close co-operation among the three, which was also praised in numerous rallies. Accounts of the May Day celebration held soon thereafter took note of the "masses accord[ing] a very warm welcome to representatives of the worker-militia, people's police, and PLA guards" who participated in the annual parade and celebrations.[27]

Mao's death in September 1976 and the arrest of the Gang of Four a few weeks later were accompanied by rumours that Deng would again be rehabilitated. Gossip that was later confirmed had it that Deng had taken refuge in south China, where he was being protected by several military leaders. Those names most often mentioned as his supporters were Defence Minister Ye Jianying of Guangdong province; newly-appointed head of the GPD, Guangxi native and head of the Guangdong revolution-

20. Beijing Radio, 12 June 1976, in *FBIS-CHI*, 14 June 1976, pp. K1–2.

21. Beijing Radio, 18 June 1976, in *FBIS-CHI*, 21 June 1976, pp. G3–4; Inner Mongolia Radio, 19 June 1976, in *FBIS-CHI*, 21 June 1976, pp. K3–4.

22. Theoretical Study Group of the Workers of the Wuhan Shipyard, "The traitorous behaviour of worshippers of things foreign as seen from Li Hongzhang's navy building," *Guangming ribao*, 17 June 1976, p. 3.

23. Beijing Radio, 12 June 1976, in *FBIS-CHI*, 14 June 1976, p. K2.

24. Shanghai Radio, 20 June 1976, in *FBIS-CHI*, 22 June 1976, p. G6.

25. Kunming Radio, 22 June 1976, p. J2.

26. *Renmin ribao*, 15 April 1976, p. 4.

27. *XH*, 1 May 1976, in *FBIS-CHI*, 3 May 1976, p. E2.

ary committee Wei Guoqing; and Guangzhou Military Region commander Xu Shiyou. Those most prominently listed as Deng's enemies were
Beijing Military Region commander Chen Xilian, Beijing mayor Wu De,
and Wang Dongxing, head of the country's security apparatus.[28] Ye's
support for Deng was rumoured to be qualified by his insistence that
Deng make a self-criticism for his role in instigating the Qingming
disturbances[29]; on the other hand, he was believed to have protected Deng
from Chen Xilian, allowing Deng to circumvent roadblocks and escape
unscathed from Beijing after the demonstrations.[30] A visiting British-Chi-
nese author was told that Deng's biggest mistake while in office was not
in his opposition to the Gang of Four (or, by inference, his military
policies) but in his desire to rehabilitate cadres who had been purged in
past mass campaigns too quickly.[31]

At the same time, under the aegis of Hua Guofeng, who held the top
positions in Party, government, and military simultaneously, pronouncements on the PLA were consonant with ideas Deng had expressed
previously. For example, a series of lectures on Shanghai Radio stressed
the importance of modern weaponry ("when a people's army armed with
Mao Zedong Thought is equipped with high-technology weapons, it will
be invincible – like a tiger with wings").[32] The lectures also advocated
reducing the number of troops, and cutting administrative and personnel
expenditures so as to devote more money to economic projects.[33]

Deng's reinstatement in mid-July 1977 to his previous positions,
including head of the GSD, was accompanied by no startling changes of
military policy – indeed, most of his ideas with regard to the PLA had
been implemented by Hua Guofeng ever since Hua assumed office after
Mao's death. While Taiwan intelligence sources reported that there was
a furious power struggle going on between Deng and Hua,[34] Deng was
telling visiting author Han Suyin that he was "only an assistant, a helper
of Chairman Hua; I don't want anything else."[35] As after his previous
rehabilitation in 1975, Deng's role in the military was again, at least
publicly, invisible. News about the PLA seemed ostentatiously to ignore
him. For example, the September 1977 issue of *China Reconstructs*
praised Hua Guofeng's military expertise, describing him as an "excellent
tactician in guerrilla warfare," and the much-praised Hard Bone Sixth
Company of the PLA wrote an article for *Hongqi* praising Mao, Ye

---

28. See, for example, Yasuaki Ishikawa, "Delayed rehabilitation for Deng," *Sankei shim-
bun* (Tokyo) 4 April 1977, p. 3; AFP, 29 March 1977, in *FBIS-CHI*, 30 March 1977, p. E1.
29. "Bandit Ye Jianying opposes bandit Deng's return," *Lien-ho pao* (Taipei), 22 April
1977, p. 1.
30. "Peiping posters attack Chen Xilian," *Chung-kuo jih-pao* (Taipei), 20 December
1977, p. 3.
31. Han Suyin's account of her conversations with Chinese officials in AFP, 14 February
1977, *FBIS-CHI*, 15 February 1977.
32. Shanghai Radio, 15 February 1977, in *FBIS-CHI*, 17 February 1977, p. E1; see also
Nigel Wade, "Debate over Chinese bill for defence," *The Daily Telegraph* (London), 2
March 1977, p. 2.
33. *FBIS-CHI*, 17 February 1977, p. E2
34. CNA (Taipei), 15 December 1977.
35. Quoted in *Der Spiegel* (Hamburg), 21 November 1977, p. 189.

Jianying, He Long, and a long list of other leaders for their military acumen; Deng was conspicuous by his absence.[36]

Beginning in October, Deng made some cautious moves in the military sphere, meeting the commander of the Swedish armed forces and addressing a delegation of retired high-ranking Japanese Self Defence Force officers. But the battle between Hua and Deng was not publicly joined, and even then only allegorically, until the following year. On 4 January 1978, the official military newspaper *Jiefangjun bao* carried a scathing article entitled "Initial Analysis of Those Who Follow the 'Wind'." Its pseudonymous author Dao (way) Xin (new) heaped scorn on the wind-following tendencies of a statesman of the Five Dynasties of a millennium ago who sounded remarkably like Hua Guofeng. In light of Hua's vow to "support firmly whatever decisions Chairman Mao had made," there could be little doubt in anyone's mind whom Dao Xin was really criticizing. *Renmin ribao* gave the article added cachet by reprinting it two days later.[37] Deng posed his counter-slogan "seek truth from facts," which was also a quotation from Mao. By November, ten of the PRC's eleven military regions had held high-level meetings affirming the importance of seeking truth from facts. The sole resister was the Beijing Military Region, thus confirming rumours that its commander, Chen Xilian, was in the forefront of military opposition to Deng.[38]

Deng's re-presentation of the four modernizations at the Third Plenum of the Eleventh Central Committee in December left little doubt as to his pre-eminent position in the PRC, lack of formal title notwithstanding. The four modernizations, however, put the military last in line for funding. This prioritization is believed to represent the successful culmination of a major effort to convince PLA leaders that a modernized defence force could not be grafted on top of a backward economic and scientific base. Not until agriculture, industry and technology had been modernized could the country's military expect to be really strong.

Whether by accident or design, the PLA's performance in the February 1979 attack/"pre-emptive counter-offensive" on Vietnam fully confirmed Deng's prediction that it was "not a crack outfit that will make a good showing in combat." Chinese infantry forces fought without air cover; radio communication between tanks broke down; units invaded in columns without securing the areas between the columns, and so on. Publicly, the media proclaimed a great victory, even alleging that China had "touched the tiger's backside" (that is, annoyed Vietnam's ally, the Soviet Union) with impunity. Privately, there were indications of concern. AFP quoted a military commission document of 18 February as saying that there had been two serious problems with the war. First, the PLA had not fought in a long time, and the co-ordination of troops had not been satisfactory. Secondly, the army was not used to the mountains

---

36. "Chairman Mao's great banner guides our struggle forever," *Hongqi*, September 1977.
37. Translated in *FBIS-CHI*, 11 January 1978, pp. E1–3.
38. "Provinces and army back Deng," *China Record* (London), November 1978, p. 4.

and climate of south China, and hence there had been only "limited advancement."[39] Deng's own assessment was reportedly that the political and diplomatic aspects of the war were favourable, but that "the actual military side of the operation had not gone so well."[40] Yang Dezhi, commander of the Kunming Military Region and deputy commander of the Vietnam incursion, commented tersely that the operation "had brought up a number of new questions for our military, political and logistical work, and also provided us with new experiences."[41]

In March, a picture of Deng, dressed in military uniform and seated astride a white horse, went on sale in Beijing. Seemingly aimed at calling attention to Deng's role in the victorious battles of the late 1940s, when the original photograph had been taken, it showed Liu Bocheng at his side, Liu's head turned toward Deng in what seems a deferential pose.[42] However, Deng's public role with regard to the military remained muted until 1980, when he assumed Hua Guofeng's position and ensconced Yang Dezhi in his former position of head of the General Staff Department.[43] Actual military policies showed no break with those being implemented since 1977; the difference was that Deng was now publicly credited with them. They encompassed the following.

A reworking of strategic doctrine which replaced People's War with People's War Under Modern Conditions. Though described as an adaptation of Mao's principles to present-day conditions, most analysts feel that it represents a sharp break with the past, with retention of the original name intended to blur the ideological impact of the discontinuity. People's War Under Modern Conditions is characterized by greater attention to positional warfare, modern weaponry and combined arms. The concept of luring an enemy deep into Chinese territory with the intention of surrounding and destroying him was amended to include the possibility of forward defence: many Chinese strategists felt that, by the time the enemy had been lured far enough into the PRC for this to work, they would have destroyed much of the country's vital industries and transport links. In addition, China's incursion into Vietnam must have sharpened planners' awareness that future confrontations were apt to involve engaging the enemy *outside* the territory of the PRC.

More attention to training. Troop training programmes were ordered to be reorganized. Less time was to be given to political study sessions and more to the study of strategy and tactics. Training exercises were adapted to the sort of real-life situations that combat troops might actually be expected to face, and to reflect the conditions of weather and terrain of particular geographic areas.

39. AFP (Hong Kong), 20 February 1979.
40. Reuters (London), 20 March 1979.
41. Beijing Radio, 16 May 1979, in *FBIS-CHI*, 17 May 1979, p. Q2.
42. AFP (Hong Kong), 6 March 1979. Liu was Deng's superior at this time, both nominally and in reality.
43. "Peking names new chief of staff as Deng Xiaoping yields the post," *New York Times*, 1 February 1980, p. A6.

Efforts to acquire advanced weaponry. Both foreign and indigenous sources would be utilized. The National Defence Science, Technology and Industry Commission was charged with supervising research and manufacturing for the PRC's seven industrial ministries that deal with defence production. Military procurement missions were sent abroad to examine a wide variety of foreign weaponry and related items, including tanks, trucks, helicopters, warplanes, missiles, lasers and computers.

Reorganization of the PLA into a smaller, younger and more responsive force. With the perception of threat from the Soviet Union much reduced after 1981, plans were announced to diminish the size of the military by one-quarter, or a million people. The number of military regions was reduced from eleven to seven, thereby cutting down on the number of headquarters and their personnel. The new military regions were authorized to command tank and artillery divisions and other specialized service branches; in the past, these branches had been directly under the armed forces supreme command. Field armies were replaced with smaller group armies. New regulations provided for the reinstitution of a rank system and set limits for time in grade. Older officers, many of whom were in their 70s or 80s, were encouraged, and in some cases forced, to retire. This made it possible to promote younger, more vigorous people to command positions.

More stringent educational qualifications for the military. Units at and above the corps level were ordered to sponsor classes to bring PLA cadres up to the level of senior middle school or technical middle school. Self-study was encouraged as well. Those willing to enrol in night school, or in television or correspondence courses, were given assistance to do so. Tests of general and specialized knowledge were instituted. People who could not or would not meet the required standards might be denied promotion or be demoted. The Young Communist League was told to persuade outstanding college graduates to join the PLA.

A three-tier system was created to train junior, mid-level and senior officers, with more than a hundred military academies participating. The apex of the system is the National Defence University, which was founded in December 1985 by merging three PLA academies – military, political and logistical. Each had previously been operated by the relevant general department of the PLA. One motive behind consolidating the resources and expertise of the formerly separate institutes was the obvious one of producing a more efficient instructional system. Another, unstated, reason was to reduce departmental compartmentalization and the factionalism that separate institutions had reinforced.

Creation of a military that was more clearly differentiated from Party and government. There was a marked decrease in the number of individuals holding positions in either two or all three of the Party, government and military hierarchies. Statistical data show that there were 122 such individuals in 1960, 445 in 1973 and only 73 in 1982.[44] Top military positions were increasingly held by people who had spent the majority of their working lives in the PLA, as opposed to individuals shuttling between civilian and military positions (as Deng Xiaoping, among many others, had done). By late 1992, all three directors of the PLA's general departments were career soldiers, as were all members of the Central Military Commission except for its titular head, Party leader Jiang Zemin.

Augmenting the military's role in support of economic development. With the threat of war much reduced, military production lines, which had typically worked at far below maximum capability anyway, could be re-geared to produce goods for civilian consumption. Military-affiliated corporations not only produced such items as food, clothing and consumer electronics for domestic and foreign sales, but also manufactured weapons for export. The PRC quickly joined the ranks of the world's top arms merchants. At the same time, military units were expected, insofar as possible, to raise their own food and build and maintain their barracks. PLA units operated guesthouses and manufactured furniture. The military also went into the tourist business, flying groups of foreign visitors to points of interest in its planes, and even, for an extra fee, allowing members of these groups to discharge weapons on its firing ranges.

As might be expected, most of these reforms met resistance from one or more directions. Those who distrusted forward defence pointed out that the PLA might be outflanked and overrun. Those about to be demobilized resisted in a variety of ways ranging from armed rebellion[45] to using personal connections to avoid discharge.

For the first time since the founding of the PRC, conscription became a problem. While the Party was having trouble convincing older soldiers to retire, it was simultaneously experiencing difficulties in persuading younger people to volunteer. The success of Deng's privatization of the rural economy made it more profitable for peasant youth, who had been the mainstay of the PLA, to stay on the family farm. City youth tended to prefer unemployment to military service, and were in any case regarded by commanders as undesirable recruits: they were less inclined to obey orders than young peasants, and unused to the hard physical labour that military training demanded. Work units tried to foist their least desirable members on the military, and officers worried that the PLA would become an army of the unfit and unwilling.

Educational requirements could be circumvented by cheating on exams or using "back door" connections to certify one's proficiency in a subject one was actually quite deficient in.[46] Arguments between indigenous

44. See Monte Bullard, *China's Political-Military Evolution: The Party and the Military in the PRC, 1960–1984* (Boulder: Westview Press, 1985.)

45. See, e.g. *Chengming*, December 1981, in *FBIS-CHI*, 14 December 1981, p. W1; *Asia Record* (Hong Kong), January 1982, p. 17.

46. See, e.g. *Jiefangjun bao*, 27 November 1988, p. 1; AFP, 24 October 1988, p. 30, in *FBIS-CHI*, 24 October 1988, p. 30.

design and production bureaucracies, who had a vested interest in not buying foreign weapons, and those who wished to purchase from abroad, slowed down weapons procurement, as did seemingly endless haggles over the level of technology to be purchased and the price to be paid.

Giving the military a larger role in the civilian economy also facilitated a large increase in military corruption. Guesthouses functioned as brothels, while the PLA in Tibet denuded large belts of trees in that ecologically fragile area in order to manufacture and sell furniture for its members' personal profit.[47] Soldiers removed substantial quantities of goods from PLA storehouses to dispose of privately; storehouses could also be used to stockpile smuggled items, which could then be transported elsewhere in military vehicles.

Efforts were made to deal with these problems, some of which proved quite efficacious. While Deng's first effort at demobilization, from about 1981 to 1984, must be considered a failure, a second effort, from 1985 to 1987, was more successful, possibly because it dealt better with the problems that had emerged. Dual-use training programmes were set up within the military to teach soldiers skills that would ease their entry into the civilian job market, and efforts were made to match prospective employers with soldiers eligible for discharge. By the end of 1992, 7.4 million PLA members had taken part in these programmes, and 2.68 million had received civilian jobs.[48] Although these statistics do not reveal the fate of the other 4.72 million servicemen, the programme does seem to have blunted resistance to demobilization.

The knowledge that they would be able to learn a marketable skill while in military service may have served as well to reduce resistance to joining the PLA. Military authorities also devised a variety of innovative schemes such as assessing a fee of approximately 5 per cent of the income of every draft-age male in a district, with the resulting fund to be divided among the families of those who actually served.[49] An expected serious shortfall in recruitment in reaction to the use of the military to put down demonstrations in the spring of 1989 did not materialize: the contraction of the economy later in the year provided an impetus for many young men to enlist.

Other problems have been confronted, but with less satisfactory results. Military corruption remains a problem, and one that appears to be growing rather than diminishing despite efforts to curb it. Factionalism in the military is mentioned far less often than in the late 1970s, when Deng began to assert himself with regard to the defence forces. But, as the recent purge of members of the "Yang family village" within the PLA shows,[50] it continues to be a concern in 1993. There are also hints of

---

47. Lhasa Radio, 13 February 1982, in *FBIS-CHI*, 16 February 1992, pp. Q1–2.
48. Beijing Radio, 26 November 1992, in *FBIS-CHI*, 3 December 1992, p. 33.
49. *Jiefangjun bao*, 1 March 1988, p. 1.
50. Tai Ming Cheung, "General offensive: Yang's protégés fall as army shake-up continues," *Far Eastern Economic Review* (Hong Kong), 10 December 1992, p. 14, details a summary of these changes.

central leadership concern that growing regionalist tendencies in the economic sphere may spread to the military.

Conclusions

The Chinese military in 1993 is considerably more proficient than in 1976. Its capabilities are far from the level of the United States or the former Soviet Union, although there is no real evidence that the PRC aspires to a superpower-level military. A glance at the seven characteristics outlined above that comprise military reform under Deng's leadership hardly shows them to be brilliant or innovative: better training, weapons, education, organization; the shaping of the military as a more professionally distinct institution; and the periodic updating of strategy, are simply common sense. The final characteristic, the military's increasing role in civilian production activities, may arguably prove a drag effect on military modernization, though it can also be rationalized as a practical expedient, given the low likelihood of an attack on China's territory and the country's urgent need for economic modernization. Moreover, since most of these ideas were being pursued during Deng's period of disgrace in 1976–77, it is not clear that he alone should be credited with them.

It may be that Deng's real genius lies not in inventiveness, but rather in his ability to impose common sense standards on the military prior to Mao Zedong's death, which had seemed devoid of all common sense. Endless polemics on the desirability of taking class struggle as the key link or on the need to damn the theory that weapons decide all, while definitely weakening the fighting capabilities of the military, simultaneously masked the vested interests of leftist forces. Under the direction of Hua Guofeng, these forces were mortally weakened after October 1976, and more sensible attitudes toward improving the PLA emerged. It took Deng, however, to make these operational, often against massive bureaucratic resistance. The demobilization and reorganization of the 1980s is perhaps the most outstanding example of this. There have been personal and professional costs to these actions: within five years of his return to power, Deng had strained relations with all three of the PLA leaders who had championed his rehabilitation: with Wei Guoqing over the liberalization of PLA literary and cultural work (1982), with Ye Jianying over demobilization (1983), and with Xu Shiyou over appointing Hu Yaobang as head of the Central Military Commission (1985).

Deng has had failures. For example, he never was able to overcome the PLA's resistance to accepting Hu Yaobang as head of the Military Commission. An attempt in 1982 to abolish the Party's Military Commission after creating an equivalent body under the State Council was also a failure: the two commissions continue to exist, with overlapping memberships. After the evident hesitation that certain PLA units had shown over enforcing martial law during the demonstrations of 1989, it was alleged that many officers had become infected with bourgeois liberal views that the army must be separated from politics.[51] Clearly there were concerns that Deng's efforts to differentiate Party, government and army had gone too far. But in the end, it is Deng's military successes that will be remembered rather than his failures.

51. See, e.g., Liu Huaqing's 18 August 1989 speech to the Sixth Plenary Session of the navy's Sixth Party Committee, carried in *Renmin ribao*, 19 August 1989, p. 2. The proposal for greater army–Party separation was attributed to Zhao Ziyang, former CCP General Secretary and CMC Chairman, following his purge after 4 June. For further analysis see David Shambaugh, "The soldier and the state in China: the political work system in the People's Liberation Army," *The China Quarterly*, No. 127 (September 1991), pp. 527–568.

Deng Xiaoping: The Statesman

Michael Yahuda

Alone of the world's Communist leaders, Deng Xiaoping has charted a course that has combined for his country rapid economic development, successful economic reform and openness to the capitalistic international economy with continued dictatorship by the Communist Party. Under his leadership Communist rule in China has survived the demise of Communism in Eastern Europe and the disintegration of the Soviet Union – the motherland of Communism. In the process the regime has weathered the ending of the Cold War and has become more engaged with the Asia-Pacific region. But Deng's reputation at home and abroad has been badly tarnished by his ruthlessness in masterminding the Tiananmen massacre of 4 June 1989. But that ruthlessness is absolutely central to Deng's political philosophy and strategy. For him it is the basis of order at home which alone ensures that the economic policies of reform and openness can be carried out without undermining Communist Party rule through the spread of liberal influences. In so far as statesmanship requires moral dimensions it will be necessary in assessing the quality of Deng's statesmanship to consider the meaning of statesmanship itself.

Before addressing that broad issue it is also necessary to identify the extent of Deng's responsibilities for China's foreign policy and clarify the character of his contribution to that policy. It is argued that in addition to placing economic development at the centre of Chinese foreign policy interests he also gave that policy a clearer and perhaps stronger nationalist character. The wise conduct of foreign policy does not depend only upon the successful mastery of the relevant domestic factors, but also requires an understanding of the forces at work in international society. Accordingly, Deng's record of adapting to the changes in international politics is also evaluated. Many of the economic reforms and China's deeper engagement with the outside world associated with Deng's leadership raise fundamental issues about the character of the Chinese state itself, issues which first arose as the result of its encounter with Western power and the forces of modernization in the 19th century. Some aspects of that are considered before concluding with an assessment of Deng's claims to statesmanship.

Deng's Leadership in Foreign Affairs

Deng Xiaoping may well be the last Chinese Communist leader to leave a personal imprint upon the making of Chinese foreign policy. Although he has not sought the despotic personal powers exercised by Mao and despite the broadening of the number of institutions involved in the conduct of foreign policy, Deng has nevertheless been able to determine matters that he has regarded as crucial. It was he who set the terms for the conduct of relations with the Soviet Union (and its successor states) and the United States, and who made the key decisions to attack Vietnam in 1979. Above all it was he who set the general course of a foreign policy designed to serve the interests of economic reform and opening to the international economy. It is therefore fitting that he should be considered as the architect of China's foreign policy since 1978 and as such be judged as a statesman.

Deng's basic viewpoints may be said to have been formed long before he became paramount leader, but it was not until Mao's death that Deng became free to articulate his views and chart his preferred course without having to defer to Mao's final imprimatur. Unlike some of his other Politburo colleagues Deng Xiaoping did not pen his name in the 1950s and 1960s to essays on foreign affairs that took a different line from Mao's. In fact he was entrusted by Mao to carry out a number of foreign engagements notably in confronting the Soviet Union during the dispute in the early 1960s. As will be seen, there is some indication that Deng was never favourably disposed towards the Soviet Union, but it would be unwise to take his role in Sino-Soviet polemics as evidence for this. Other leaders such as Zhou Enlai, Liu Shaoqi and Peng Zhen were also prominent in the conduct of the dispute and Mao would not have tolerated any significant departure from his views on an issue that was so important to him. This article, therefore, will focus primarily upon Deng's leadership from 1978 onwards.

Assessing Deng Xiaoping's statesmanship presents a difficulty as he is still very much active and the course of his career even at the age of 89 is unpredictable. Timing is of unusual significance in evaluating the quality of a statesman. Perspectives change and, since statesmen are often judged in the light of subsequent developments, any judgment made of one in his lifetime is likely to be partial and transient. For example, those generous evaluations of Deng Xiaoping made before the Tiananmen killings that saw him nominated on two separate occasions as the *Time* magazine "Man of the Year" now appear to reflect more upon the observers than the observed. The following aspires no more than to make a preliminary assessment in the hope that it will not immediately become out of date.

How should Deng's statesmanship be assessed? The brutal and deliberate massacre of unarmed civilians by armoured troops on the night of 3–4 June 1989 will inevitably weigh against him in historical judgments. That is an issue which will be considered once the broader questions of his conduct of China's foreign affairs have been addressed. The existing literature on how to measure successful statesmanship is not very helpful. As a prominent international relations theorist has noted, the question of statesmanship and its allied subject statecraft has been neglected in social scientific writings.[1] But there is more extended treatment by Western writers in the realist tradition that focuses on statesmanship and the promotion of the national interest. Statesmanship is usually considered even within that tradition to require more than concern for one's own

1. On the latter point see David A. Baldwin, *Economic Statecraft* (Princeton: Princeton University Press, 1985) pp. 9–12.

national interest narrowly defined. As Martin Wight has argued in discussing the views of George Kennan and Hans Morganthau, "the great aim of statecraft, of foreign policy, is to pursue and safeguard the national interest within the setting of a respect for the interests of others, or of international society as a whole."[2] Perhaps the most notable contemporary realist scholar with his own claims to statesmanship, Henry Kissinger, has consistently argued that successful foreign policy requires paying attention to both the maintenance of equilibrium (or balance of power) and to acting with restraint.[3] In other words he too recognizes the importance of moral considerations.

But Deng is heir to two rather different traditions. He is the last in line to a Chinese tradition of statehood that unlike any other contemporary state traces itself back continuously for nearly 3,000 years. Indeed there is evidence that both Mao and Deng consulted regularly the 11th-century massive compilation, *Zi Zhi Tong Jian* (*The General Mirror for the Aid of Government*), that detailed for the emperor in 294 chapters how his predecessors in the previous 1,300 years had handled difficult questions.[4] However useful that may have been for the conduct of domestic politics, the international circumstances of China's distant past that involved managing threats from nomadic barbarian peoples to the north and conducting tributary relations with notionally deferential neighbours could hardly be compared with the modern condition. Nevertheless the impact of the weight of the past is a factor in assessing Deng's statecraft.

The other tradition to which Deng is an heir is that of Marxism–Leninism and particularly the Chinese variant of it. Despite the massive corpus of Marxist writings on most other subjects there is very little on statesmanship or statecraft. In this respect it is perhaps best to regard Deng as the heir to Mao. It is worth recalling that despite finding "mistakes" in Mao's record in domestic matters the lengthy 1981 Party *Resolution* devoted just one sentence to foreign affairs to express support for his policies.

Writing 15 years ago about a similar assessment of the recently deceased Mao Zedong, John Gittings suggested that there were three different sets of criteria for assessing his statesmanship:

(i) by measuring Mao's contribution to "world peace," or to the maintenance of some sort of international stability preserving the present order.

(ii) by measuring the contribution to the building up and strengthening of the socialist

---

2. Martin Wight, "The theory of the national interest" in Gabriele Wight and Brian Porter (eds.), *International Theory: The Three Traditions* (Leicester & London: Leicester University Press, 1991), p. 126.

3. See his many statements to that effect in his memoirs *The White House Years* and *Years of Upheaval* (London: Weidenfeld & Nicolson, respectively 1979 and 1982). To take one example from the former: "If history teaches anything it is that there can be no peace without equilibrium and no justice without restraint" (p. 55).

4. Harrison E. Salisbury, *The New Emperors: China in the Era of Mao and Deng* (Boston: Little, Brown and Company, 1992), especially pp. 9 and 325–26. But see also the book as a whole, based largely upon interviews, for a graphic, if not entirely accurate, portrayal of the extent of the influence of the Chinese imperial past upon the conduct of especially Mao, but also Deng.

state in China, with well-defined interests and a social and political system secure from outside interference; or

(iii) by measuring Mao's contribution to the building of socialism not only in China but abroad, and to the advancement of the proletarian revolution.[5]

It was the last, involving contradiction between the pursuit of socialism within China and proletarian internationalism, that Gittings suggested was of most interest and raised the important questions.

With Deng's accession this ceased to be of current significance – at least not in that form. Instead the contradiction was transformed into one between the upholding of socialism within China and the engaging in ever deepening ties with the international capitalist economy. The central thrust of Deng's policies has been to call for the development of the productive forces through economic reform and openness while maintaining Communist Party rule. Indeed he reaffirmed them in his address to his military commanders immediately after the Tiananmen killings. In other words even at the point of China's deepest domestic and international crisis when Deng was under pressure from his less reformist colleagues to draw up the socialist barricades against the capitalist world he insisted upon adherence to his central strategy. While he argued that "we should not have an iota of forgiveness for our enemies" he also declared that "our reforms and opening up have not proceeded adequately enough."[6]

By switching the focus of Chinese politics from concern with class struggle to the development of the productive forces, Deng initiated a significant transformation in China's engagement with the outside world. In the words of a Chinese commentary, since December 1978 "Deng Xiaoping and the Party Centre already began to abandon the constraint of the 'leftist' confrontationist approach."[7] In Mao's lifetime, after the break with the Soviet Union the engagement with the rest of the world was limited to strategic matters deemed necessary to sustain the security of the state from external enemies and to trade designed to fill gaps in the domestic economy. Beyond these questions lay the issue of the nature of the Chinese obligation to support revolutionary movements and other Third World countries. Under Deng's leadership that engagement has widened to include a broad range of economic linkages with social and political consequences that have made the country interdependent with the international capitalist economy and many of the institutions that underpin it.

Within China it may be argued in Marxist terms that Deng's strategy of developing the productive forces will necessarily have consequences for the superstructure, including of course how China is ruled. Indeed it may be argued that the tension between the two is at the heart of many

5. See John Gittings, "The statesman," in Dick Wilson (ed.), *Mao Tse-tung in the Scales of History* (Cambridge: Cambridge University Press, 1977), p. 247

6. See Deng Xiaoping's speech of 9 June 1989 in *Beijing Review* (henceforth *BR*), Vol. 32, No. 28 (10–16 July 1989), pp. 14–17.

7. Jin Yu and Chen Xiankui, *Dangdai Zhongguo da silu – Deng Xiaoping de lilun yu shijian* (*The Big Themes of Contemporary China – Deng Xiaoping's Theory and Practice*) (Beijing: The Chinese People's University Press, 1989), p. 186.

of China's domestic problems. But in its external relations too there has developed great tension between holding on to the political and organizational structures of Communist rule and the deepening interdependencies with the outside world. It is therefore important to consider how Deng has sought to redefine Chinese state interests in this new context.

The Re-drawing of China's National Interest

Deng's strategy has had a two-fold effect upon China's position in the international community. On the one hand, it has brought the country into a multi-faceted engagement with the different forces at work in international society. But on the other, it has also caused Chinese policy to focus more narrowly on Chinese national or state interests. The impact of this narrower focus has been felt in many spheres including relations with Third World countries and revolutionary movements, ideology, the character of international obligations, and the cultivation of a diplomatic style of entitlement.

Upon his assumption of the reins of power in December 1978, Deng virtually brought to an end China's remaining practical support for revolutionary movements abroad and significantly reduced China's aid to Third World countries. Almost immediately China changed course from being a net aid giver to becoming a net aid receiver.[8] During his tour of South-east Asia in November and December of that year he indicated to his hosts that, while he could not entirely disavow the Communist insurgent parties of the region lest the Vietnamese and Soviets take over the patronage, he could nevertheless assure them that China's support for these parties was confined to propaganda and that material support was negligible or non-existent.[9] While several South-east Asian governments remained sceptical, there is no available evidence that in the 1980s the Chinese authorities gave material aid to Communist insurgent forces in the region other than Burma and those engaged in resisting Vietnam in Cambodia.

The theme of "building socialism with Chinese characteristics" implies that it is a form of what used to be called "national Communism." As articulated by Deng, Chinese Communists alone can work out what is socialism and the forms it can take in accordance with their own experience and understanding of Chinese conditions. In explaining his adherence to Marxism Deng declared that "by Marxism we mean Marxism that is integrated with Chinese conditions, and by socialism we mean socialism that is tailored to Chinese conditions and has Chinese characteristics."[10] It follows that China cannot look to others for a model and nor

8. Samuel S. Kim, *China In and Out of the Changing World Order* (Princeton: World Order Studies Program Occasional Paper No. 21, Princeton University, 1991), p. 37.

9. Robert S. Ross, *The Indo-China Tangle, China's Vietnam Policy 1975–79* (New York: Columbia University Press, 1988), pp. 221–22.

10. Deng Xiaoping, *Fundamental Issues in Present-Day China* (Beijing: Foreign Languages Press, 1987), p. 54. For his first mention of the concept see his talk of 12 January 1983, *ibid.* pp. 10–13.

can it be one for others. But, more importantly, it meant that no outsider could legitimately query the ideological integrity of that socialism.

This "national Communism" was also reflected in an approach to relations between Communist parties that form the core of what used to be called "proletarian internationalism." A visit by a West European Communist leader on 7 June 1982 provided the occasion for putting forward four principles that have since been advanced as the only acceptable basis for inter-party relations, and effectively precluded the possibility of arriving at a collective understanding of what principles of Marxism–Leninism might have universal validity. The four principles were "independence, complete equality, mutual respect and non-interference in each other's affairs in developing party-to-party relations." They were reiterated with considerable publicity four years later on the eve of the re-establishment of relations with the East European parties with the Soviet Union very much in mind.[11] The "national Communist" character of the formula is plain. Had it applied in the Maoist era it would not have been legitimate for Mao to have accused the CPSU of ideological deviation.

This nationalistic approach was soon to be applied to inter-state relations with the revival by Deng Xiaoping in 1988 of Zhou Enlai's Five Principles of Peaceful Co-existence (or FPPC).[12] This was originally conceived as a means to facilitate relations with the non-Communist states of Asia and it became the formal basis for the general conduct of inter-state relations. It was generally associated in Mao's lifetime with the more moderate phases of foreign policy. But as used by Deng in 1988, and especially after the Tiananmen events, FPPC has been used to promote a concept of absolute state sovereignty that in the past had applied to the more revolutionary periods. It seemed anachronistic in the late 1980s to apply it in a more interconnected and interdependent world that faced global environmental problems that transcended state borders in their application and means for resolution. The formulation was designed to deflect international and particularly Western criticism of the Chinese government's human rights record. It was a defensive, perhaps even truculent, reaction of a regime that felt increasingly beleaguered.

The FPPC was offered alongside the rather tired rhetoric of Third World oratory from the 1970s as a formula for a new international political and economic order. Characteristically, it was self-serving and it conveniently overlooked the fact that China was at the same time making demands upon the international community and the Western countries in particular for economic transactions on favourable terms that could only

11. *BR*, Vol. 29, No. 41 (13 October 1986), p. 7

12. Wu Xiuquan, *Eight Years in the Ministry of Foreign Affairs (January 1950–October 1958): Memoirs of a Diplomat* (Beijing: New World Press, 1985), pp. 42–43 describes how Zhou initiated the proposal in 1953 as "guiding principles for development of the ministry's work in Asia." The principles were first made public in the Sino-Indian agreement negotiated by Nehru and Zhou in 1954 and provided the official guide for all China's state relations ever since. They are: (1) mutual respect for each other's territorial integrity and sovereignty; (2) non-aggression; (3) non-interference in each other's internal affairs; (4) equality and mutual benefit; and (5) peaceful co-existence.

be granted if those concerned followed international norms and principles of obligation that the Chinese government was not prepared to have applied to itself.

This may be considered as the diplomacy of entitlement or what Samuel Kim has described as the *"maxi/mini principle* in the conduct of multilateral diplomacy – maximizing China's rights and interests and minimizing China's responsibility and normative costs." The particular instance he had in mind was China's abstention on UN Security Council Resolution 678 which authorized the use of "all necessary means" to compel Iraq to implement the previous resolutions. Kim described it as "an unprincipled quest to make the best of all worlds." The effect was to countenance the American use of force while pretending otherwise.[13] No wonder President Bush used the occasion to break his own sanction against meeting Chinese leaders by receiving Foreign Minister Qian Qichen in Washington personally. Other examples of a Chinese sense of entitlement may be seen from its expectation of favourable treatment from Japan by invoking war-time guilt or from the United States by demanding generosity as of right.[14]

Broadly speaking China's conduct of international economic relations has been rightly described as neo-mercantalist.[15] Despite the promptings of the World Bank China has not opened its domestic markets to foreign competition. There has been no question of adopting the liberal arguments of Adam Smith and the other classical economists. As Deng has argued repeatedly, and as he pointed out again to his doubting comrades in the course of his famous 1992 Spring Festival visit to southern China, there is nothing to be feared from extending the operations of foreign funded enterprises:

As long as we keep ourselves sober-minded, there is nothing to be feared. We still hold superiority, because we have large and medium state-owned enterprises and township and town enterprises. More importantly, we hold the state power in our hands.[16]

At the same time it is important to recognize that Deng's economic nationalism has not led him, like many of his elderly colleagues, to advocate a new kind of isolationism. Deng has consistently opposed that. In a speech in 1984 he went so far as to put the blame for China's poverty and ignorance upon the isolationism followed by the country for 300 years from the middle of the Ming Dynasty until its defeat in the Opium

13. Kim, *The Changing World Order*, pp. 25–27.

14. On Japan see Allen S. Whiting, *China Eyes Japan* (Berkeley: University of California Press, 1989) and Laura Newby, *Sino-Japanese Relations* (London: Routledge, 1988). On the United States, see Michel Oksenberg, "The China problem," *Foreign Affairs*, Summer 1991, p. 12.

15. See Robert Kleinberg, *China's "Opening" to the Outside World: The Experiment with Foreign Capitalism* (Boulder: Westview Press, 1990), especially pp. 254–268.

16. See Central Document No. 2 (1992) as carried in *Zhengming* (Hong Kong, 1 April 1992) in *BBC Summary of World Broadcasts, Part 3* (henceforth *SWB*), FE/1346/B2/2.

War of 1840.[17] The standard Chinese Nationalist and Communist explanation for China's weakness was to blame it upon imperialism. While
Deng has acknowledged that openness to the capitalist world will bring
in "undesirable things," he has consistently argued that these are manage-
able and that they should not be used as an excuse to close China's open
door. Thus in his 1992 spring offensive he criticized those on the left who
used the threat of the alleged American policy of "peaceful evolution" to
try to limit the open door policy as constituting a greater danger than
those on the right. His advocacy of openness has been central to his
overall strategy and it has played a large part in China being the only
Communist or former Communist country to have succeeded in raising
significantly the standard of living of the general population in the
process of economic reform. Indeed Deng has argued that part of the
reason for the collapse of the Soviet Union was the economic failure of
the Gorbachev regime. It follows that in Deng's view socialism will
survive in China only if it continues to provide growing economic
prosperity.

The corollary of Deng's stress on reform and openness has been his
emphasis upon the need to uphold the "Four Fundamental Principles."
His two successors in the 1980s, Hu Yaobang and Zhao Ziyang, both fell
for their alleged failure to take a sufficiently strong line against
"bourgeois liberalization." Deng envisages a future in which China will
continue with Communist political dictatorship at home while engaging
in both economic reform and ever-widening economic engagement with
the West. Whether that is compatible with China's international environment remains to be seen, but it is a future that offers no respite to
continuing domestic tension between, on the one hand, those seeking to
uphold Communist Party rule and the ideology that sustains it and, on the
other, those directly engaged in carrying out economic reform and
conducting foreign economic relations. It is a future that will challenge
the Party to adapt continually to the social and political consequences of
reform and openness. It is difficult to envisage how Communist Party
members would not seek to resist the continual diminishment of their role
in Chinese society that is entailed in such a future. In fact it would seem
highly likely that the more traditionally minded among them and those
with deeply embedded vested interests in the status quo would seek to
resist these trends by evoking nationalistic themes with which to castigate
the foreign connections so as to undermine or at least slow down the pace
of economic reform.

Deng's Adaptation to the Changes in International Politics

Deng's reorientation of China's foreign policy in support of the
fundamental drive for economic development must be seen within the
context of the enormous changes in the country's international security
environment. It was the pursuit of economic goals that gave credibility to

17. Deng Xiaoping, *Fundamental Issues*, p. 79.

Deng's claims that China needed a period of "international tranquillity,"[18] but as China's leaders discovered in the 1950s, the search for a peaceful environment was no guarantee that superior adversaries would respond accordingly.[19] In other words, China's foreign policy was to a large extent dependent upon a strategic international environment that it could not hope to control. Since that environment has been totally transformed since 1978 it is important to examine how Deng has perceived these changes and how he has adapted to them.

From Deng's perspective China's international situation may be said to have changed from the late 1970s when the country was endangered by strategic military encirclement to the early 1990s when the survival of the regime was at risk because of political pressures. The transition from military to political threats has been accompanied by the decline of the country's global strategic significance as a major player in the so-called "great strategic triangle" and by its marginalization to being a country of primarily regional significance. If the end of the Cold War and the collapse of the Soviet Union has ushered in a period of relative peace and freedom from military threat after 40 years of pressure, it has also ushered in a period of great political uncertainty about the durability of its Communist political system.

The new international situation has also profoundly changed China's own region so that it promises to be an even more propitious environment within which to realize Chinese hopes for economic development: the major regional conflicts in Indo-China and Korea are being diffused, with China playing a significant role in helping to resolve them. The reduction of tensions has facilitated the continued expansion of Chinese economic relations in the region. Moreover since the mid-1980s this has been reflected in closer ties with South Korea, Taiwan, Hong Kong and the countries of South-east Asia. Moreover (with the half-hearted exception of Japan) the countries of the region did not as a whole join the West in imposing sanctions in the wake of the Tiananmen events. But the easier relations within the region have so far not materially helped the Beijing regime to manage its deep crisis of political survival in which domestic and international factors are closely linked. Deng's 1992 strategy to accelerate economic development through deepening the ties with Hong Kong and the rest of East and South-east Asia is designed to overcome that political crisis through economic means.

In reviewing more broadly Deng's perceptions and responses to China's changing international environment it is useful to distinguish between three broad phases of the change: first, the search for an alignment to resist alleged Soviet expansionism, 1978–81; secondly, the management of independence between the two superpowers, 1982–89;

18. See Deng's speech of 16 January 1980, "The present situation and the tasks before us," *Selected Works* (henceforth *SW*), p. 226: "we really need a peaceful environment, and thus, for the interest of our own country the goal of our foreign policy is a peaceful environment for achieving the four modernizations."

19. See the brief account in Michael B. Yahuda, *China's Role in World Affairs* (London: Croom Helm, 1978), pp. 66 and 80–81.

and thirdly, the challenge of the end of the Cold War, 1989–92 (and beyond).[20]

Deng's initial perceptions of China's international strategic situation in 1978 were similar to those of Mao before his death two years earlier.[21] For both men the crucial questions centred on the two superpowers and in particular on how to counter the perceived Soviet threat of encirclement. It is fruitless to speculate on whether Mao, like Deng, would have attacked Vietnam in the spring of 1979 to "teach it a lesson" after it had invaded Cambodia to replace the Pol Pot regime with one of its choosing. But in important respects Deng's management of the episode was similar to those occasions when Mao had resorted to the use of force. Like Mao, Deng proved himself to be capable of swift, ruthless and decisive action in which decision-making was concentrated in his hands as he strove to keep the initiative in the military and diplomatic aspects of the conflict. Perhaps too the way he apparently calculated the risks of possible military intervention by the principal superpower adversary and took steps to minimize them owed something to the legacy of Mao. A limited evacuation of people from key points near the Soviet border and the suggestion that the United States and Japan were aligned with China coupled with the careful and deliberate signalling to the Soviet Union that China's punitive attack was limited in both scope and duration all combined to suggest that the Soviet threat had been carefully considered and that Deng did not seek to provoke the Soviet leadership to the point that it would feel compelled to respond.[22] Deng's Vietnam war exposed Chinese military weaknesses to the extent that many observers regarded it as a defeat.[23] But seen as part of a much longer-term strategy to dislodge Vietnam from Cambodia, Deng's approach must be judged to have been a success. The war was accompanied and followed by a successful diplomatic campaign to keep Vietnam isolated internationally in economics and politics. Vietnam's support by the Soviet Union enabled it to invade and occupy Cambodia, but it was its dependence upon the Soviet Union that proved its undoing in the long run. As the Soviet Union weakened and changed course under Gorbachev Deng was able to sustain sufficient pressure upon Vietnam until it withdrew its armed forces from Cambodia in 1989 and eventually made its peace with China on substantively Chinese terms in 1991.

It was the consequences of the Soviet invasion of Afghanistan in late

20. Interestingly, Chinese accounts of China's foreign policy have subdivided the period in similar ways.

21. For accounts of Mao's views of international politics at this time see Gittings, "The statesman," and Michael Yahuda, *Chinese Foreign Policy After Mao, Towards the End of Isolationism* (London: Macmillan, 1983) ch. 3.

22. For analysis of Mao's approach see Allen S. Whiting, *The Chinese Calculus of Deterrence* (Ann Arbor: University of Michigan Press, 1975).

23. See for example, King C. Chen, *China's War Against Vietnam, 1979: A Military Analysis* (Baltimore: University of Maryland, Occasional Papers/Reprint Series in Contemporary Asian Studies, No. 5, 1983); and Harlan W. Jenks, "China's 'punitive' war on Vietnam: a military assessment," *Asian Survey*, Vol. XIX, No. 8 (August 1979); and Gerald Segal, *Defending China* (Oxford: Oxford University Press, 1985) ch. 12.

1979 which had initially seemed so threatening that paradoxically turned the tide and made the prospects of war seem more distant. That in turn enabled Deng to preside over a shift towards a foreign policy more balanced between the two superpowers that was called "an independent foreign policy" at the 12th Party Congress in September 1982. It soon became apparent that the Soviet Union would face a newly determined American response that began in the last year of the Carter presidency and was carried still further by the Reagan administration. That, combined with the pressure from the Afghani resistance forces, the diplomatic isolation of the Soviet Union in the Third World and its growing domestic economic problems, persuaded Deng and his advisers that the Soviet Union was overstretched. In other words the immediate danger had receded.[24] It was now possible to take a more measured approach to understanding the international environment and China's place within it. At the time of greatest danger in 1978–79 Deng Xiaoping went so far as to suggest publicly alliances with both Japan and the United States. In December 1979 Deng told a foreign journalist "if Japan and China co-operate, they can support half of Heaven." A year earlier, in an interview with *Time* magazine, he specifically called for an alliance with the United States.[25] Within a year such talk had faded away. Although the shift to the stance of independence had been facilitated by Chinese dissatisfaction with Reagan's handling of the Taiwan issue, the relaxation of the Soviet threat was the critical factor that reduced the Chinese need to stress the strategic link with the United States.[26] The essence of the policy of independence was that China would not ally itself with any major power and that undoubtedly suited the broader Chinese psychological outlook on international affairs.

It was perhaps in the period from 1982 to 1989 as the Soviet threat waned that Deng displayed his creativity as a statesman.[27] It was during this period that he put forward his well known concept of "one country two systems," described by Mrs Thatcher at the time of the signing of the Anglo-Chinese Joint Declaration on Hong Kong in 1984 as an "idea of genius" (of which more will be discussed later). This was also the period in which Deng concluded that not only was a new world war no longer inevitable, but that it could be postponed indefinitely. By 1984 he was

24. See Carol Lee Hamrin, "China re-assesses the superpowers," *Pacific Affairs* (Summer 1983), pp. 209–231.

25. Yahuda, *Foreign Policy After Mao*, pp. 205 and 216.

26. For interpretations that give greater weight to problems in Sino-American relations see Jonathan D. Pollack, "The opening to America" in Roderick MacFarquhar and John K. Fairbank (eds.), *The Cambridge History of China*, Vol. 15, Part 2, *Revolutions Within the Chinese Revolution 1966–82* (Cambridge: Cambridge University Press, 1991), pp. 457–469; and Harry Harding, *A Fragile Relationship: The United States and China Since 1972* (Washington, D. C.: The Brookings Institution, 1992) pp. 119–125.

27. For a Chinese account that emphasizes the themes of peace and development as exemplified by the positive linkage between East–West and North–South issues, the prospects for a comparatively long period of peace, the "core" significance of North–South relations and the continuing need to resist hegemonism, see Tao Chuanwang, Zhang Changyun and Luo Zhangfu (eds.), *Deng Xiaoping zhuzuo zhuanti yanjiu (Researching the Main Themes of the Writings of Deng Xiaoping)* (Beijing: People's Press, 1990), pp. 318–339.

arguing that "world peace" could be safeguarded, though he claimed that this could only be done if "we oppose hegemony."[28] Such a view had never been advanced by Mao, for whom conflict and struggle were fundamental. Deng went further to argue that a link existed between peace and development. He argued that the East–West military conflict was linked to the North–South economic relations. Problems in one could spill over into the other. But for a self-styled Marxist it was remarkable that he argued that the interests of the North and South were compatible. Perhaps echoing China's basic approach to Western countries, Deng claimed that the North required markets and the South needed advanced technology. He further developed a view of China's special role in this regard: "I can state positively ... that China seeks to preserve world peace and stability, not to destroy them. The stronger China grows, the better the chances are for preserving world peace."[29] This argument was put forward to domestic as well as foreign audiences.[30] Such arguments about the compatibility of North and South, the desirability and possibility of international stability and Deng's assertions about the ideologically neutral quality of technology and management facilitated the opening of Special Economic Zones, special cities and regions and, more broadly, to an ever deepening engagement with the international (capitalist) economy.

But at the same time Deng kept a wary eye on relations with the two superpowers in terms of manoeuvring within the strategic triangle. Like most of the other leaders involved in the subtleties of its operations, he tended to play down its significance in public: "Some people are talking about the international situation in terms of a big triangle. Frankly, the China angle is not strong enough."[31] But in practice he sought to utilize it as a means of putting pressure on and gaining concessions from the other two. In 1982 the Reagan administration came under great pressure from Beijing on several bilateral issues including aspects of the Taiwan problem. The prospect of the "regression of Sino-American relations" was continually put forward as a possibility if Beijing were not to get its way (which tended to be put in the form of an unbreakable principle). The implied "threat" involved a corresponding improvement in Sino-Soviet relations or at least a deterioration in American standing vis-à-vis the Soviet Union because of problems with China. The fact that Deng Xiaoping involved himself personally in apparently trivial matters such as the fate of a Chinese tennis star suggested that important issues were at stake from a Chinese perspective. In the end, however, the Chinese side backed down when it became clear that the American side would not make further concessions. It was apparently recognized in Beijing that a shift in the larger balance of power had taken place that reduced China's significance for Washington in the "great triangle." The Reagan adminis-

28. Deng Xiaoping, *Fundamental Issues*, p. 46.
29. *Ibid.* p. 95.
30. For example see his speech to an enlarged meeting of the Military Commission, *ibid.* p. 116.
31. *Ibid.* p. 98.

tration no longer needed the "China card" and this was reflected in the change from Haig to Shultz as Secretary of State.[32]

Yet Deng was slow to recognize that accommodation between Reagan and Gorbachev on nuclear strategic issues meant that the significance of the "great triangle" was coming to an end and that this would involve a corresponding marginalization of China in global affairs. Thus China was not involved in the process leading to the signing of the 1987 INF agreement, nor in many of the negotiations that led to Soviet disengagement from many of the regional conflicts in the Third World. China was not even involved in the making of the 1988 Geneva agreements that led to the Soviet military withdrawal from Afghanistan even though Deng had long called for that as one of the conditions for normalizing Sino-Soviet relations.[33] Prior to normalization, as marked by the Gorbachev visit to Beijing in May 1989, Deng went to considerable lengths to assure the United States and President Bush in particular that this would not affect Chinese relations with America and would not entail a return to the alliance with the Soviet Union of the 1950s.[34] He seemed oblivious to the fact that Bush and his administration had long anticipated and indeed welcomed the Sino-Soviet rapprochement.

The truculent and defiant tone of the response of Deng and his elderly colleagues to the criticisms of the Western world, particularly the United States, to the Tiananmen massacre and its aftermath was perhaps to be expected. Deng's brusque rejection of these as interference in China's internal affairs had already been foreshadowed by his resurrection of the FPPC as the basis for a new world order the year before. Not surprisingly, at a time when the survival of Communist rule in China was seen to be at stake, Deng regarded the clamour about human rights abuses in his country as less a sign of the existence of international norms of behaviour than as evidence of a dark plot by Western forces to undermine socialism in China and elsewhere by a sinister subversive policy of "peaceful evolution." This was confirmed for him first by the collapse of Communism in the East European countries in 1989 and finally by the collapse of the Soviet Union itself in 1991 after the failure of the August coup.

In April 1990 the CCP circulated among its members Deng's "very

32. For analyses of these events see, Jaw-ling Joanne Chang, "Negotiation of the 17 August 1982 U.S.–PRC arms communiqué: Beijing's negotiating tactics," *The China Quarterly*, No. 125 (March 1991) pp. 33–54; Robert S. Ross, "China learns to compromise: Change in U.S.–China relations, 1982–1984," *The China Quarterly*, No. 128 (December 1991) pp. 742–773; and Michael B. Yahuda, "The significance of tripolarity in China's policy toward the United States since 1972," in Robert S. Ross (ed.), *The Superpowers and China: The Cold War Triangle* (forthcoming). For a somewhat different analysis that stresses Beijing's concern about American arrogance in taking China for granted see Harding, *A Fragile Relationship*, pp. 131–37.

33. For a brief account of China's marginalization even before the collapse of the Soviet Union see Michael Yahuda, "The People's Republic of China at 40: foreign relations," *The China Quarterly*, No. 119 (September 1989), pp. 519–539.

34. See for example, *BR*, Vol. 32, No. 9, 27 February–5 March 1989. See also Harding, *A Fragile Relationship*, pp. 178–79. It should be noted that the last piece of evidence cited of American concern at a possible Sino-Soviet accommodation is dated 24 March 1986 (*ibid.* p. 178).

important comments" about the consequences for China of the collapse of East European Communism and the "betrayal" by Gorbachev: "Everyone should be very clear that under the present international situation all enemy attention will be concentrated on China. They will use every pretext to cause trouble, to create difficulties and pressures for us." That combined with the aftermath of the Tiananmen events meant that what China needed was "stability, stability and more stability." He went on, "the next three to five years will be extremely difficult for our Party and our country, extremely important. If we stand fast and make it through, our enterprise will develop quickly. If we collapse, China's history will regress for several tens of years, even a hundred years."[35] But unlike some of his colleagues who reportedly sought to open polemics with Gorbachev, Deng argued in favour of avoiding ideological issues and urged that state relations be developed on a steady cordial basis: "Observe the development soberly, maintain our position, meet the challenge calmly, hide our capacities, bide our time, remain free of ambitions, and never claim leadership."[36]

There was no doubt that China's leaders favoured the more conservative, orthodox elements in the CPSU and, because of the threat of Yeltsin, they modified their critical stance against Gorbachev in the spring and summer of 1991. A stream of the more hardline Soviet leaders visited China during this period and Jiang Zemin visited Moscow. The unprecedented Chinese offer to the Soviet Union of a loan of 1 billion Swiss francs was meant to signal Chinese support. At that time China's leaders seemed to share the Soviet hardliners' view that close Sino-Soviet relations at this point made it more difficult for the United States to use its enhanced global position to exercise pressure on either.[37] The Chinese leaders including Deng welcomed the attempted Soviet coup in August and were dismayed by its failure, but under Deng's influence China maintained in public a formally correct position. Even before its failure Deng said that China should not enter into alignments, or unite with the Soviet Union to resist the United States.[38] After the failure the Politburo expected that the United States would intensify its efforts to undermine socialism in China by peaceful means. As a result it concluded that China should criticize Gorbachev's revisionism and his betrayal of socialism in its internal propaganda while refraining from making adverse comments in public.[39]

35. "Deng Xiaoping de Zhonggong suanming" ("Deng Xiaoping sees the future for the CCP"), *Zhengming*, Hong Kong, No. 151 (1 May 1990).

36. Shih Chun-yu, "China, Soviet Union establish new relations of good-neighbourliness, co-operation," *Da Gong Bao*, Hong Kong, 16 May 1991, in *FBIS-CHI*, 16 May 1991, pp. 13–14.

37. *Xinhua* reported without comment the substance of a 28 February 1991 editorial commentary in *Pravda* to that effect.

38. *Qing Bao (Intelligence)*, Hong Kong, 5 September 1991, in *FBIS-CHI*, 9 September 1991, p. 10

39. He Po-shih, "CCP issues successive emergency circulars ordering entire Party to guard against changes," *Dangdai*, Hong Kong, 15 September 1991, in *FBIS-CHI*, 24 September 1991.

Deng's longer-term reaction, as shown above, even at the at the time of the Tiananmen events included a renewed commitment to the policies of reform. He consistently rejected the proposals of his more "leftist" colleagues to draw in the horns and cultivate an anti-American coalition. Since the imposition of Western sanctions in 1989 Chinese diplomacy has overlooked the "loss of face" involved in the declared refusal of Western leaders to meet their Chinese counterparts. Instead China's foreign relations have focused on continuing and deepening the broad range of feasible economic relations so that within three years few of the sanctions remained in place, and on cultivating relations with neighbours in the Asia-Pacific.

The policy of what China's Foreign Minister has called "good neighbourliness" may be said to embody China's first attempt at a coherent regional policy that was not subordinated to the relationship with the Soviet Union and the United States. It reflected the fact that for the first time in 40 years China's leaders no longer feared attack from either. But it also arose from the recognition of the significance of the countries of the region to China's policies of economic development reform and openness. China's leaders have actively courted membership of regional institutions, so that China in 1991 became a dialogue partner of the Association of South East Asian Nations (ASEAN), a member of the Asia Pacific Economic Co-operation (APEC) – alongside Hong Kong and Taiwan – and expressed support for the controversial Malaysian proposal for a kind of East Asian trade grouping excluding the United States. Henceforth China would no longer excite suspicions by being willing to deal with its neighbours on a bilateral basis only. China has also played a new role in contributing to the diffusion of the two long-standing conflicts in the region in Korea and Cambodia. Deng retreated from his earlier proposal to settle the Korean issue on his model of "one country two systems" when China indicated to the North that it would not veto the South's application to join the United Nations. The North was in effect compelled to set aside its declared principle and apply for simultaneous membership. Such flexibility was less evident in China's handling of the Cambodian issue where the Vietnamese were given no alternative but to accept Chinese terms. The Vietnamese "pilgrimage" to Beijing having shed the two senior leaders most disliked by the Chinese, and their having to accept Chinese observer status at the Cambodian Supreme National Conference held in Beijing may be seen as the last chapters in Deng Xiaoping's long attempt to "teach Vietnam a lesson."[40]

Underlying Deng's approach, however, is still an assertive rather than a confident nationalism as may be seen from his reported reaction to his Foreign Minister's casting of a vote of abstention on the UN Security Council resolution authorizing the use of force against Iraq. According to a Hong Kong journal, he told his bridge partners Yang Shangkun, Wan Li, Song Renqiong and Chen Pixian:

40. For accounts see, Nayan Chauda, *Brother Enemy: A History of Indo-China, the Fall of Saigon* (New York: Macmillan Press, 1988).

When I saw on the television news that Qian Qichen unhurriedly raised his hand in "abstention" I nodded to him and saluted him. By holding up his hand he again showed the whole world that China has a decisive say in solving major disputes in the world. Our foreign policy is firm and principled. We will not follow any other country or act according to another people's baton; we will not threaten other countries with force, nor are we afraid of other countries' threat of force; we will not give up our principled stand by accepting exchanges or compromises. If we violate this principled stand, it will mean an out-and-out betrayal of Marxism–Leninism and a betrayal of the behests of millions of martyrs, and our posterity will not forgive us.[41]

As noted earlier, the abstention was an attempt to have it both ways. By abstaining the Chinese knew that they were leaving the door open for an American orchestrated use of force against Iraq sanctioned by the United Nations. That was why President Bush was willing to receive Qian Qichen in Washington personally (thereby ending his own sanction against meeting Chinese leaders). They also knew that it would mean acknowledging that the economic sanctions against Iraq for which the Chinese had voted would not be given the chance to work any longer. The abstention was at best an empty gesture designed to get the Chinese off the hook of neither condoning Iraq's attempt to annex its weaker neighbour by force nor supporting American military action against another Third World country. Deng's rhetoric, if truly reported, smacks of wishful thinking or even desperation. The last comments about betrayal are reminiscent of his comments on the eve of ordering the tanks to shoot the demonstrators and illustrate his deep fears about the political succession in China and the survival of the regime.

But it was not long before a more decisive and less morbid and perhaps more typically active Deng Xiaoping emerged as he developed his 1992 spring offensive. Deng envisages that it will be possible to modernize along the lines of Hong Kong and Singapore while retaining Communist rule through the coercive powers of the military and security organs.

Deng and China's Modern Problems of Statehood

It may be regarded as paradoxical, but Deng's very success in presiding over the most successful programme of economic modernization in the Communist world and perhaps in China's history has brought to the fore the problems of modern statehood that his programme was designed to solve. The questions that were supposedly solved by the establishment of the PRC in 1949 have been re-opened. The policies of reform and the growing regionalization of the economy have weakened the capacities of the central government, thus raising again questions about the underlying unity of the country.

At the heart of the issue is the revival of the old 19th-century problem that troubled the Confucian reformers who sought to modernize along Western lines while retaining Chinese traditional Confucian values. Deng's economic reform programme of embracing foreign capitalist

41. Kim, *The Changing World Order*, pp. 25–27.

practices so as to develop socialism with Chinese characteristics is reminiscent of their goals as epitomized in the slogan, "Chinese learning for the essentials and Western learning for the practicalities" (*Zhong xue wei ti, Xi xue wei yong*). This encapsulated the reasons for their failure, as Western technology and managerial know-how were antithetical to Confucian values. The same would appear to be true of the current attempt as applied to Chinese Communist values. Certainly there are parallels between the resistance of the more old fashioned upholders of traditional Confucianism in the 19th century to what they regarded as disruptive Western intrusions and the resistance of old fashioned upholders of traditional Communism in the current period to alleged Western subversion.[42] But it is also true that there are important differences between the two situations. China is no longer as closed as it once was and there are many social forces and groups who have been permeated by modern and Western influences. As the Tiananmen events showed, China is part of the "global village."[43] Moreover the position of members of the Communist Party is highly complex as many at all levels are actively engaged in what might be called entrepreneurial activities, and others at middle levels of the bureaucracy and especially in the state owned enterprises fear and resist many aspects of the reforms. The internal position is also very different. The centrifugal forces within are not really matched by interventionist forces of superior military strength.

Nevertheless Deng's China is confronted with a legitimacy crisis of gigantic proportions as the very things which sustained it in 1949 had been degraded 40 years later. The inner confidence of a Party imbued with a sense of mission and belief in itself as a unifying revolutionary force backed by the support of the bulk of the people, proven in a long series of revolutionary and civil wars, was no more. Similarly, the stimulus of belonging to a world-wide movement that constituted the future for mankind had gone. Internally, the "crisis of faith" at the end of the Cultural Revolution has been superseded by cynicism, corruption and nepotism. Party rule was maintained in the end by the tank and the armed police. The success in the economy has been derived from the non-socialist sector as even in the industrial realm the value of the industrial production of the favoured state-owned medium and large enterprises has been by-passed by the collective and private firms. In 1978 the state-owned sector accounted for 90 per cent of the value of industrial output, but by 1991 it had been surpassed by the combined value of the industrial production of the collective, private and foreign related enterprises. The sources for economic reform no longer come from the Communist Party or the Marxist canons of political economy, but are derived from the private sector and more particularly from capitalist external influences. Even Deng's initiative of seeking to base continued Party rule on the

42. For the classic account of the former see, Mary C. Wright, *The Last Stand of Chinese Conservatism: The T'ung Chih Restoration, 1862–1874* (Stanford: Stanford University Press, 1957)

43. See David S. G. Goodman, "Reforming China: foreign contacts, foreign values?" *The Pacific Review*, Vol. 5, No. 1 (1992).

provision of economic prosperity carries within it its own seeds of destruction. The new economic sprouts and the new social forces to which they give rise will inevitably regard the Party and the order it claims to provide as an obstacle to rather than the facilitator of entrepreneurialship and economic development. Sooner or later the question of the Party's capacity to undertake political reform of itself seems bound to arise again.

It is against that backcloth that Deng's "brilliant" idea of "one country two systems" must ultimately be assessed. Initially it was put forward as a means for unifying the socialist motherland with capitalistic Taiwan and Hong Kong by peaceful means. It had been thought that Deng developed the idea as an inspired response to an unexpected British request to review the treaties affecting Hong Kong (these were not formally recognized by the PRC as they were the most infamous of the "unequal treaties" that bore testimony to China's previous "century of humiliation" – but nor were they effectively challenged by Beijing). But more recently Chinese sources have claimed that the concept was first introduced by Deng at the end of 1978.[44] If so it would explain Deng's extreme annoyance at Mrs Thatcher's initial insistence on her 1982 visit to China that treaties were binding whether one liked them or not, and if the Chinese refused to honour those treaties what credence could be placed upon their honouring any new ones. Deng reportedly cursed her and declared that he would not be "another Li Hongzhang."[45] In any event he articulated his concept in public for the first time and that became the organizing framework for the Sino-British Joint Declaration on Hong Kong that was signed in 1984.

Both the concept and the Joint Declaration to which it gave rise were unprecedented in international diplomacy. Not only did it envisage the operation of two mutually opposed socio-economic systems within the bounds of one state sovereignty, but it also called for a transition period of 13 years in which the British were entrusted with preparing the basis for the exercise of "a high degree of autonomy" by Hong Kong under Chinese sovereignty thereafter. This involved great risks for the Chinese side as well as for the people of Hong Kong in mortgaging the future to the co-operative capacities of Chinese and British leaders whose political cultures and outlook could hardly differ more, especially as these were to be tested by the uncertainties of international and their respective domestic politics. At the time of writing with less than five years to go before the reversion of sovereignty it is still too early to discuss with confidence the future of Hong Kong itself. But it is already apparent that the issues involved are highly divisive within China. From the outset it was clear that the evolution of Hong Kong would affect China's international

44. See Tao Chuanwang *et al.*, *Deng Xiaoping Zhuzuo*, p. 290.
45. The famous 19th-century high official who suffers, perhaps unfairly, from the reputation of having sold out his country's sovereignty to buy peace and better relations with foreign imperialists.

reputation for good or ill within the Asia-Pacific region and in the international economic community. It was also understood that the territory would become even more important in the country's economic development at provincial, national and international levels. But the Tiananmen events and the impact of the collapse of European Communism has underscored the view that Hong Kong could be politically subversive to the socialist mainland. Moreover since Deng Xiaoping himself in the early spring of 1992 put Hong Kong forward as a model for Guangdong province and indeed for other parts of China he has ensured that the Hong Kong issue will be central to the debates within China about the country's fundamental orientation. It may well become part of the factional rivalries that are bound to attend the struggle for the political succession that cannot be long delayed.

Meanwhile Deng must be credited with having come up with an imaginative concept to resolve the dilemmas inherent in the problems of reuniting both Hong Kong and Taiwan. The concept is consistent with older traditions that allowed alien enclaves to exist within Chinese administered territories and it may also be said to have built on the Communist approach to national minorities who on paper at least enjoyed a degree of local autonomy. But at the same time Deng has deepened his country's entanglement with the more cosmopolitan world of international capitalism that so menaces his conservative (or leftist) colleagues as it menaced their Confucian forebears more than a hundred years before.

Conclusions

Perhaps the more pertinent questions to be asked of Deng's statesmanship are the conventional ones traditionally applied to Western leaders.[46] How has the statesman defined his country's national interest? What values have underpinned that definition? How conscious has he been of the interests and values of others and to what extent has he sought to accommodate them? How has he sought to give effect to these concerns?

Timing is of unusual importance in evaluating the quality of a statesman. That is because any such evaluation must involve a historical judgment. For "what distinguishes statesmen from mere politicians is that they succeeded in leaving a mark on the history of their respective states, as well as on world history, commensurate with the importance of their states."[47] There is therefore a moral and philosophical dimension to be added to the criteria for assessing statesmanship. In the words of Martin Wight, "in this [historians'] endless debate different people and generations strike different balances between the criterion of technical success, mere expertise, and the moral criterion. This latter itself is twofold,

46. See for example the erudite discussion in Wight, "The theory of the national interest," pp. 111–136.
47. Ghita Ionescu, *Leadership in an Interdependent World: The Statesmanship of Adenauer, De Gaulle, Thatcher and Gorbachev* (Harlow, Essex: Longman, 1991) p. 1

involving the judgement of loftiness of motive, and the judgement of the ultimate contributions to human good."[48]

Few would question Deng Xiaoping's entitlement to be considered a statesman. Even though the precise meaning of the term may be elusive, he certainly possesses the qualities most usually associated with it. For example, Ionescu might almost have had Deng in mind when he added the following to his historical requirements, "courage and decisiveness [and] consistency of political aims."[49] Similarly, in a memorable phrase about the need of a statesman to be active, Henry Kissinger argued that the statesman "owes it to his people to strive, to create, and to resist the decay that besets all human institutions."[50]

Questions do arise however, about the quality or art of Deng's statesmanship. For example, Kissinger, paraphrasing Bismark, held that "the art of statesmanship is to listen carefully until one can perhaps discern the footsteps of history and follow for a brief period in their train."[51] In other words, a statesman should be one who leads the way to the future rather than someone who makes a last ditch stand for the past.

With these considerations in mind, it is fair to say that contrary to Chinese claims on his behalf, Deng Xiaoping, like Mao Zedong before him, could not be regarded as a creator of international order who was alert to the interests of other countries and was sensitive to the operations of their domestic systems. His curt dismissal of Western liberal democracy is remarkable for its mixture of condescension and ignorance:

In developing our democracy, we cannot simply copy bourgeois democracy, or introduce the system of a balance of three powers. I have often criticized people in power in the United States, saying that actually they have three governments. Of course, the American bourgeoisie uses this system in dealing with other countries, but when it comes to internal affairs, the three branches often pull in different directions, and that makes trouble.[52]

There is no evidence here of familiarity with West European systems where the executive commands a majority in the legislature. Yet Deng had spent five years in France during the impressionable age of 16 to 21. But, like many Chinese both before and since, Deng spent his sojourn abroad largely among his own countrymen and did not gain a close familiarity with the local culture. It will be recalled that Deng was very poor during this period and he spent most of his time either at work in menial jobs or as a writer and stenographer for the local Communist journal. However, like many of the other Chinese Communists from France who later attained prominence, Deng did not put himself forward as a Marxist theorist. Those who had been trained in the Soviet Union and those who remained within China, perhaps being less troubled by

48. Wight, "The theory of the national interest," p. 121.
49. Wight and Porter, *International Theory*, p. 1
50. Henry Kissinger, *The White House Years* (London: Weidenfeld & Nicolson, 1979), p. 55.
51. Henry Kissinger, *For the Record, Selected Statements 1977–1980* (London: Weidenfeld & Nicolson, 1981), p. 261.
52. Deng Xiaoping, *Fundamental Issues*, p. 163.

reflections upon the variety and the comparatively advanced and complex character of Western economies, felt freer to engage in abstract discourse. But the explanation could hardly lie in their supposed ignorance of Chinese conditions as insinuated by Deng Liqun in early 1992 as a response to Deng Xiaoping's "Spring Offensive." Among Deng's associates from those years in France are some of the most hallowed names in Chinese Communism, notably Zhou Enlai, Nie Rongzhen and Li Fuchun. Interestingly, they have all distinguished themselves by their practical accomplishments. None, of course, is more famous in this regard than Deng himself.

It may also be that Deng's brief stay in the Soviet Union in 1926 may have soured him towards that country, as unlike many of his colleagues it is difficult to find favourable mentions of it in his writings. Indeed in his three visits there in the course of the developing Sino-Soviet dispute Deng appeared to distinguish himself by the virulence of his criticisms.[53] As late as March 1988 a distinguished Soviet scholar at the Institute of Oriental Studies in the Soviet Academy of Sciences privately reflected that the normalization of relations with China had been held up because of Deng's personal antipathy. Certainly, Deng's personal style has not been noted for its diplomatic smoothness. Having been charmed by Zhou Enlai, Henry Kissinger is said to have recoiled from a particularly bruising encounter with Deng by dubbing him "a nasty little man."

Deng's claims to statesmanship can hardly be made on the basis of his diplomatic charm. But more to the point they cannot rest either on moral grounds. He cannot be regarded as the epitome of the revolutionist who seeks to recast the world in the name of a doctrine for whose ends no sacrifice is too great. The cold-blooded killings of peaceful demonstrators that he ordered in June 1989 had more to do with survival and retribution than the upholding of a moral order.

Deng's claims therefore must rest on his reinterpretation of China's national interest and on engaging his country once again with the rest of the world. His countrymen owe him a heavy debt for steering them from the xenophobic fruitless destructiveness of perpetual class struggle towards the path of economic development and growing prosperity. His advocacy of reform and openness may be enough to satisfy the Bismarkian demand that as a statesman he should follow however briefly in the footsteps of history. But by his simultaneous insistence upon Communist Party rule Deng may be remembered in the end as one who in Mao's terminology "walked on two legs" with one directed towards the future and the other towards the past.

The legacy Deng has bequeathed his successors in foreign affairs is mixed. On the positive side he has pointed the way for China to emerge in due course as a newly industrializing economy closely linked with the

53. The best accounts of Deng's younger years are to be found in Uli Franz (trans. by Tom Artin), *Deng Xiaoping* (Boston: Harcourt Brace Jovanovich, 1988) especially pp. 21–75; and in Ching Hua Lee, *Deng Xiaoping: The Marxist Road to the Forbidden City* (Princeton: The Kingston Press, 1985) pp. 25–35.

international economy and increasingly integrated within the Asia-Pacific region. The country is on the brink of becoming a major force in the region with a capacity to project naval and air power throughout East Asia. But Deng's successors will have to learn to exercise that power with restraint lest they agitate their neighbouring states to find security through seeking countervailing power. On the negative side, Deng will have left his successors with extraordinarily difficult problems in sustaining the Chinese state as a unitary actor. His own legitimacy which rests on belonging to the generation of the founding fathers of the revolution is personal rather than institutional and it cannot be passed on. His successors are likely to be men of narrower outlook and bound by their bureaucratic and personal allegiances. They are likely to experience greater difficulties in holding on to Communist Party rule and to restraining the centrifugal tendencies of growing regionalism.

In bringing China more into the world Deng has solved certain problems only to open the door to many more. Perhaps his most important act of statesmanship has been to lead China towards modernity beyond the point of possible return to the period of isolation and dark totalitarian rule. But in doing so he has perhaps reached the limits of his vision.

Index